MONEY, POWER, RESPECT

HOW WOMEN IN SPORTS ARE SHAPING
THE FUTURE OF FEMINISM

MACAELA MACKENZIE

SEAL
PRESS

NEW YORK

Seal Press
Hachette Book Group
1290 Avenue of the Americas, New York, NY 10104
www.sealpress.com
@sealpress

Printed in the United States of America
First Edition: June 2023

Published by Seal Press, an imprint of Perseus Books, LLC, a subsidiary of
Hachette Book Group, Inc. The Seal Press name and logo is a trademark of
the Hachette Book Group.

The Hachette Speakers Bureau provides a wide range of authors for speaking
events. To find out more, go to www.hachettespeakersbureau.com or email
HachetteSpeakers@hbgusa.com.

Seal Press books may be purchased in bulk for business, educational,
or promotional use. For information, please contact your local bookseller or
Hachette Book Group Special Markets Department at special.markets@hbgusa.com.

The publisher is not responsible for websites (or their content) that are not owned
by the publisher.

Library of Congress Cataloging-in-Publication Data
Names: MacKenzie, Macaela, author.
Title: Money, power, respect : how women in sports are shaping the future of
  feminism / Macaela MacKenzie.
Description: First edition. | New York, N.Y. : Seal Press, 2023. | Includes
  bibliographical references and index.
Identifiers: LCCN 2022050319 | ISBN 9781541600898 (hardcover) | ISBN
  9781541600904 (ebook)
Subjects: LCSH: Sports for women—Social aspects—United States. | Women
  athletes—Political activity—United States. | Feminism and sports—United States.
Classification: LCC GV709.18.U6 M327 2023 | DDC 796.082—dc23/eng/20221219
LC record available at https://lccn.loc.gov/2022050319

ISBNs: 9781541600898 (hardcover), 9781541600904 (ebook)

LSC-C

Printing 1, 2023

For Emmi and June. Girl Power.

CONTENTS

AUTHOR'S NOTE

TO BEST UNDERSTAND THE WAYS WOMEN IN SPORTS ARE SHAPING our cultural conversation, I interviewed dozens of athletes, academics, and activists. Unless otherwise cited, the information in this book is drawn from those conversations.

INTRODUCTION

Twenty-three women set out to get a raise. They were outperforming their male colleagues—had been for years—despite unequal working conditions, lackluster promotional efforts, and performance bonuses nothing short of pathetic. They wanted more. To be paid fairly. Equally. But to those in power, equality often feels like a threat. The women were met with a firestorm of resistance. Their bosses claimed publicly that the pay gap was all in their heads, that they deserved to be paid less because their job was easier, that really, they, and not their male counterparts, were the lucky ones. They were gaslit, condescended to, told to keep quiet and simply be grateful for what they had. And through it all, they were expected to keep doing their job: winning.

By the time the twenty-three women of the US Women's National Soccer Team (USWNT) stepped onto the field for the 2019 World Cup final, they had come to represent the ambitions and frustrations of every woman who's ever been told she's worth less—less money, fewer opportunities, less acknowledgment. Their fight drew a big crowd: 1.1 billion viewers globally tuned in to their World Cup run (including 22 percent more US viewers for the final match than the men's World Cup final attracted the year prior).[1] Politicians and celebrities from Barack Obama to Tom Brady tweeted their support. Almost overnight, the women had become global icons of gender equality. And when the team clinched the championship title, a stadium filled with fifty-nine thousand men and women spontaneously erupted into chants of "Equal Pay!"

These women had played by all the rules and succeeded. And still, they didn't get paid.

Most women, whether they've ever seen a soccer game or not, know this story. They know it because they've lived it. Across industries, women are expected to make a living under the constant pressure that they'll have to do more with fewer resources—and then settle for a smaller paycheck with a smile. It's about money, but it's also about what the money represents: power and respect. In going public with their fight for equal pay, the USWNT had touched a primal nerve. These women had done everything that was asked of them and more: They had become the best women's soccer program in global sports history, overcoming subpar training conditions and ignoring misogynistic media coverage that downplayed their skill. They'd won a record four World Cup titles—the most in women's soccer history—bringing glory to their country at a time when the United States' global reputation felt especially precarious. And as a thanks, their employer hired lobbyists to argue against their case in Congress and filed embarrassing court documents arguing the women had their own biological inferiority to blame for the pay gap.[2]

What more do women have to do to be valued equally? And why did it feel like it was up to a group of men to decide?

As Megan Rapinoe told me, "That's bullshit."[3]

I first spoke to Rapinoe the morning after the team's pay negotiations with US Soccer imploded. I was a senior editor at *Glamour,* profiling Rapinoe as a 2019 Woman of the Year. She had, in the span of a summer, become one of the most recognizable voices in the history of the fight for equal pay, crossing firmly from the arena of soccer fan fame into the cultural zeitgeist, becoming a pink-haired, champagne-popping, Twitter-trending feminist icon. She and her teammates were fresh off their World Cup victory, which had ended in a crescendo of public support for equal pay. At the team's victory parade in New York City, just a few days prior, there had been a palpable sense of optimism in the air. The streets were more packed than I'd ever seen them (despite it being the middle of a workday in the Financial District), filled with men and women, boys and girls, who had all shown up in starry-eyed support of their team. In a speech in front of New York's City Hall, US Soccer's then president Carlos Cordeiro said, "In recent months, you have raised your voices for equality. Today, on behalf of all of us at U.S. Soccer, I want to say, we hear you. We believe you. And we're committed to doing right by you."[4] It felt like a turning point. But just weeks later, news broke that the negotiations between US Soccer and the women of the USWNT had fallen apart after just two days. It was a gut punch.

By this time, it was already clear that the team's fight was much bigger than a pay dispute in soccer. But the rage so many women were feeling at this latest insult was a sign of just how closely linked the fight for women's equality in sports was becoming to the fight for women's equality more broadly. Women were pissed—including Rapinoe. By the time I met her and her entourage before her Woman of the Year photo shoot, she had already done the rounds on the morning shows; it was barely 10 a.m. and she'd already had to defend her value on *Good Morning America*, *CBS This Morning*, and the *TODAY Show*. She seemed weary. It all felt very familiar. We know the stats: In the United States, women make just 83 cents for every dollar men bring home—for Black women it's just 63 cents, Native and Indigenous women bring home an estimated 60 cents, and for Latina women it dwindles to an abysmal 58 cents. As a group, Asian American, Native Hawaiian, and Pacific Islander women bring home 95 cents to the dollar, but that number varies widely by ethnicity: Vietnamese women earn 64 cents, Cambodian women 60 cents, and Burmese women just 50 cents to the white male dollar. When you include full- and part-time workers, capturing more women in economically insecure and low-wage jobs, the pay gap widens to 77 cents earned to the dollar of white men.[5]

The gender pay gap hits LGBTQ women particularly hard. Women in same-gender couples bring home less than hetero couples, despite the fact that they are more likely to be dual-income households. Research on the pay gap for transgender women specifically is limited, but one recent analysis found transgender workers overall make 32 percent less than their cisgender colleagues, even when they have similar or higher levels of education.[6]

In sports, where the money is big and the bias against women even bigger, the gender pay gap grows exponentially. In basketball, for example, the NBA's highest-paid player Steph Curry earned a $48 million salary in the 2022–2023 season. In the WNBA, the league's highest-paid players made just $228,000 (a historic high).[7] So for every dollar Steph Curry brought home, the Seattle Storm's star power forward Breanna Stewart earned less than half a cent. *Half. A. Cent.* Put another way, the *combined* salary of all 144 WNBA players—the majority of whom are Black women—was less than a third of what one single NBA player made.

~ ~ ~

THE FIGHT FOR equal pay in sports got under my skin. Before I began covering the USWNT's road to the World Cup in 2019, I wouldn't have considered myself a die-hard sports fan. But as a lifelong athlete, I knew the power of sports in my own life, and as a journalist I had always been interested in challenging the biases and taboos that held women back. I began to think of sports not just as entertainment, but as a mirror of what's happening in other industries. The more I learned, the more inequalities I saw reflected.

Sports are particularly good at illustrating the gender gap when it comes to the resources invested in women, for example. In other industries, the lack of capital and support granted to women can be easy to obscure—you don't see the women-led businesses that never get funded, rarely hear about the women who don't get promoted. But in sports, the investment gap is as obvious as the arenas women play in and the uniforms on their backs. While their male counterparts fly private, train in state-of-the-art facilities, and enjoy multimillion-dollar marketing budgets, women in sports wear hand-me-down uniforms, play in public parks, and fly back from championships in economy. In sports, we see a glaring reflection of the lack of women in leadership positions, the worst of sexist media coverage, the penalty women pay for trying to become moms while having a career. We're subject to routine debates about women's supposed biological inferiority. There isn't a single facet of the fight for women's equality that isn't currently playing out in the world of sports, where equal opportunity and equal pay are impossible to separate.

Women athletes fight the same discrimination women are facing in all levels of work every day. But they do it with something most of us don't have: influence. Women's sports are the literal arena in which we see women's ambition and skill on display, and witness their fight for equality play out. When women athletes call bullshit, it's often from a big platform. But making sexism and misogyny concrete and visible isn't the only thing women's sports have to offer in the fight for gender equality. The more I talked to women athletes, and the more I followed their campaigns for equal pay and equal treatment, the more I came to realize that sports aren't just the way to understand the problem—they're a way to solve it.

Sports are perhaps the most powerful tool our culture has for defining gender roles. "There are few institutions that are more revered and more ubiquitous than sport," says Mary Jo Kane, director emerita of the Tucker Center for Research on Girls and Women in Sport at the University of Minnesota. They give us heroes to worship and rivalries to cheer, help define our shared values, and shape our understanding of gender roles, positioning men as the playmakers and women as the cheerleaders standing on the sidelines. When the modern Olympics began in 1896, women were not allowed to compete because it would be "impractical, uninteresting, unaesthetic and indecent," according to Baron Pierre de Coubertin, the founder of the International Olympic Committee. The Olympics were all about male excellence, he said, with "female applause as a reward."[8]

But while sports have historically enforced sexist stereotypes—men are strong, women are irrelevant—that same culture-defining power is also what makes sports a compelling agent of change in the fight for gender justice. "Sports provide an arena that can completely destabilize our notions of women's physical, mental, and emotional competence," says Kane. Watch Simone Biles, the greatest gymnast of all time, defy perceptions of what the human body is capable of; watch runners Allyson Felix and Alysia Montaño win championships after becoming mothers; watch gymnast Aly Raisman powerfully testify before Congress on behalf of sexual abuse survivors—and the sexist stereotypes about the competence of half the population immediately wither. "Sport can be a force to amplify women's voices and tear down gender barriers and discrimination," said Lakshmi Puri, former UN assistant secretary-general and deputy executive director of UN Women. "Women in sport defy the misperception that [women] are weak or incapable."[9]

The reality is, sports are less like a mirror and more like our social media feeds; they reflect our attitudes and our biases, but they also have the power to shape them. They tell us through testosterone-pumped Monday Night Football promos how to see men as dominant, God-like rulers of the universe and through second-class stadiums how to see women as less than. Sports influence us. It's time to use that to women's advantage.

~ ~ ~

I WROTE THIS book during a particularly hard time for women. A global pandemic forced millions of women out of the workforce, causing a generational setback for women's economic equality; transgender rights became an increasingly frequent target of right-wing persecution, stripping trans women and girls of their personhood; *Roe v. Wade* was overturned, which makes having a uterus in America a life-threatening liability. Nearly every woman I interviewed for the book spoke about the greater significance this moment in history had given her work; she may have just been playing basketball, or fighting to run a race according to her gender identity, or working to make sure pregnant women didn't lose opportunities, or hustling to get women athletes more media coverage, but her work in sports was often about something bigger. It was about the belief that securing more power for women in one corner of the world would have ripple effects everywhere.

Signing your daughter up for Little League or buying season tickets to your local WNBA franchise won't solve centuries of systemic discrimination against women. But decades of research shows it will help, beginning with the personal effect playing sports has on girls' sense of power. Girls who play sports have more confidence and higher self-esteem. They are more likely to graduate and more likely to end up in the C-suite. Sports give girls ownership over their bodies, providing a space to test their limits and forge their identity on their own terms. "As a girl competing in the sport I loved, it was a way to tune out all the noise in my head and just be free," says CeCé Telfer, an NCAA Division II champion runner. "Taking to the track showed my full potential. I was like, *oh my gosh I do well under pressure.* This is my place. This is where I live, where I am." The liberation in sports is so powerful that author and former pro basketball player Mariah Burton Nelson wrote in her book *The Stronger Women Get, the More Men Love Football* that there is "an actual fear on the part of many men that women's growing athleticism somehow threatens not only men and men's sports but the very nature of things: men on top."[10]

I've experienced the emancipating effects of sports in my own life. I grew up as a competitive dancer and in my twenties took up running. Like CeCé, and so many women before and since, it was here I too found something radical. Running was about what my body could do, not what it looked like. Any success I found on the pavement or track was due to my effort and my effort alone. When I pushed harder, I was rewarded. No one could tell me my body was inferior or incapable or not my own. Running became a place to challenge all the assumptions I had about myself—and that changed the way I showed up in the world.

I am by no means unique here. There are as many stories about personal liberation in sport as there are women who have ever played. And more importantly, those intimate revolutions have impacted entire communities. In Mexico's Yucatán Peninsula, an indigenous women's softball team—Las Diablillas, the "Little Devils"—barefoot and in traditional Mayan dresses, have completely redefined gender norms in their town (and won global recognition in the process). "Here a woman serves the home and is not supposed to go out and play sports," Fabiola May Chulim, the team captain and manager, told the *New York Times*. "When a woman marries, she's supposed to do chores and attend to her husband and kids. We decided a few years ago that's not going to impede us anymore." Their team has shaped family dynamics and changed the perceptions of women in the community. "I used to really only leave the house to help my husband with our crops. Now, thanks to softball, I have permission to leave the house, enjoy myself with friends and visit new towns," said pitcher Alicia Canul Dzib. "It motivates me to keep playing and set an example for my daughter."[11]

Women's sports have the power to be deeply subversive, challenging the most basic perceptions of how women should show up in the world. So intimidating is the power of sports that in some places, playing can be life-threatening for women. When the US-backed government in Afghanistan fell to Taliban rule in 2021, women athletes emerged as some of the most endangered, fleeing the country in fear. "Our names and photos are on social media," cyclist Sediqa Sidiqi told *The Lily* after a Taliban official told international media that women in the country would no longer be allowed to play sports. "If they find out that we are cyclists, they will kill us." Sidiqi had been the captain of the Bamiyan Women's Cycling Team, finding freedom and a precarious sense of equality in the ability to do something as simple as ride a bike to school. In the wake of the Taliban takeover, Sidiqi's father took a photo of her many medals and cycling certificates—a single piece of digital proof of the many accomplishments of her cycling career—before planning to burn them out of fear. "I worked so hard and had such big dreams," she said. "Now I have only a picture."[12]

~ ~ ~

THIS IS A book about power and the unique role women's sports play in shaping who has it. In these pages, we'll examine how women's sports influence culture and widen our understanding of what's possible for women and others whose genders have been marginalized. (A note on terminology: Not everyone playing women's sports necessarily identifies as a woman, though they suffer from the sexism that impacts women's leagues regardless. Throughout this book, unless as part of a direct quote or in reference to a nonbinary individual, I'll use the term "woman athlete" rather than "female athlete" to recognize the diverse spectrum of bodies and gender identities who identify as women in sports.)

We'll start with the money. It's how we indicate value, and as long as we live in a capitalist society, closing the pay gap will remain a vital part of closing the power gap. In Part I, we'll look at the biggest pay battles being waged by women athletes, including the USWNT's ultimately successful campaign, and about how the fight for equal pay in sports mirrors the frustrations of women across industries. We'll also look at the gulf in investments in women, from venture capital checks to sports sponsorships, and how women-led endeavors are redefining value and return on investment, building an impossible-to-ignore case for investing in women. Finally, we'll face the motherhood penalty, digging into the very real costs of motherhood (for actual moms and for women without children, who suffer from an assumed motherhood penalty). Through the stories of women whose bodies are their jobs, we'll challenge assumptions of what the birthing body is capable of and follow the caregiving revolution being led by moms in sports.

In Part II, we'll see exactly how influential the fight for equality in women's sports is in shaping our perceptions of power—starting with an up-close look at how labor movements in basketball and hockey have harnessed the power of the collective voice to build new, more equitable systems. We'll learn how women coming together to fight for their own economic rights makes them damn good at fighting for other social justice issues, influencing elections, bringing down abusers, and fighting for transgender inclusion. And we'll explore why athletes make such effective leaders—there's a reason 94 percent of all women C-suite executives once played sports—and why seeing women in ownership positions in sports and across industries has the power to rebalance the scales.

After money and power comes the final piece of the equity puzzle: respect. In Part III of this book, we'll look at the stories we tell about women and how they check women's potential. We'll start with the impulse to sexualize women and how the objectification of women in sports undermines us all. We'll tackle the myth of women's so-called natural inferiority that we routinely see in the not-so-ancient rules barring women from athletic activity; in the comments of endless internet dickheads who claim that they could definitely take twenty-three-time Grand Slam champ Serena Williams in a game of singles (really?); and, apparently, explicitly stated in legal documents filed by a major US employer. It's the idea at the core of gender discrimination, and we'll take it down once and for all.

~ ~ ~

WHEN I STARTED writing this book, I asked Rapinoe why she thought her team's fight for equal pay had set off a broader women's movement, their team motto "LFG"—Let's Fucking Go—becoming a rallying cry. Without hesitation, she said that by waging their fight for equal pay so publicly, the team had made women across industries feel seen. In a country where wage discrimination is technically illegal, it's easy to think that closing the pay gap would be as simple as presenting evidence that a male counterpart was making more and getting the raise you deserve. But "that's not how inequality works," says Rapinoe. She and her team had called bullshit on the idea that women should patiently wait for change and issued women the world over an urgent summons: "Don't ever underestimate the power of people holding on to power," Rapinoe says. "You have to pry it from their death grip."

So . . . LFG.

PART I
MONEY

The secret point of money and power in America is
neither the things that money can buy, nor power for
power's sake but absolute personal freedom.

—JOAN DIDION

CHAPTER 1

EQUAL PAY FOR EQUAL PLAY

Missy Park was twelve when she first realized her rights as a woman were being decided, not just on Capitol Hill or in a court of law, but on the tennis court. It was 1973, and tennis superstar Billie Jean King was playing former world number one Bobby Riggs in the Battle of the Sexes—a spectacular showdown of men's vs. women's skill. The outcome wouldn't just give the winner the ultimate tennis bragging rights, it would either confirm or challenge the most deeply ingrained assumptions about women's power and worth: Were women really the weaker, less valuable sex? Millions of girls like Missy, a sports-loving tomboy from South Carolina, were watching closely.

The climate was ripe for this kind of head-to-head, winner-take-all gender face-off. Women were entering the workforce in record numbers, the Supreme Court had just codified a woman's right to bodily autonomy with the passage of *Roe v. Wade*, and Title IX—the landmark law that banned discrimination on the basis of sex in federally funded programs—was about to go into effect. But there was a long way to go: women still couldn't get a credit card in their own name, could be fired for getting pregnant, and earned just 56 cents for every dollar men made. So when Bobby Riggs—a fifty-five-year-old retired tennis pro and self-proclaimed "male chauvinist pig"—approached King about playing an exhibition match to settle the question of who was the stronger sex once and for all, she knew it would be about far more than tennis. "My job in the match, and I remember this being very clear, was to change the hearts and minds of people," King later said.[1] King had been a vocal supporter of women's equality throughout her career, but she knew that laws and policies don't necessarily change people's biases or behaviors. She saw the Battle of the Sexes as key to validating and celebrating what was happening legislatively in the United States and rooting equality firmly into cultural consciousness.

As the palatable poster girl for the women's liberation movement, King was perfect for the job. While fighting for equality in tennis, she'd become an icon in the fight for women's rights while initially avoiding calling herself a feminist—a term then loaded with stigma. "At that time, people thought it meant you hated men, which was so far from the truth," she tells me nearly fifty years later. Toeing the feminist line to avoid alienating people made her "crazed," she says, but it worked. As a kid, Park wasn't exactly thinking about these nuances, but she knew how she felt about Billie Jean King—the tennis superstar wasn't one of those "angry" women but "a woman making her way in the world." And Park liked that. King, for her part, knew she had a rare platform as a popular athlete, and she intended to use it to reach as many people as she could. "If someone is too uncomfortable, they usually don't hear you at all," she says. "I never wanted to lose my audience—ever."

The Battle of the Sexes drew one hell of an audience. King and Riggs (mostly Riggs) hammed it up when they arrived for the match, held at the Houston Astrodome, leaning into the pageantry of it all. Riggs entered the stadium in a rickshaw pulled by a pack of "Bobby's Bosom Buddies" (local Houston hotties who had been chosen for the occasion in a contest that included measuring their bust size) wearing a jacket emblazoned with the logo of his new sponsor: Sugar Daddy lollipops. King arrived via a feather-festooned golden litter carried by a hunky male harem à la Cleopatra. It all made for extremely good TV. (ABC paid $750,000—nearly $5 million in today's dollars—for the broadcast rights.)[2] Park was one of a record ninety million people watching. "I remember my parents and I were invited to this huge watch party at somebody's house," she recalls. "There were TVs in every room playing the match—even in the bathroom—and the men all wore little snouts, you know, because they were male chauvinist pigs."

It was a fantastically entertaining spectacle, but there was an edge to the campy excitement. The idea that a tennis match would decide the future of gender equality was hyperbolic, sure, but it wasn't baseless. Riggs spent the weeks ahead of the match trashing women, saying women belonged "in the bedroom and in the kitchen" and bragging about the fact that his certain victory over King would "set the women's lib movement back about another 20 years." He questioned whether women were constitutionally fit to be athletes and even showed up to a prematch practice (packed with reporters) wearing a T-shirt with holes cut out to expose his nipples, quipping that the style would look much better on Billie Jean.[3] The nation was balancing on a knife edge in the fight for women's economic and social rights—and millions of women and girls were looking to King to push them forward.

For Park, it was the first moment in her life that all the times she'd felt less than because of her gender suddenly fell into context. "It was like, Oh my gosh, I'm not the only one that's treated like this," she says now. "I realized this thing that I thought was a personal problem was actually a much larger problem." She was growing up at a time where women were beginning to loudly challenge a system in which they were second-class citizens, but it wasn't until she saw Billie Jean King taking on the patriarchy that night in 1973 that she realized the sports she loved so much were "a stand-in for a larger fight," she says. Sports, "the last bastion of male power," could do something that no law could, she realized: they could change people's beliefs.

It was a "moment of truth," King says. "I thought about what would happen if I won. I thought about what would happen if I lost. I visualized the realities. I knew this match could change the hearts and minds of people. I knew it was a moment in time that could maybe help women have a better life." She would never have an audience this big again. "This was my one chance," she says. "I had to win."

King prepped for the match like her liberation depended on it, doing two hundred sit-ups and four hundred leg extensions every day and meticulously studying Riggs's game.[4] "He was one of my [tennis] heroes, so I knew a lot about him," she says. Riggs, in all his chauvinist bravado, didn't show King's game the same respect ("So typical," she says) and showed up totally unprepared for what he was about to face. It was a bloodbath: King trounced Riggs in straight sets: 6–4, 6–3, 6–3.

King's overwhelming victory proved that women were not the weaker sex, were not less valuable, and were capable of many things outside "the bedroom and in the kitchen." In winning a tennis match, King had changed hearts and minds. "In just under two hours, she forced a reexamination of what it meant to be female and an athlete," feminist historian Susan Ware wrote. As the *New York Times* would later put it, "In a single tennis match, Billie Jean King was . . . able to do more for the cause of women than most feminists can achieve in a lifetime."[5] In the fifty years since the match, not a single day has gone by that someone hasn't told King about how the Battle of the Sexes impacted their lives, she says.

For Missy, King's victory gave her permission to play to her full potential. Playing tennis, basketball, and running track with boys growing up, there was always one question weighing on her mind, holding her back: *Was it okay to beat them?* "Because they had the power," she explains. "If you beat them, it could be very tricky." Not only had Billie Jean beat the boys in dazzling fashion, but she'd earned national adoration and respect as a result. The way Park—and millions of other women and girls—saw her place in the world began to shift.

~ ~ ~

FOR ALL KING has accomplished to change perceptions of women's value and worth, she likely won't see the final fruits of her labor— equal pay—in her lifetime. Neither will you or I. It will be another 151 years before the global gender pay gap is closed, according to the World Economic Forum (WEF).[6] If nothing changes to accelerate the glacial pace of the gap closing, your children and your grandchildren will *still* be fighting to see women receive equal pay for equal work.

Pay is just one piece of the global gender gap—the complicated web of systemic biases that hold women back simply because they are women. The WEF counts four metrics in its measure of global gender equality—political empowerment, economic participation and opportunity, educational attainment, and health and survival— but pay proves to be a particularly impactful piece of the puzzle. Globally, 2.4 billion women of working age are without equal economic opportunity; there are still ninety-five countries that don't guarantee equal pay for equal work and eighty-six countries where women are restricted from certain jobs, according to the World Bank. "In every type of work in every sector, every occupation and every country, women are paid less than men; every source of pay information, collected by every method, ends in this conclusion," writes economist Linda Scott. It adds up to an economic chasm between men and women—globally, women are valued at just 65 percent of the average man—one that isn't easily solved, even by laws that mandate pay equity.[7]

In many parts of the world, such laws have technically been on the books for decades: Iceland mandated equal pay in 1961, the United States passed its Equal Pay Act in 1963, and by 1980, at least six other countries, from Australia to India, had followed suit.[8] It has been illegal, in other words, to pay a woman less than a man for the same work in much of the world for over half a century. And yet, here we are, still miles away from parity.

The most obvious problem with equal pay laws is that they are nearly impossible to enforce because there's typically no one who is actually responsible for doing so. This places the burden on women to be their own watchdogs and advocates. "Even if you know it's happening, do most women have the time, bandwidth, financial stability, and career stability to file a lawsuit?" asks Megan Rapinoe. "I doubt it." Even for women who do have the resources to identify a pay gap in their salary and hire a lawyer, taking your employer to court can often prove to be a fruitless endeavor. In the UK, for example, "the employer's risk [of penalty] is so minimal that it makes economic sense to pay women lower salaries and bet that nothing will ever come of it," Scott writes. It wasn't until very recently that lawmakers around the world began making an effort to close these gaps with a second round of antidiscrimination laws that mandate pay gap reporting and enforcement: The US Paycheck Fairness Act, passed by the House of Representatives in 2021, would increase penalties for companies in violation of federal equal pay laws and ban employers from retaliating against employees for seeking equal pay. The European Union proposed similar enforcement measures, which would ban companies from asking for a prospective employee's salary history and require those with over 250 employees to publicly report the difference in pay between men and women.[9]

The main reason pay equity laws haven't closed the pay gap—as Billie Jean King knew so acutely as she prepared for the Battle of the Sexes—is that there is a difference between policy change and cultural change. To understand this fully, it helps to understand what causes the pay gap in the first place. It's not as simple as a hiring manager shaving off 17 percent of the approved salary for a given role as soon as a woman walks into a job interview instead of a man (though such explicit bias does play at least some role). The pay gap is a far more slippery thing to measure, driven by a set of nuanced, stubborn, and often interconnected factors economists lump into two creatively named categories: explained and unexplained.

In the first category, we have all the systemic variables that "explain" the fact that women working full-time make cents for every dollar full-time working men make. These include education level, experience, age, hours worked (particularly relevant as women are more likely to work fewer paid hours as they take on the burden of caregiving responsibilities at home), and occupation (relevant because women tend to be clustered in lower paying industries).[10] These are what some economists call "nondiscriminatory" factors—terminology that implies these things rationalize the pay gap (though, as we'll see throughout this book, sexism and misogyny are alive and well here, too). By this reasoning, if a woman steps back at work to have a baby or care for young children, for example, it is perfectly logical that it would impact her earnings. Likewise, if a woman chooses to go into a low-paying industry, it's no mystery why she'll make less than her male classmate who opted to go into a more lucrative job. In other words, if women are making less money, it's because of the choices they have made.

Not even these "explained" factors, however, account for the entirety of the wage gap. The second set of factors contributing to the pay gap is made up of unmeasured variables and labor market discrimination, which typically takes two forms, economists Fatma Abdel-Raouf and Patricia M. Buhler explain in their book

The Gender Pay Gap: wage discrimination (a woman with the same skills in the same job is paid less because of her gender) and occupational segregation (a woman with the same skills is pushed into lower-paying jobs or roles with less responsibility because of her gender).[11]

When economists adjust for the explained factors of the pay gap—hours worked, type of job, etc.—the wage gap, measured in median earnings, narrows. The "adjusted" or "controlled" gender pay gap, as it's sometimes called, was about 1 cent in 2022.[12] If you compare the earnings of men and women *in general*, in other words, women earn around 83 cents to men's dollar, but if you were to compare the median earnings of men and women in the same job, with the same resume, working the same hours, women would earn 99 cents to men's dollar. This is useful for pointing out the fact that there is some portion of the gender pay gap driven by the pure belief that women are simply worth less. But the adjusted gender gap can also be a harmful and misleading way to talk about discrimination. The "explained" variables captured in the unadjusted gap are vitally important, each shaped by discrimination in their own way, and factoring them out makes room for the argument that women are to blame for their own economic subordination.

This complex ecosystem adds up to a whole lot of lost cash for women—$1 million in lifetime earnings for college-educated millennials, according to an analysis from the Institute for Women's Policy Research. (Since the size of the pay gap varies by race, so do the total estimated losses in lifetime earnings, with Latina women losing somewhere in the ballpark of $1.2 million, Black women losing $946,000, and white women missing out on $555,000 in earnings, according to data from the National Women's Law Center.) The pandemic drove up these costs significantly. As women were forced out of the workforce by the millions, a new variable in the gender gap emerged. Time out of the workforce is a particularly pernicious driver of the pay gap; real-time lost earnings are compounded by less tangible losses women face during time off, including training and experience, as well as opportunities for promotion. For the average American woman earning a median wage of $47,000 pre-pandemic, these pandemic-induced losses alone could add up to an eye-popping $600,000 in total lost life-time earnings, according to an analysis by Center for American Progress economist Michael Madowitz published by *Newsweek*. Women making six figures pre-pandemic stand to lose an *additional million* on top of what they were already losing to the pay gap. Collectively, *Newsweek* reported, women in the United States will lose $885 billion.[13]

~ ~ ~

EVERY DAY THAT women get paid less, they are worth less—financially but also culturally. "The pay gap is sending the wrong message to women about who they are, and how they're valued, and what they can or cannot become," NBA player Steph Curry, the highest paid athlete in the league and the father of two daughters, wrote in an essay for the *Players' Tribune*. "I want our girls to grow up knowing that there are no boundaries that can be placed on their futures, period. I want them to grow up in a world where their gender does not feel like a rulebook for what they should think, or be, or do. And I want them to grow up believing that they can dream big, and strive for careers where they'll be treated fairly. And of course: paid equally."[14]

Curry's dream for his daughters acknowledges that the pay gap is about more than what shows up in paychecks. As women continue to be undervalued, they lose something else: time. As women get paid less, they are able to invest and save less, creating a significant wealth gap—11 percent for customer-facing workers, 31 percent for women in technical and professional jobs, and 38 percent for women in senior and leadership positions, according to the WEF. The wealth gap leads to a retirement gap, putting women in the position to either work longer or retire with less—35 percent less when it comes to pensions and 20 percent less in Social Security income. "When we talk about what the pay gap costs us, let's be clear," Abby Wambach, the two-time Olympic gold-medal-winning soccer legend said in her viral 2018 commencement speech at Barnard College. "It costs us our very lives."[15]

After the 2015 women's World Cup, Wambach walked off the field and into retirement with sports god status. She'd cemented her team's legacy as the greatest in the sport and its players as champions in the fight for women's equal pay. When she stood onstage at the 2016 ESPYs to receive the Icon Award alongside Kobe Bryant and Peyton Manning, she'd earned the right to be there. "We had just won the World Cup. We had been received like champions back here in the United States, and I kinda fancied myself. I was like 'Wow, we're really doing it, us women,'" she said at ESPNW's Women in Sports Summit in 2020. But as the lights turned off and the three sports icons turned to walk offstage, reality hit. "Their biggest concerns were where they were going to invest their hundreds of millions of dollars—that they rightfully earned—but my biggest concern was how I was going to find a new job to pay a mortgage. This was the moment I realized I am not immune to the things all women experience."

Wambach was lucky not to have to worry about this until her playing career was over. She made enough money to be able to focus solely on soccer, but that's not the case for many professional women athletes, who—like all women—are more likely to have to supplement their income to stay afloat. In the United States 3.7 million women work multiple jobs to make ends meet, and thanks to the pay gap in sports, a surprising number of professional women athletes are among them.[16] Kendall Coyne Schofield is a three-time Olympic medal–winning professional hockey player—but most people she meets assume that must be more of a hobby than a career. "I am getting tired of standing next to my husband [NFL player Michael Schofield] and no one asks what his [real] job is," says Coyne Schofield. She gets asked all the time. Being a professional athlete is of course a full-time job—Coyne Schofield puts in at least six hours of training a day to stay on top—it just doesn't pay like one. So as degrading as it may feel, most professional women athletes have to find a second stream of income, which can range from coaching or broadcast gigs to working retail. In addition to being the captain of the US Women's National Hockey Team, Coyne Schofield works as a player development coach for the NHL's Chicago Blackhawks.

Jessica McDonald, a member of the 2019 World Cup–winning US Women's National Team squad, has spent most of her career as a professional soccer player hustling in second and third jobs to make ends meet. In her first few years in the National Women's Soccer League (NWSL) she was making about $15,000, she says—far below minimum wage. "I probably could have filed for food stamps, honestly," she says. As a single mom, she did everything she could to provide for her son while continuing to work toward her dream of making the US National Team. Any time she wasn't training, she was coaching, running soccer camps, training kids on the side. One year, she got a full-time job in an Amazon warehouse. She would train in the morning, clock in for an eleven-and-a-half-hour shift—"You're on your feet all day packing boxes, scraping tape off the floor," she says—and then sometimes train again at night. "I was exhausted," McDonald says. "Those were some brutal times."

Stories like McDonald's are common in sports, where the pay gap is several times larger than the one most women face. In golf, for example, the average man PGA golfer makes ten times the average woman LPGA player. In soccer, men MLS players make nine times what women NWSL players make. Women in those sports have it good. In hockey, NHL players make ninety-four times what Premiere Hockey Federation players make. In baseball and softball, the pay gap skyrockets: men in the MLB made 705 times what women in the National Professional Fastpitch League made (before the women's league folded in 2021). And of course you'll recall the ridiculous pay gap in basketball, where legend and five-time Olympic gold medalist Diana Taurasi, who makes the WNBA's supermax salary of $228,094, earns just marginally more at the pinnacle of her epic career than the mascot for her city's NBA franchise, the Phoenix Suns.[17]

The WNBA is a particularly potent example of how we as a society value women. The league (which is half owned by the thirty franchises of the NBA) is one of the most popular and successful women's major league sports: the league boasts household names like Sue Bird and Candace Parker and in recent years has seen a "massive jump" in viewership. Yet the pay gap women in basketball face at every level remains enormous, and the way it manifests often feels like a slap in the face to the extremely talented and hardworking women who make up the league. Take, for example, the story of Miami Heat player Duncan Robinson, who by all accounts started his career as a fairly mediocre basketball player. Robinson had no Division I offers to play college basketball (he played for a Division III school before eventually transferring to Michigan's DI program) and went undrafted by the NBA, playing for the NBA's minor league after graduating. In the underdog story of the century, Robinson worked hard on his game and eventually signed a $90 million five-year contract with the Miami Heat—the largest in history for an undrafted player.[18] That's awesome for Robinson— it's a great story about perseverance that coaches will share with kids for generations. Go Duncan.

But also, what the hell. *So many* WNBA players have better resumes. So many women *did* get DI offers, *did* have standout college careers, *did* turn pro as first-round draft picks. So many women have been exemplary in every moment of their career. And the same industry that funded Robinson's $90 million deal gives them crumbs. In 2022, the NBA's number one draft pick Paolo Banchero signed a four-year $50 million contract for an average annual salary of $12.5 million. The WNBA's best rookie player Rhyne Howard, meanwhile, got a three-year deal with an average yearly salary of $75,000, meaning Banchero will make more playing one-half of a game than Howard will earn in her entire season. That astronomical imbalance persists all the way up to the highest levels of the league, regardless of the skill of the players in question. In 2020, basketball icons Sue Bird and LeBron James both won their fourth championship—but James did it while earning a $38 million salary while Bird only brought home $215,000. Over her epic, nearly two-decade professional career, Bird had reportedly only gotten a 1 percent raise before the WNBA's most recent contract bumped salaries by over 50 percent.[19]

If there is a silver lining in the state of pay in women's sports, it's tennis, where athletes have the opportunity to earn equal prize money—key compensation in a sport that offers no salaries—at all four of the sport's Grand Slam events. This is thanks in large measure to Billie Jean King, who was instrumental in organizing women tennis players in the 1970s to create their own tennis tour, giving them unprecedented leverage and laying the groundwork for equal pay in all sports. In 1973, the US Open became the first major tournament to offer equal prize money to men and women (Wimbledon, the last Grand Slam to close the pay gap, did so in 2007). Pay still isn't entirely equal in tennis—some lower-tier tournaments still offer men bigger prizes—but thanks to this legacy, women tennis players, even those who are relatively unknown, now have the opportunity to earn more in a single Grand Slam than King did over the course of her thirty-one-year professional career. In 2022, Elena Rybakina, ranked seventeen on the tour, took home $2.5 million for her first win at Wimbledon (same as men's champion Novak Djokovic), earning nearly 30 percent more in one tournament than King did over thirty-nine major championships.[20]

Today, it's easy to look at how financially flush women tennis players are—until 2021 when women athletes in diverse sports started to get more global name recognition, almost all of the highest-paid women athletes were tennis players—and forget exactly what it took to get here.[21] Enter women's soccer, with a forceful reminder of just how ugly things can get when women fight for more.

The fight for equality in soccer has been simmering for decades. From the moment the US Women's National Team was created in the 1980s, players were expected to accept a laundry list of insulting inequalities and to do so with a thank-you-I'm-just-so-happy-to-be-here attitude. Their pay was particularly laughable: "When we won the World Cup in 1991, we made $15 a day. That was the per diem, no salaries. No bonuses," said former USWNT player Linda Hamilton when she was inducted into the National Soccer Hall of Fame. Before 2007, there was no prize money for the women's World Cup; today's women do compete for prizes, but the gap remains enormous.[22]

Things incrementally improved over the years, but the women were still playing on a vastly unequal field (literally—synthetic turf at women's games, which can increase the risk of injury compared to real grass fields, has been a point of contention for years). In 2016, the women of the USWNT reached a breaking point. They were underpaid, underresourced, and underwhelmed by the fact that their exploding popularity after their 2015 World Cup win hadn't changed anything. (Sound familiar? History has a way of repeating itself in US soccer.) Frustrated with the lack of progress, five of the most recognizable players in the world—Megan Rapinoe, Alex Morgan, Carli Lloyd, Hope Solo, and Becky Sauerbrunn—decided to make their grievances public, filing a complaint with the Equal Employment Opportunity Commission (EEOC)—a necessary first step in the path to filing a gender discrimination lawsuit.[23]

While the complaint worked its way through government administration, it was time for the players to negotiate a new collective bargaining agreement (CBA)—the contract between a federation and a players' union that dictates the terms of their employment. Despite the growth of the women's game, and the growing cultural conversation on the pay gap, "equal pay just wasn't an option" at that point, says Becca Roux, the executive director for the US Women's National Team Players Association. "[US Soccer] wasn't going to agree to it." The new CBA, ratified in 2017, made incremental gains. "It was not a loss. We closed the gap dramatically," says Roux, including successfully negotiating the right to a share of revenue. But even those piecemeal gains were painful to obtain, the entire process feeling "hurtful" and "personal," says Roux. "Negotiations in 2017 were mean," she recalls. The experience was enlightening. So many women are met with gaslighting and brutality when they fight for equality. "I had this naive, probably privileged, perspective that if you just show them data and be like, 'Look, you're being discriminatory assholes. Let's change.' that maybe they would," Roux says. "You always had to have some sort of hope that there will be some sort of change. You keep fighting and you keep pushing and trying to find the angle."

In the meantime, the gender discrimination complaint filed by some of the players was working its way through the EEOC process, passing through an independent investigation of the players' claims and an attempted mediation between the parties. In 2019, the EEOC told the players they had a "right to sue" their employer.[24] So on March 8, 2019—International Women's Day—that's exactly what they did.

The lawsuit called out various forms of alleged gender discrimination, including unequal working conditions and promotional efforts, but the most glaring issue was pay. A key point of contention was that the men's and women's teams were paid via completely different structures; the men earned money through

game appearance fees and performance bonuses—no salaries—
while many players on the women's team earned guaranteed salaries, prioritizing stability while the professional women's soccer
landscape remained shaky. (The Players Association agreed to this
structure in their 2017 CBA, alleging in their lawsuit that US Soccer refused to offer them the same bonus fees offered to the men
in an alternative structure.) The result, the players of the USWNT
alleged, was that in some cases they were being paid just 38 percent
of what their male counterparts would have made if they were as
successful as the women.[25] (The lawsuit doesn't address the astronomical pay gap in World Cup prize money, a related but separate
issue controlled by FIFA, the global governing body of the sport.*)

While they were playing under a structure they felt limited
their earning potential, the USWNT was actually generating more
revenue for US Soccer than their male counterparts. Reporting by
Rachel Bachman for the *Wall Street Journal* revealed audited financial reports from US Soccer showed the revenue gap—a critical
part of US Soccer's defense in the lawsuit—had all but evaporated.
In 2016, following the USWNT's World Cup win, the women's
team had generated $1.9 million more for their employer. In the
three-year post–World Cup period from 2016 to 2018, the women's
team generated a total of $50.8 million for US Soccer to the men's
$49.9 million.[26]

We know what happened next: the women of the USWNT won
their fourth World Cup in 2019 in such glorious fashion that they
became their own global movement for women's equality. Their

---

* The pay gap in prize money, which is set by FIFA—the global governing body
of the sport—is immense. And growing. In 2014, the winners of the men's World
Cup took home a cool $35 million—more than double the entire prize pool for the
women's World Cup a year later. After the world cried "bullshit," FIFA doubled the
total prize pool for the 2019 women's championship, adding $15 million in funds (for
a total of $30 million)—only after they upped the 2018 men's prize pool by $42 million, widening the gap. For the 2022/2023 World Cup cycle, men will compete for a
total prize pool of $440 million while the women compete for a meager $60 million.

employer publicly toasted their victory and then promptly turned around and hired not one but two lobbying firms to convince lawmakers in Washington that the women's claims of unequal pay were inaccurate, refusing to move forward with an equal pay structure at the negotiating table.[27] "It was just a gut punch," says Roux.

In 2020, it got worse. Federal judge R. Gary Klausner dismissed the team's claims of unequal pay on the grounds that the women had earned more total compensation than the men (by being more successful and thus earning more prize money) and that, more importantly, the women had agreed to this pay structure. "The [Women's National Team] was willing to forgo higher bonuses for other benefits, such as greater base compensation and the guarantee of a higher number of contracted players," Klausner wrote in his decision. "Accordingly, Plaintiffs cannot now retroactively deem their CBA worse than the MNT CBA by reference to what they would have made had they been paid under the MNT's pay-to-play structure when they themselves rejected such a structure."[28]

By dismissing their suit, Klausner had essentially said that "pay is equal if a woman can obtain the same amount of money as a man by working more and performing better. . . . The women had to be the best in the world to make about the same amount per game as the much less successful men," according to a subsequently filed appeal. The sexism of blaming the women for their own economic suffering was so blatant even the US Men's National Team, who have been supportive of the women's fight for equal pay, spoke up. In the appeal, USMNT players argued that the women had been "pressured" to accept the unequal pay structure, adding that they had been "stunned" that US Soccer hadn't granted the women equal pay when they negotiated their 2017 collective bargaining agreement. "The women deserved better from the Federation," lawyers for the men's team wrote. "And a lot more money."[29]

~ ~ ~

THIS IS TYPICALLY the part where some dude chimes in with all the reasons why women in sports don't deserve equal pay: *they couldn't last two seconds in a competition against men, no one wants to watch them play anyway, they generate less revenue.* For these men, fighting for equal pay, opportunity, and respect isn't just illogical, it's an idiotic thing to suggest. As one of the many men who take the time to write to me with their misogynistic musings recently put it, "It is only possible to reach the plane your [sic] on through institutionally induced brain damage." (Thanks for your input, Tim.)

We'll address the flawed thinking and simple-minded misogyny behind the first two arguments—biological inferiority and weak viewership numbers—in detail throughout this book, but it's important to understand the revenue argument up front. Of all the reasons opponents use to justify the pay gap, this one probably seems the least objectionable. It's easy to dismiss guys like Tim, who make blatantly sexist pronouncements about the capability of women, but harder to brush off those who argue that most men's sports generate more revenue for sponsors, leagues, and teams, and, therefore, their players deserve to make more money. It's not sexist—it's just business, right?

Not so fast. "The revenue differences all go back to sexism," says David Berri, a sports economist who specializes in gender issues in sports. As we'll see throughout this book, women's sports are shortchanged in almost every way possible—women athletes receive fewer opportunities to play, fewer resources to play with, and fewer chances to reach potential fans through media coverage. "When you're talking about equal pay in women's sports, the rebuttal is always, 'But the revenue!' And my response is always, 'But the investments!'" says Roux.

The most fundamental flaw in the men-generate-more-money-so-they-should-make-more-money argument is that men's sports have had decades to develop, grow fan bases, and build up multimillion-dollar revenue streams, while women's sports are just getting started. "We're in our infancy. Men's sports have gone through all these growing pains that women's sports have not been allowed to," says Billie Jean King. From a sports economics standpoint, you just "can't make the comparison" between a league that's twenty-seven years old (like the WNBA) and a league that's seventy-seven years old (like the NBA), says Berri. It takes patience, time, investment for a league to get off the ground. "Let's put it this way," he says. "If you go back in time to when professional football started it was the middle of the Great Depression—investing in a football franchise was a very bad way to spend your money." In the early days, the NFL seemed doomed—the majority of new teams failed within a few years, and the league certainly wasn't making any money, Berri says. Had investors pulled the plug or blamed the players for the league's lack of early financial success, "a league—an industry—that is now worth $11 billion in annual revenue doesn't exist," says Berri. The NBA has a similar story. "Initially, the NBA was this little rinky-dink league on the East Coast of the United States that didn't have any fans—they were putting games after high school games because they figured someone would show up for the high school game [and then stay]," Berri says. "You have all these men saying, 'Well, we earned it.' But they are winning a race that they were given a giant head start with."

~ ~ ~

CONSIDERING THE AMOUNT of attention given to equal pay in recent years, it seems like the pay gap should be on its way toward extinction. There are more women than ever leading Fortune 500 companies, and athletes like Naomi Osaka are setting all-time earnings records in women's sports. A 2022 report from the Pew Research Center even suggested that millennial women had vanquished the pay gap in their demographic. Their analysis of US cities found that in twenty-two metropolitan areas women under thirty made just as much if not more than their male colleagues.[30]

But while there is much to be hopeful about, progress in closing the pay gap has been achingly slow—since the Equal Pay Act was passed in the United States in 1963, the gender wage gap has narrowed by less than half a cent per year, according to the National Committee on Pay Equity. And while some groups are making notable gains, we're a long way from meaningful systemic change. The flipped gender gap identified in the Pew report, for example, likely won't last for many of the under-thirty women who currently benefit. It's well documented that the pay gap widens as women age, thanks largely to a motherhood penalty that limits women's wage growth—whether they choose to have kids or not.[31]

By allowing the pay gap to persist, we collectively lose a lot.

The gender pay gap costs the global economy $160 trillion in lost wealth every single year, according to the World Bank. That's twice the global GDP.* One hundred sixty *trillion* dollars left on the table because markets refuse to pay women equally even when it's in their own economic interest to do so. The US alone could add $4.3 trillion to the country's economy by 2025 if it supported women attaining full gender equality.[32]

Securing the economic rights of women in minority groups has the power to be even more impactful for the global economy. In 2020, economist Dana Peterson, moved to action by the murder of George Floyd, combed through decades of data to quantify the cost of racism. She found that closing racial gaps over twenty years would have added $16 trillion to the US economy. "It is the sum total of what Black Americans might have spent on

---

* For econ novices, GDP, or gross domestic product, is the total amount that households, businesses, governments, and individuals spend in a given economy. Think of it as a measure of an economy's overall health. Inequality is hugely impactful for GDP—when any given group experiences income and wealth discrimination, it lowers their spending power and, therefore, brings down the overall GDP.

goods, services, and housing, as well as what Black-owned business might have earned in profits if racial barriers to housing,
education, equal pay, lending, and access to credit were not present," Peterson explains. That's nearly the size of China's entire
2021 GDP.[33] "The metric that most people in the world of finance
understand is GDP growth . . . so putting dollars and cents to
social endemic problems is one way to speak to this group who
hold the keys to the kingdom in terms of access to money, investments, savings and wealth," Peterson says. "People can usually
grasp money left on the table."

Black women's labor is a particularly important part of the
unaccounted-for value being left on the table. "I have a theory that
if someone were to try and account for the exact amount of labor Black women have forcefully and freely contributed to the U.S.
economy and culture, if America had to match us cent for sweat
drop, it would be a number so great it would bankrupt all of this
country's resources," poet and author Camonghne Felix wrote in
her powerful 2021 profile of Simone Biles for *New York Magazine*.
According to the work of economist Nina Banks, former president
of the National Economic Association, she's not wrong. Banks has
devoted much of her work to highlighting the unpaid and unrec-
ognized labor of Black women—specifically, the community work
and activism that Black women uniquely face when government
and public policies fail to support racialized populations. Banks
argues that economists should be accounting for Black women's
collective community labor—everything from publicizing issues
facing minority communities, to organizing neighborhood pa-
trols, to lobbying elected officials—the same way feminist economists have begun to quantify the unpaid labor women perform in
the home. "If these *community* activities were channeled through
the market—if other people were paid to do them—they would
be counted as 'work' and their value included as part of national
income accounting," Banks argues.[34]

As Peterson puts it, "this has been a problem for a long time and we're wasting money and missing out on growth that could benefit all people by allowing these gaps to persist."

～～～

IN A CAPITALIST system where money equals value, women getting paid is a revolutionary act in itself. "I think women should get all the money that they possibly can get, every single bag," says Rapinoe. But closing the pay gap would also have profound effects beyond getting more cash into women's pockets. "If the global community chose to dissolve the economic obstacles facing women," writes economist Linda Scott, "an unprecedented era of peace and prosperity would follow."

More than an individualistic pursuit of women's wealth, paying women lifts communities. "In many cultures, women are the predominant breadwinners of their families, so access to capital is not just access to capital for them, but also for their children and for their households," says Sarah Marchal Murray, chief strategic partnerships officer at Kiva, a microfinance nonprofit that connects women around the globe as lenders and borrowers. "When you think about economic development goals and the ways in which we talk as a society about wanting to evolve, it all comes back to starting with the woman at the center of communities." Women are in fact more likely to invest their earnings in their communities, according to the Organisation for Economic Co-operation and Development.[35]

So, why not just pay women equally? If the gender wage gap is costing the global economy trillions of dollars each year, and closing it would benefit us all, why don't we just agree to pay women?

In a word: power. Keeping women and other marginalized genders down is priceless for the group in power. "When women's sports has been kiboshed, it was because somebody felt threatened," says Roux. She points to the infancy of women's soccer, which was actually *banned* in England for decades because the sport became too successful in the early 1900s. As women stepped into roles traditionally held by men during World War I, women factory workers began playing soccer against their male colleagues during breaks, according to soccer historian Gemma Clarke. One group, the Ladies of the Dick, Kerr munitions factory, began gaining notoriety, attracting crowds of thousands to their games and raising money for wounded soldiers. The Football Association was not happy about this. The women were becoming "too powerful, too political, and worst of all, too popular," Clarke wrote, so the FA began waging a campaign to push women out of the sport, even hiring medical experts to "make detailed public statements declaring that soccer did terrible things to women's bodies, that women were not biologically designed to play soccer . . . and that it was inherently dangerous." When that didn't work, they prohibited women from playing in professional stadiums—a ban that stood until 1971.[36]

Rapinoe was right when she said gender equality needs to be pried from the "death grip" of those in power—a feat the USWNT finally accomplished in 2022, six years after filing their gender discrimination complaint with the EEOC. Through all the obstacles—the lobbyists, the failed negotiations, the public claims that they didn't deserve more—the players never wavered from their commitment to equality. In February 2022, they got it, reaching a $24 million settlement with US Soccer in their lawsuit and signing a new CBA with the Federation that guarantees the players equal pay with the men's team through 2028. The deal creates a new compensation model for both the men's and women's teams, featuring an equal revenue-sharing structure, and pooling all future prize money won by either team to be split evenly, cutting the women into the huge prize pool enjoyed by all teams who qualify for the men's World Cup.[37]

The settlement was a victory for the team, but it's not the everything-is-peachy win for women that headlines made it out to be, says Rapinoe. "Ultimately we had to file a lawsuit for gender discrimination against our employer, which is a national governing body—that's terrible," she says. The USWNT may have finally gotten paid, but did the culture of the sport really shift? Did hearts and minds really change? The very public resistance to paying the women equally, the attempts to undermine them in the media (and in Congress)—"those things don't just go away because we had a civil rights uprising and reached a settlement," Rapinoe says. She's left wondering if things will really be different, if her employer really believes she's equal. "When the top brass is around the men's game, their fricking hair is falling out [in excitement]. They're having the time of their life," she says. "That's what I see as equality. It's not just in the numbers. It's not just in how much we're paid. It's in the attitude and the way both teams are taken care of on and off the field."

Like Billie Jean King, the women of the USWNT know their fight is bigger than them. They're after culture change—not paychecks. And on that front, "I mean, literally all of the work needs to be done. That's how I look at it," says Rapinoe. "I feel like this is the beginning."

CHAPTER 2

PUT YOUR MONEY WHERE YOUR MOUTH IS

I F PAYCHECKS AND PRIZE MONEY WERE THE ONLY SYMPTOMS of financial inequality for women, this would be a much shorter book. But in many ways, the pay gap is just the most visible sign of a more systemic issue of underinvestment—a multipronged beast of a problem that keeps women down while often remaining obscure enough not to raise any red flags. While the investment gap can certainly be tangible (think the abysmal fraction of venture capital dollars that go to women founders) it's often more abstract, showing up in a mentorship gap for women across industries or a lack of opportunities for women to even get in the game in the first place. This is what makes it so dangerous—you don't see the startups that never get funded, and until the pandemic, nobody really paid much attention to the millions of women making ends meet through a patchwork of jobs or quietly disappearing from the workforce. Sports is a venue where sponsorship investments are often public and the differences in resources are as obvious as the stadiums women play in and the uniforms on their backs—and it offers those trying to shortchange women fewer places to hide.

In March 2021 Stanford sports performance coach Ali Kershner made that explicitly clear when she Instagrammed a photo of a lone weight rack, its contents capping out at thirty pounds, standing pathetically next to a pile of limp yoga mats.[1] It looked like the kind of home gym you might have assembled during the pandemic in an effort to maintain some paltry level of fitness. But this was not a photo of a panic-purchased amateur home gym. This was a photo of a weight room, if you can even call it that, in the closed campus bubble site for the National Collegiate Athletic Association (NCAA) Division I Basketball Championships. You might know it as March Madness.

March Madness is a big deal in the world of sports. The tournament generates hundreds of millions in revenue for the NCAA. They could afford, in other words, to splash out on a state-of-the-art weight room (even during a pandemic). And they did—for the men.

Kershner's photo was of the weight room in the *women's* tournament bubble in San Antonio, Texas. For these athletes, the NCAA had provided a training facility that looked like it could have been assembled for about $400 on Amazon while absolutely balling out on the men's competition facility in Indianapolis, Indiana. The boys' weight room sprawled across the expanse of a hotel ballroom, boasting state-of-the-art weight racks as far as the eye could see. The side-by-side optics for the NCAA were brutal, and initially, the organization tried to blame the disparity on "limited space" at the site of the women's tournament bubble. That excuse quickly fell apart thanks to Sedona Prince, a forward for the Oregon Ducks, who shared a video of an unused space the size of a football field located just a few steps away from the women's practice court. It afforded more than enough room for a decent training facility. "If you aren't upset about this problem, then you're a part of it," she said in a viral TikTok that quickly turned the investment gap in sports into headline news.[2]

What the NCAA thought of its women athletes has been made crystal clear. An apology tour followed—Dan Gavitt, the man responsible for overseeing both the men's and women's tournaments, expressed his regrets at "dropping the ball"—but the damage to the NCAA's reputation was done. And now, with the eyes of social media focused on the tournament, it quickly became obvious that NCAA organizers had fallen short on more than just the weight room for the women's tournament: there were concerning reports of subpar pandemic safety protocols, lousy food, and in the pettiest slight of all, even lame swag bags. Both the men and the women got puzzles to help pass the time while they were in quarantine for the duration of the tournament, but while the men reportedly received 500-piece puzzles, the women were given simpler 150-piece puzzles. Seriously. It's hard to believe the food, the quality of the COVID tests, or the intelligence-insulting puzzles were an innocent coincidence in the context of an even more disturbing gender discrepancy pointed out by journalist Brenna Greene: with both tournaments well under way, the NCAA had shared over a thousand photos from the men's games to its media hub but hadn't gotten around to uploading any images from the women's competition even after several teams had played.[3] With no photos, how were media supposed to cover the women's game?

Moments like these that make women feel small, that suffocate their potential to excel, usually don't get so much attention. (Even when they do, they rarely go quite so viral.) What weight-gate showed with stunning clarity was just how much of an afterthought women in sports are—even to the very organizations that are supposed to be promoting them, investing in them, and ultimately benefiting from growing their revenue-generating capabilities.

The entire embarrassing debacle put a spotlight on the investment gap in sports and opened a discussion on how deeply systemic it is across industries. What was perhaps most unsettling about the NCAA's actions was that there was no obvious fall guy, no cartoonish misogynist cackling late at night over his plans to make women's basketball players weak while packing up all the good puzzles to send to the men's bubble. The sexism of this moment was institutional, made possible by dozens of seemingly innocuous planning decisions, and that made it even more dangerous. "With the obvious disparity between the women's and men's tournaments," Stanford women's basketball head coach Tara VanDerveer said in a statement, "the message that is being sent to our female athletes, and women across the world is that you are not valued at the same level as your male counterparts."[4]

This is the part where men like Tim typically chime in with something about how the men's college basketball championship generates more money for the NCAA so they deserve to have better stuff. The point about revenue is true: the 2019 men's tourney reportedly brought in over $917 million in income while the women's competition generated just $15 million in total income.[5] But the Tims of the world often fail to finish the thought. The outputs for men's basketball are naturally greater because the inputs are greater: the NCAA pours vastly more resources into men's basketball, which already had a decades-long head start. That's how investment works: put resources in to get money out. And to illustrate that point, there's no better metaphor than the weight room. Imagine that you took two equally capable weight lifters and gave them each a month to train for a deadlift competition. To one, you grant access to a state-of-the-art gym, a nutritionist, a physical therapist, and an endless supply of protein shakes. At the same time, you throw the other lifter in a gym with a couple of thirties, a grilled cheese sandwich, and an offhanded "good luck." Who do you think is going to have a stronger performance?

In the wake of the outrage surrounding the weight room, the NCAA hired an outside law firm to conduct a review of gender discrimination in the organization's basketball operation. It turns out, the weight rack seen 'round the world was merely the tip of a multimillion-dollar iceberg. The NCAA was not only operating a system in which "broadcast agreements, corporate sponsorship contracts, distribution of revenue, organizational structure, and culture all prioritize Division I men's basketball over everything else in ways that create, normalize, and perpetuate gender inequities," according to the report, but also poisoning the water of women's sports. The NCAA's actions directly limited the growth of women's basketball, according to the report, and perpetuated "a mistaken narrative that women's basketball is destined to be a 'money loser' year after year."[6]

The truth, the report found, is that the potential for college women's basketball is huge. The legal review included the analysis of an independent media expert who assessed the value of the women's tournament based on broadcast rights alone. He found that with the growing fandom surrounding women's basketball, the annual broadcast rights would be worth between $81 and $112 million by 2025, which is several times more than what ESPN currently pays for them (as part of a deal that also includes the rights to twenty-eight other NCAA championships). The "expert analysis shows that pursuing gender equity is not only the right thing to do, but also has real and significant long-term financial value—and therefore strategic importance—to the NCAA overall," the report concluded.

If there was any remaining doubt that the NCAA had treated women's basketball as a second-class product, a damning report from the *Wall Street Journal* erased it when reporters Rachel Bachman, Louise Radnofsky, and Laine Higgins found there was at least one major investment the NCAA could have made in women's basketball for little or no cost and yet repeatedly declined to do so. In addition to being denied the right to equal training facilities, food, and, yes, even puzzles, the women's Division I basketball players were denied the right to play under the official March Madness moniker. This is more than a matter of semantics. The extremely recognizable "March Madness" branding was used to market the men's college basketball tournament into the billion-dollar behemoth it is today, and, according to the *Wall Street Journal*, the legitimacy and recognizability the label confers were deliberately withheld from the women's tournament. There's "no question" the value of the women's championship would increase "dramatically" if the March Madness branding were extended, an expert in brand creation and protection told the *Wall Street Journal*.[7]

In other words, the NCAA doesn't even need to invest additional money in the women's game to see the cash start flowing—they just need to get the hell out of the way.

~ ~ ~

THE FIASCO OF the 2021 NCAA Division I Men's and Women's Basketball Championships unfolded nearly fifty years after a watershed victory for women in college sports: the passage of Title IX, the civil rights law that prohibits gender discrimination in federally funded programs and is best known for the revolution it sparked in women's sports.

Passed in 1972 as part of the Education Amendments Act, Title IX holds that "no person in the United States shall, on the basis of sex, be excluded from participation in, be denied the benefits of, or be subjected to discrimination under any education program or activity receiving Federal financial assistance." (That includes all public schools and universities and any private school where students are eligible for federal student loans.)

It began, as it so often does, with a misogynistic remark and a fed-up woman. In the case of Title IX, that woman was Bernice Sandler, a part-time lecturer at the University of Maryland who was denied a tenure-track position on the grounds that she came on "too strong for a woman." In true strong-woman fashion, she did something about her situation, filing a complaint against her university and eventually teaming up with Congresswoman Edith Starrett Green—leader of the fight to pass the Equal Pay Act of 1963—to write what would become a landmark law for all women in the United States. The budding legislation found many champions in Congress, including Rep. Shirley Chisholm, the first Black woman elected to Congress, and Rep. Patsy Takemoto Mink, the first woman of color elected to Congress, who fought for the law as a pillar of feminist progress, seeing it through to passage. (Mink's advocacy for Title IX was such a central pillar of her work as a lawmaker that the law was renamed in her honor after her death in 2002.)[8]

Brief but mighty in scope, Title IX guarantees women the most basic kind of investment: the opportunity to show up and compete on a level playing field. Covering all school operations, the law opened academic and extracurricular doors for women en masse. Law schools, medical schools, broader entrance to higher education—all of these things became accessible to large numbers of women for the first time. "One of the most significant impacts was the creation of generations of women who have benefited from access to opportunities in various parts of the society that had been very difficult for them to access before," says Ellen J. Staurowsky, a professor of sports media at Ithaca College in New York.

Sports may not have been the original focus of the law, but because nearly all of the high schools and colleges that Title IX applied to had sports teams, this is where the law's implications quickly became the most visible. Title IX guarantees women not only the opportunity to play but equal resources from locker rooms to promotion (at least in theory).[9] Altogether, Title IX's protections meant girls' and women's sports suddenly had a federally protected right to thrive. Billie Jean King saw it coming from the start: "Women would absolutely bust through the doors," she says of the sports revolution that followed Title IX's passage. "My generation had

gotten the door ajar, but the next generation was going to completely smash it down."

Before Title IX, the participation rate of boys to girls competing
in high school sports was twelve to one. This was certainly not
for lack of talented girls with the desire to play but due to the lack
of opportunities. (Many schools had few, if any, women's teams.)
And just 2 percent of all funding for college athletic budgets went
to women's sports programs the year before Title IX was passed.[10]
Title IX proved that if you build it, girls will come, triggering
the Cambrian explosion of women's sports. Once the legislation
passed in 1972, the participation rate of girls in high school sports
more than tripled, and by 1975 (the year Title IX's rule officially
started being enforced), the gender gap in sports participation had
narrowed to two to one, handily doing away with the bogus idea
that girls, with their delicate constitutions, either wouldn't want
to or shouldn't be allowed to play sports. Today there are over
eleven times more high school sports participation opportunities
for girls than there were in the seventies, and women's collegiate
sports have grown sevenfold—girls went from being just a fraction
of school athletes (7 percent in high school and 15 percent in college) in 1972 to nearly half of all high school and collegiate athletes
today.[11] Thanks to Title IX, girls playing on their school's varsity
soccer team not only have fields to play on but college scholarships
to look forward to and generations of role models to look up to,
changing the trajectory for generations of girls and women.

The access to sports that Title IX afforded also seeded a bigger
revolution for women and girls. For the first time, women had
widespread access to spaces where they were free to explore their
own physical power and develop a sense of bodily autonomy—
particularly relevant in a political environment where a woman's
right to make private decisions about her own body was being
very publicly decided by the Supreme Court (an environment that,
sadly, persists). "At a societal and cultural level, women were ex-

periencing what it's like to have fair treatment, access to power, to money, and to the opportunity to exert their voice," says Staurowsky. The ripple effects were epic. Title IX began an era in which women's power and the liberation of women's bodies were becoming visibly and publicly linked. And girls are still reaping the benefits of that investment five decades later. Girls like Molly Dreher, a Division I runner in California, whose ability to play sports in school taught her early that traditionally "masculine" spaces were for her too. "It's important for women to be competitive, to be fully invested in sports, so that they know that they don't have to be on the sideline," they say. "[Sports are] a chance for women to understand that they can do anything they put their minds to via something tangible."

For girls from highly stereotyped and further marginalized communities, sports are even more revolutionary, providing opportunity for self-knowledge and greater inclusion in spaces that break down stigma through teamwork and community building. As Delia Douglas, director of the Office of Anti-Racism at the University of Manitoba, a sociologist who studies the intersection of race, gender, and sport and was a basketball player in college, puts it,

> Sport is an opportunity to demonstrate your intellectual acumen, physical competence, your excellence, and your freedom. It expands horizons. It's a space for you to grow, to connect, to live, to seek and possibly secure a full expression of yourself in an area that you enjoy, that you excel at. In sports, you seek to see what your limits are and what your achievements can potentially be. The knowledge that comes with that in terms of your strength, your courage, your vulnerability, your resilience, your determination, your resolve, carries you through the rest of your journey. That and the connection and the potential solidarity that we get in sport are absolutely tied to a more just, equitable world, both in the realm of sport and beyond.

Beyond the individual implications, activists who fought so hard for the passage of Title IX knew from the beginning that such a clear and public investment in women's sports would ultimately make the fight for gender equality in the United States extremely tangible, turning the radical ideas of the women's lib movement into something as simple as who got better equipment in gym class. "There is nothing abstract about men getting twenty new basketballs while women get the hand-me-downs, or female athletes piling into their coach's station wagon while men travel by chartered bus or plane," historian Susan Ware writes.[12] Title IX put the gender investment gap front and center in a way that was impossible to ignore—much like the NCAA's actions would nearly half a century later.

Like every legislative action that has ever sought to improve the position of a marginalized group, Title IX has attracted fierce opposition. In 1974, two years after Title IX passed but one year before federally funded programs were expected to comply, the NCAA launched a "tremendous lobbying campaign" against Title IX, worried about the existential threat to the (male) college sports status quo.* As *Sports Illustrated* put it, the fear was that the "extreme" proposal for equality could "emasculate college sport."[13]

In a way it did. Title IX ended a system in which nearly 100 percent of the resources and investment went to men. And once girls had the opportunity to play, they dominated. The first generation of girls to grow up entirely under Title IX's protections—its cohort included all-time greats like Mia Hamm, Jackie Joyner-Kersee, and

---

* The NCAA, for the record, was partially successful in its lobbying campaign against Title IX, which it took all the way to the Supreme Court; at the time, the Court ruled in the NCAA's favor on the grounds that the dues the organization received from member schools exempted it from Title IX's reach, but crucially left the door open for the law to apply on other grounds—like the organization's control over schools' federally funded athletic programs. After weight-gate, a coalition of senators introduced a resolution stating the NCAA is indeed subject to Title IX's rule and needed to shape up.

Lisa Leslie—went on to monopolize the 1996 Olympics so spectacularly it was dubbed the "summer of women,"[14] minting a new generation of role models and marking the beginning of a new era in the fight for equality.

~ ~ ~

THE PASSAGE OF Title IX empowered millions of women and girls in the United States and influenced generations of athletes around the world, but it didn't magically erase sexism and discrimination in sports, just as the Equal Pay Act of 1963, which made gender-based pay discrimination illegal in the US, hasn't exactly solved the pay gap.

There are still "dramatic shortfalls" in Title IX compliance, Staurowsky says. In a comprehensive report commemorating the fiftieth anniversary of Title IX in 2022 for the Women's Sports Foundation (WSF), Staurowsky and a team of researchers analyzed sports participation opportunities at the high school and college levels and found, on average, girls today receive just 42 percent of all athletic participation opportunities despite accounting for 48.5 percent of enrolled students. That might seem like a fairly small six-point gap, but it represents 1.1 million varsity sports positions. That's 1.1 million girls across the country who, because of persistent gaps in investment, don't have the chance to play, to see themselves as equals, to seek and secure a full expression of themselves. In total, the 3.4 million available spots on girls' teams in the 2018–2019 academic year (the latest for which data were available) in high schools across the US were still fewer than the number of opportunities available to boys before Title IX was passed (3.6 million in the 1971–1972 academic year). Using data from the National Center for Education Statistics and the Civil Rights Data Collection, the WSF found forty-three states fell short on offering proportional athletic opportunities to girls in schools. For girls with disabilities, access to sport is even more challenging. Boys with disabilities "consistently" participate in adaptive sports at higher rates than girls, according to findings from the US Government Accountability Office, and less than half of all student athletes playing adaptive sports at the high school level are girls.[15]

In college, a similar gap persists; women comprise nearly 60 percent of enrolled college students yet have fewer than 44 percent of the sports participation opportunities. Across NCAA-affiliated schools and the smaller athletic programs affiliated with the National Association of Intercollegiate Athletics and junior colleges, women athletes had "more than 80,000 fewer opportunities to play and compete than if their athletic programs had offered them opportunities proportional to their enrollment," the WSF found.[16]

For further marginalized girls, opportunities to play are fewer. As a single-axis law, Title IX addresses discrimination through the single lens of gender, meaning its benefits aren't exactly evenly distributed. The experiences of women of color, athletes with disabilities, and transgender women and girls who face multiple frameworks of oppression are often left out of the narrative and off the playing field. The overwhelming majority of college women athletes are white—in the NCAA, Black women represent just 11 percent of all women athletes in the conference, Hispanic women comprise 6 percent, women identifying as biracial represent 5 percent, Asian women are 2 percent, and Indigenous women are registered at just 0.05 percent. That aligns with the relatively fewer number of opportunities for girls of color to play sports in high school. In "heavily minority" schools, girls have fewer opportunities to play—just 67 percent of athletic participation spots offered to boys—while in the "heavily white" schools across town, the gender gap is much narrower; there, girls have 82 percent of the sports opportunities boys have, according to a report by the National Women's Law Center and the Poverty and Race Research Action Council.[17] It makes the ongoing work of organizations like Athlete Ally and the Black Women in Sport Foundation (BWSF), which advocate for an even playing field for minorities in sports, even more vital. "I didn't think that we would need the foundation at this point," says Tina Sloan Green, who cofounded the BWSF in 1992 to create more opportunities for Black women and girls in sport. "Now, I know we need it more than ever."

For transgender women athletes, opportunities to play are almost nonexistent. And in a cruel twist, the law meant to prevent discrimination against girls in sports is being used as a weapon against trans girls, thanks to conservative politicians and antitrans activists who argue that Title IX should be used to "protect" school sports for cisgender students (a deeply flawed argument that we'll address in depth in Chapter 5).

It doesn't stop with fewer opportunities. The women and girls who do get the opportunity to play do so under the restrictions of a smaller budget. Paradoxically, after the passage of Title IX, men's sports budgets increased dramatically. In 1978, the average athletic budget for women's sports was $276,000—which was less than half of the *increase* made in the average athletic budgets for men's sports.[18] Those years set a clear tone for the future of investment in women's sports: women would only be allowed to rise insofar as they didn't dip into resources for men.

This attitude has continued to prove true across time, sports, and geographies. It shows up in donations to athletic programs—one report found that for every $1 women's basketball programs in the Southeastern Conference receive, men's basketball receives $6.02 (and football programs receive a whopping $67.03). It shows up in resources spent on recruitment—just 30 percent of the over $241 million dropped on recruiting athletic talent at the college level was spent on recruiting women. And it shows up in scholarships. According to a WSF analysis, men athletes received a mind-bending $252 million more in athletic scholarships than their women counterparts. That's in absolute dollars—were

women athletes to benefit from athletic scholarship funds proportional to their enrollment in college (where women now outnum-
ber men in the US), schools would have to award an additional
$750 million in athletic scholarships for women.[19] That's $750 million of educational opportunities for women lost in the cavernous
investment gap.

~ ~ ~

THREE MONTHS AFTER the NCAA was held accountable for the
discrepancies between the men's and women's basketball facilities, the *New York Times* reported on the second-class treatment of
women in the NCAA college softball and baseball championships:
"One sport's players get showers, off days, massages and a festive
dinner, while the others get doubleheaders and sweaty bus rides
back to a hotel." One guess as to which is which. This treatment
would be inexcusable even if no one tuned in to watch the women
play, but the truly twisted thing is that the women's softball tournament handily surpassed the viewership numbers of their male
counterparts. The women drew an average of 1.2 million viewers
for every game in the 2021 Women's College World Series—59
percent more viewers than the Men's College World Series pulled
in—and still endured the humiliation of riding back to their hotel
in sweaty game gear. Things don't get much better in women's pro
sports. Crappy playing conditions have been a major sticking point
for years in negotiations between US Soccer and the USWNT; in
addition to being paid unequally, the women spent years training
on artificial turf fields, which are recognized as being worse for
playing and increasing risk of injury, and endured punishing travel
conditions (like flying back from the 2011 World Cup in Germany
in economy middle seats as Megan Rapinoe did).[20]

The lack of investment is a demeaning way to let women know
where they rank. "All of those micro examples add up to this over-
arching sense of not feeling heard, not feeling seen and ultimately,

affecting what you believe you can accomplish in the world," says Stef Strack, a former Nike executive and founder of VOICEINSPORT, a mentorship and advocacy organization aimed at increasing girls' power through sport. Molly Dreher, the cross-country runner, also played soccer in high school, and remembers watching the boys' soccer team at her school get new jerseys every year while her team was stuck with the same scuffed kits. "[The school] invested in what they wanted to parade. They rallied the school to go see the games for the boys' team and it was the boys' team that got flashy new jerseys and new gear," they say. The same issues exist at the professional level. Pro women's sports have a history of asking players to wear sized-down men's uniforms. Or in the case of the very first US Women's National Team, to literally wear men's hand-me-downs. The night before heading to their inaugural tournament in 1985, the team was reportedly up late cutting and sewing men's cast-off kits to make them fit. It wasn't until 2019 that Nike finally designed World Cup uniforms specifically for women, rather than just resizing jerseys designed for men. (That meant professional women's soccer players finally got a jersey with enough give in the neckline to easily slide on over a ponytail.)[21]

Playing with old equipment on a high school team seems like a small thing, but when you're the one in the worn-out jersey it hits different. Dreher was encountering the investment gap for the first time and quickly understood where it led—if the boys' team drew bigger crowds at their games, it was not because they were inherently better but because that's where her school was funneling its resources, from jerseys to promotion. Without a lot of resources coming from the school, Molly and her teammates tried to raise money for the team on their own, lobbying the community for donations and going door to door selling local coupon books for $20 a pop. They were good fundraisers—her sophomore year, the girls raised over $10,000 for the team, she recalls. "And then suddenly, some of it disappeared," she says. "The boys' head coach demanded that they get 'equal pay' from our money that we raised on our own. That was the biggest wake-up call for me."

Fewer opportunities to play, pitiable promotional efforts, inferior playing conditions—"When you add all that up, it's like I'm not surprised that pro leagues are struggling," says David Berri, the sports economist. Men in sports have been reaping the advantages of investment for decades, while women's sports have been set up to fail and then criticized for not turning their scraps into a multibillion-dollar business overnight. "When spreadsheets are pulled out the conversation is 'You guys don't bring in money. You guys aren't successful. You should be grateful that you have a place to play,'" says Kendall Coyne Schofield, captain of the US Women's National Hockey Team and three-time Olympic medalist. To grow a team, or a league, or a company, you have to put resources in. You have to invest. That's how it has (mostly) worked when it comes to men's teams, leagues, and companies—money goes in based on the hope that potential will turn to profit. In a system not shaped by decades of misogyny, that's how investment would work for women's endeavors too, but getting stakeholders to realize that "takes a leader," Coyne Schofield says. Instead, women athletes are routinely made to feel either like politically correct boxes to check or charity cases allowed to exist at the benevolence of men. Megan Rapinoe summed up the attitude perfectly in a 2019 appearance on *Anderson Cooper 360*: "It's like, 'How cheap can we do this while sort of keeping them happy?'"[22]

~ ~ ~

THIS IS WHERE the pay gap starts. Behind the shortfall that shows up in women's paychecks lurk decades of underinvestment. When we talk about the pay gap without recognizing that fact, we preserve the myth that the blame somehow lies with women. Girls like Molly don't get new jerseys because they don't attract bigger crowds. Women have lower starting salaries because they don't negotiate. You didn't get the raise because you didn't lean in hard enough. Particularly in Western if-you-can-dream-it-you-can-do-it societies, the blame for inequality is too easily pinned on those who are experiencing it. The same flawed logic keeps the investment gap in place: just as the NCAA okayed giving women's basketball players a worse weight room because they don't generate the revenue of men's basketball, those with access to wealth justify not investing in women by saying they've failed to make it to the top.

Nowhere is this more apparent than in venture capital dollars invested in startups where you can literally put a number on how much sexism costs women. In 2021, women founders received $6.4 billion in capital—the most in history and an 83 percent jump over the previous year. In one context, this number represents a victory scenario. "When I started Female Founders Fund almost ten years ago, the concept of the female founder as an entity didn't really exist," says Anu Duggal, a venture capitalist and founding partner of FFF. But the progress promised by that historic $6.4 billion is misleading. That $6.4 billion represented just 2 percent of all startup investments in 2021, a drop from 2.2 percent in 2020 and the lowest share since 2016. It's the share of resources that matters, not absolute dollars. (An overall boom in the VC market in 2021 explains the seemingly paradoxical fact that the most cash women founders had ever received was still the smallest share of funding that had gone to women as a group in years.) Mixed-gender founding teams fared only marginally better, earning just under 16 percent of the overall VC pie. Globally, the pattern holds.* A similar gulf exists for women founders of small businesses—the average size of small-business loans granted to women owners is 31 percent less than the average loan given to a male proprietor. Funding

---

* In Europe there's a similar investment gulf: 93 percent of VC funds go to all-men teams, with 5 percent going to mixed-gender founding teams and a measly 2 percent going to all-women-led teams. In Africa, the gender funding gap for entrepreneurs stands at $42 billion, according to one estimate.

for women entrepreneurs of color is even more contemptible: 0.27 percent of VC dollars went to Black women and just 0.37 percent went to Latinx women in 2019.[23] This bears repeating: a *fraction of a percent* of the billions of dollars invested every year is invested in women of color.

There are billions of dollars on the table. And between nearly 98 and 100 percent of that vast financial resource pool is going to mostly white, mostly straight and cis men, keeping the funds that seed success almost entirely out of women's pockets.

The VC market may be especially visible, but it is not unique. Women routinely face underinvestment in less tangible ways at work every day. Not only are women less likely to receive career mentorship than men, they're also less likely to receive put-your-money-where-your-mouth-is sponsorship—a more active form of mentoring that involves a sponsor ponying up their investment in a mentee by putting them up for promotions, advocating on their behalf for raises, and generally devoting real resources to their growth. One particularly illuminating survey of "high potential" MBA graduates from around the world found that men benefit more from these types of relationships than women. Men with mentors were more likely to get higher-ranking jobs right out of grad school than women with mentors and made nearly $10,000 more in that role.[24]

～～～

LIKE WOMEN IN any workplace, athletes rely on investments to grow their game. And just like women founders, women in sports receive a diminutive share of the cash. Closing the systemic investment gap is an incredibly complex problem—in all but a few extreme cases, there's no magic wand a company or a league can wave to instantly poof women higher paychecks. The money has to come from somewhere, and changing the way resources are allocated takes time and a lot of negotiation. But for brands who sponsor athletes, the solution is much simpler. All they have to do is rethink the way they write checks.

Sponsorship deals, more than paychecks or prize money, are in many sports the biggest determinant of how much money an athlete makes (and by extension how much time they can devote to their performance vs. having to work a second job). It will likely come as no surprise that the gender gap in sponsorship dollars is colossal—just 7 percent of the $30 billion that's spent each year in the global sports sponsorship market is estimated to go to women athletes. That partially explains why only two women have ever made Forbes's list of the top fifty highest-earning athletes—Naomi Osaka and Serena Williams. Osaka became the highest-paid woman athlete in history in 2019. In 2022, she was the nineteenth highest-paid athlete overall, with $59.2 million in earnings—$58 million of which came from a lucrative roster of sponsorships including deals with Louis Vuitton, Airbnb, Levi's, Nike, Mastercard, and Sweetgreen. But Osaka and Williams (who ranks thirty-first with $45.3 million in earnings) are the outliers. Sportico, a sports industry news and data platform, estimated that no other woman athlete could even crack the top one thousand. Male tennis star Roger Federer, meanwhile, made $90.7 million in the 2021–2022 fiscal year that Forbes used for its annual list. Less than $1 million came from his earnings on the court. Injuries kept Federer from playing his sport for most of the year (which is, in theory, the thing he gets sponsored to do), yet he still earned tens of millions in endorsement deals from brands including Uniqlo and Rolex.[25]

The annual Forbes list shows just how far women athletes have to go to prove themselves in order to be paid even remotely closely to the way male athletes are paid. It wasn't until 2017 that a woman even made the list of the hundred highest-paid athletes. By that point in her career, Serena Williams had been a tennis champion for decades—with twenty-three Grand Slam wins—but perhaps even more important for sponsors, she'd crossed firmly into the cultural zeitgeist, becoming a household name the way some of her higher-ranked male colleagues (Fletcher Cox, Mike Conley, Dustin Johnson—ring any bells?) had not. What more could sponsors want from an athlete? The reluctance to bet on women the same way sponsors bet on men is obvious to the sports agents brokering these multimillion-dollar deals. With male athletes, the attitude from sponsors is "We're going to take a risk and we're going to bet big," says Lindsay Kagawa Colas, an executive vice president at Wasserman who represents many top WNBA players. "With women, what I hear a lot is 'We just want to make sure it's going to be successful.' It's rarely approached as an investment. We have to convince them it's going to be a sure thing." In shoe deals alone, first-round NBA draft picks routinely score ten times more money on average than her women clients of the same caliber, she says.[26]

∼ ∼ ∼

IN MOST INDUSTRIES, the personal toll of the investment gap is easy to obscure, but in sports, the never-stop hustle risks players' health and compromises their careers. "I can only imagine how long I could play if I had LeBron James's money, and I could also give a million dollars to my recovery," says Hilary Knight, a forward for the US Women's National Hockey Team and four-time Olympic medalist. (Actually, James reportedly spends closer to $1.5 million a year keeping his body in peak condition.)[27] Instead, even the best women athletes in the world are spending their extra time and energy hustling to convince the people writing the checks of their worth. "I know how much better and more skilled the sport is going to become when we don't have to do all this," Knight says. "My attention when I wake up tomorrow could just be, 'Oh, I get to go train. I get to skate with the teammates that I love. We get to go play a hockey game, and earn a livable wage doing it.'"

The pay gap–induced grind has gotten particular attention in the WNBA, where the investment gap means many WNBA players feel "obligated to play basketball 24/7," says Chiney Ogwumike, a forward for the Los Angeles Sparks and former vice president of the WNBA Players Association. While LeBron is off taking million-dollar ice baths, or whatever recovery treatments it is he spends his $1.5 million on, the top women in basketball routinely spend their off-seasons playing overseas where they can earn six to seven times their WNBA salary. Bluntly, the money is "hard to turn down," says Elizabeth Williams, a center forward for the Washington Mystics. The economics are so enticing that Diana Taurasi, one of the greatest basketball players of all time, went so far as to sit out the 2015 WNBA season, where she earned just over $100,000, to rest up for the upcoming season in Russia, where she earned $1.5 million to play. (Overseas teams operate on completely different financial structures—they pay so much more for a variety of reasons that vary based on country and team. In Russia, for example, women's basketball teams are often owned by oligarchs who prioritize championship prestige over profitability.) With a salary gap like that, playing at home would have been "irresponsible," Taurasi explained to fans in a letter. Ironically, the hustle limits players' ability to be available for sponsorship opportunities at home that could lead to bigger investments in the future, says Colas. As it stands, the majority of the league is still working overtime. Fifty-five players—that's nearly 40 percent of the league—missed WNBA training camp sessions before the start of the 2021 season due to overseas commitments, and a dozen missed their opening games.[28]

As is too often the case, things had to get exceptionally bad before the public began paying attention to the toll this system takes on the women of the WNBA. In February 2022, as the Russian war in Ukraine began, Phoenix Mercury player Brittney Griner was detained near Moscow while traveling to rejoin her Russian team UMMC Ekaterinburg in what appeared to be trumped-up drug charges. The US government declared her "wrongfully detained" and assigned a negotiator specializing in hostage affairs to fight for her release. In August, Griner was sentenced to nine years in a penal colony. In a statement, the WNBA Players Association said, "She is very clearly a hostage." After nearly eleven months in custody, Griner was returned home in a prisoner swap.[29]

Griner's ordeal brought the financial insecurity created by the investment gap to global headlines. Why would a top professional athlete—Griner is a three-time All-American, seven-time WNBA All-Star, two-time Olympian—"need to leave the United States to find offseason work," Colas, Griner's agent and friend, wrote in an op-ed for the *LA Times*.[30] The inequality is impossible to deny. "The same system that rendered a woman who is a generational talent nearly invisible until she was detained in Russia offers a rich ecosystem of income opportunities that are almost exclusively available for men," Colas wrote. "Now we have a high-stakes example of how economic disparity can have terrifying consequences."

~ ~ ~

IN 2022, THE NCAA at last made some changes. Women's college basketball was finally brought under the lucrative March Madness marketing umbrella, and the tournament was expanded to include sixty-eight teams (instead of the previous sixty-four) to match the men's field. The player experience improved too: all teams in the women's Final Four got dedicated hotel players' lounges as well as a family lounge to share the experience with loved ones—both amenities that the men's Final Four players have had for years. The fan experience also benefited from increased investments with small but meaningful changes, including Instagrammable photo-op backdrops akin to those long featured at the men's championships, which made the women's tourney feel like an exciting and shareable moment. (And yes, the players finally got swag bag equality too.)[31]

It was a turning point in NCAA history. But to be clear, the organization didn't make these investments because they suddenly had a change of heart about the importance of supporting gender equality—they invested because an independent investigation, based on data, told them they were potentially leaving $100 million on the table by treating the women's tournament as a second-class product. "This has always been the most annoying," says Rapinoe. Women's ventures—sports teams, companies, you name it—suffer from the same false narrative that they're inferior products. It takes an overwhelming amount of evidence (and often a little public shaming) to convince those writing the checks that women aren't destined to be money losers, especially when data provide plenty of evidence that the opposite is true. "It's totally irrational in so many ways," Rapinoe says. "But I never underestimate the power of people's biases."

Getting in on women's sports now feels a bit like getting in on Amazon when it sold nothing but books—women are on the precipice of rewriting the rules of a $500 billion industry. Eighty-four percent of sports fans around the globe are interested in women's sports (51 percent of whom are men), according to a study conducted by Nielsen, and yet, they're barely being acknowledged. Sponsors are overlooking a gold mine: the accounting firm Deloitte projected that the TV and sponsorship revenue for global women's sports would be worth "a great deal more" than $1 billion in the coming years based partially on the fact that in sports where men's and women's games benefit from near-equal investment—such as tennis—they drive "roughly equivalent" commercial impact.[32] "No one's asking for a handout," says Colas. Investing in women is just good business.

That's become clear to anyone who follows women's college basketball. Following the increased investment from the NCAA, ESPN aired all women's March Madness Final Four and championship games across all networks. That resulted in huge gains in viewership for women, from a 160 percent jump in the selection show (where the full tournament bracket is revealed live) to an 18 percent increase in viewership for the championship game, which peaked at nearly six million viewers. And that's not even counting the eighteen thousand fans who packed the sold-out Target Center in Minneapolis to see the game in person. Under the moneymaking March Madness branding, the women's tournament banked three major new sponsors (Target, Capital One, and Degree), and ESPN sold out its advertising inventory before the tournament even began. With a bigger platform, the women's Sweet 16 generated $1.8 million in social media value, as assessed by digital measuring platform Zoomph, and the women's March Madness champions garnered 146 million impressions on social media that were alone valued at $2.5 million.[33] "Those returns are sitting there," says Berri. "You simply have to go get them."

Women athletes know this. "As the product ourselves, we know that when women are given a platform and when there is proper investment, we deliver the stories, the global audiences, and the drama," said Angela Ruggiero, a four-time Olympian and CEO of the Sports Innovation Lab, a sports market research and advisory firm. In 2020, they produced what is likely the most comprehensive look ever taken at the investment case for women's sports, analyzing fan behavior on social media and TV viewership stats.[34] From the over ten billion data points (roughly half of which were collected from male fans of women's sports) a clear narrative emerged: women's sports, teams, leagues, and athletes are incredibly adept at creating community.

That community is worth a lot more than its size might indicate. For example, brands have traditionally bought sponsorship or ad time based on overall television viewership for games; in August 2020, the report found that 1.4 million households watched an NBA game, while only 782,000 households tuned in to a WNBA game—a viewership gap that seemingly justifies an investment gap. But the Fan Project report also provided another, potentially even more important metric: during that same period the NBA fans watched an average of 68 percent of a playoff game, while WNBA fans tuned in for 82 percent of a regular season game, demonstrating a much higher level of engagement per game and across the season. In other words, it's not about the size of your audience but what you can do with it.

When you consider how easy it is to be a passive fan of men's sports, this isn't all that surprising. Men's sports are in the air we breathe—it would be almost impossible to flick through TV channels at any given time of year and not catch at least half a dozen of them. Making women's sports so comparatively difficult to access has forged extremely engaged fans—if they're watching, it's because they've actively sought that content out. The 2020 WNBA season provided some additional insight into why a stronger relationship exists between women athletes and their fans. The report found more viewers tuned in to the WNBA's 2020 season following an Instagram campaign that highlighted the activist work of the players than after milestones in actual game play, including the start of the finals. In other words, fans showed up for these women because they identified with who they are as humans—not just because they were impressed by their shooting average.

"The world we live in has been marketed, measured and monetized against men's sports," says Shelley Pisarra, executive vice president of global insights at Wasserman. But women's sports aren't just a smaller, younger version of men's sports—they're something entirely new. And that calls for new forms of investment, and new ways to conceptualize value. In challenging a system that has willfully ignored anyone outside the heteronormative six-foot-four, white, male, Tom Brady "norm," women's sports are highlighting new metrics—storytelling, direct-to-consumer merchandise sales—and definitions of worth so compelling even capitalist investors are called to pay attention.

For Carly Leahy, cofounder of reproductive information brand Modern Fertility, women's sports were an obvious place to invest for exactly this reason. In 2022, the brand launched one of their most ambitious campaigns to date, partnering with Nneka Ogwumike and Candace Parker of the WNBA, Olympic gymnast Aly Raisman, and soccer stars Kelley O'Hara and Sydney Leroux to expand the brand's mission of fertility awareness and reproductive care. What excited Leahy about the idea of working with women athletes was the opportunity to break the more "glamorous" celebrity spokesperson formula. Women in sports, she knew, had an intangible "it" factor—as much as we admire their superhuman skills, we can also see ourselves in their stories. "Every single thing they are doing with their bodies is judged," Leahy says, "but they are the ones who are banging down the door, asking new questions."

That kinship and the elusive ability to make people feel seen is the new model for value that women athletes and fans of women's sports bring to the table. "When you look at metrics that are meaningful from a brand perspective—engagement, brand consideration, likelihood to buy, advocacy after participating—women crush on those metrics and fans of women's sports excel against fans of traditional, or men's, sports," Pisarra explains.

The shift in the way brands invest in sports has implications far beyond this one industry. Sponsorship deals, let's not forget, are meant to influence us—to tell us not just what to buy but whose story to pay attention to. When those deals are built by and for women, their influence naturally changes.

Since 2019, women's athletic apparel company Athleta has made two of the most significant sponsorship deals in recent history, partnering with Allyson Felix and Simone Biles. It might not seem particularly groundbreaking for an athletic brand to sponsor an athlete (both Biles and Felix were previously sponsored by Nike), but "the way we work with them is quite different," says Kyle Andrew, the former chief brand officer of Athleta. Traditional brand sponsorships are built around performance—win a certain number of championships to get paid. "That was the thing that had always been most frustrating to me," Felix tells me. "Compensation was so performance driven in these big shoe companies; it was like if you don't make a certain team, then you're cut by 50 percent." Most people, she says, don't care about the nuances of world rankings, don't follow every qualifying meet, don't know the time she ran in her last four hundred. Most people do, however, know what it means to have to balance their identity as a human with their identity as a professional. "We're working with these women because of what they stand for, what they believe in and the change they can make in the world versus how fast they can go or what medals they can win," says Andrew.

When the brand announced they were sponsoring Biles ahead of the Tokyo Olympics, in a partnership that would center her advocacy work for building girls' confidence and well-being in sport, Athleta received an outpouring of supportive press and feedback from customers. When Biles withdrew from the team final at the Tokyo Olympics, citing mental health issues, "it was so clear that was resonating with customers," Andrew says. These sponsorships, in other words, don't follow the classic transactional script. "It's not, let's write you a check and we'll put some products in store," Andrew explains. "What we're trying to say is these women are bigger than that. How do we elevate what they stand for, and how can they amplify our values?" Athleta saw an impressive 5.5 percent growth year over year in brand awareness in Q1 of 2022—a bump the company attributes in part to the partnerships with Felix and Biles. In non-marketing speak: "These women help us bring in new audiences," Andrew says. And those audiences aren't just making Athleta money but connecting with the brand.

Brands that invested in women's sports saw up to 400 percent more brand loyalty from fans of women's sports than from general sports fans, according to the Fan Project, which is likely because of the powerful emotional connections women's sports create.* And again, that's showing up in sales numbers: people are more likely to actually think about and spend money with sponsors of women's sports *because* they're sponsors of women's sports.[35] Women's sports have become so synonymous with the values of gender and racial equality that investing in them has a halo effect, giving brands a platform to engage in some serious values signaling. Showing up for women in sports puts a stake in the ground on cultural issues that Pisarra says are becoming increasingly difficult to separate from the world of sports. "Given how culturally on point and out front women's sports are, they're leading the way, able to put together the story for brands that says, 'We are the place you need to be.'"

Waking up to this reality, brands are increasingly using the equality halo of sponsoring women's sports to boost their own image. French chemical company Arkema became the first national supporter of the 2019 World Cup, positioning itself as an inclusive company ready to attract new talent. "Signing this agreement is a great opportunity for us to support and enhance the status of women both in sport and at work," Arkema's chairman and CEO explained. More recently, workforce tech company UKG bet big on the NWSL with a multiyear, multimillion-dollar sponsor deal for the Challenge Cup as part of the company's campaign to close the pay gap in business. They also made the 2023 tournament the first professional women's soccer tournament to achieve pay equity in prize money.[36]

Whether you believe the motive of the companies standing to profit from the advocacy and community of women's sports fans

---

* Based on interviews with over twenty-one thousand people in Australia and New Zealand, one study found women's sports have a "significantly higher" emotional connection score, even though more people are familiar with men's sports.

is pure or simply another case of sportswashing (using the feel-good power of sports to improve one's reputation), athletes are finally being recognized for their value. "When I was marketing women athletes fifteen years ago," Colas says, "all I heard was no." Today, we're straddling the tipping point. In 2022, Gatorade—one of the biggest legacy sponsors in sports—announced a change in strategy. Recognizing the epic potential of women's sports, the company made a $10 million donation to organizations dedicated to keeping women and minorities in sport, which it swiftly followed with an announcement that it will begin prioritizing investments in women—while pulling the plug on men's sports partnerships, including a five-year deal with the NHL. (Gatorade's parent company PepsiCo also appears to be reevaluating its investment in men's sports, ending its iconic sponsorship of the Super Bowl halftime show.) "For us, the future of sport means continuing to invest in young and diverse athlete communities, cutting edge leagues, and embracing all athletic journeys," Jeff Kearney, Gatorade's global head of sports marketing, wrote in a LinkedIn post announcing the new era.[37] "We're already seeing the impact it makes, and there's a lot more to come."

~ ~ ~

Investing in women pays for everyone. Just as the gender gap costs the global economy trillions of dollars in lost human capital, the reluctance to invest in women has historically left big money on the table.

Let's go back to venture funding. If women received the same investment and support as male entrepreneurs, the size of the global economy would increase by 3–6 percent. Put another way, not investing equally in women-founded companies is costing the world between $2.5 and $5 trillion, according to a report from Boston Consulting Group (pointedly titled "Want to Boost the Global Economy by $5 Trillion? Support Women as Entrepreneurs"). A previous report published by BCG helps explain why: women-founded companies generate more than twice the revenue per dollar invested compared to those with male founders. Over a five-year period, they generated 10 percent more cumulative revenue than companies founded by men.[38]

The proof is there. But to see the payoff, women first need to see the investment.

CHAPTER 3

THE MOTHERHOOD PENALTY

M OTHERHOOD IS A CAREER KILLER. AT LEAST, THAT'S WHAT women are told, if not in words, certainly in practice. Especially if you're a woman in sports. Alysia Montaño, an Olympian, seven-time national champion, and two-time medal-winning world champion runner, knew the deal: devote your body to your career or your pregnancy, not both. That's why at eight months pregnant she stretched a hot pink tank top over her belly, laced up her spikes, and ran eight hundred meters at the 2014 USA Track and Field Championships. By this point in her career, Montaño was a champion several times over, but she knew all too well how motherhood would devalue her in the eyes of sponsors. She wanted to prove that was bullshit, to show that a pregnant body was still a very capable one, and that women should be the ones making the rules around what balancing a career and family should look like.

Montaño couldn't have predicted this defining moment when she signed with her first major sponsor—Nike—straight out of college.

It was the holy grail for a twenty-one-year-old athlete just turning pro. Pregnancy, and how it should be addressed in her new contract, was the furthest thing from her mind—her eyes were fixed firmly on the Olympics. "You're not really thinking, Oh, where's the clause that addresses pregnancy, and is it fair?" At the time, most major sports sponsors—even the ones who humble-bragged about their support for women athletes in marketing campaigns—cut pay for athletes who became pregnant, or dropped them entirely, lumping pregnancy in with an injury clause stating if you don't compete, you don't get paid. Starting a family is not the same as getting an injury, but treating it as such created an industry norm in which there was not only zero paid parental leave but no guarantee that postpartum athletes would have a job to come back to. Compete or get cut. "Basically," Montaño says, "they had you by the ovaries."

The practice didn't exactly champion women; for athletes, the model seemed to say once you become pregnant you're "used goods," Montaño says. She began thinking about getting pregnant about four years into her Nike contract, she says. "As an athlete, your body is your business, and you think about when there's going to be an off year," she explains. When she shared her thoughts about getting pregnant with her sponsor, "they were like, 'We'll just pause your contract and stop paying you,'" Montaño recalls. (Nike declined to comment on its past treatment of athletes during pregnancy and the postpartum period, including Montaño's experience, for this book. When asked by *Glamour* about their policy in June 2019, a representative of Nike said, "We can't change the past, but we sure can change the future," in ensuring that "no female athlete is penalized for pregnancy.")[1]

Montaño saw no reason she couldn't have a family and a career, so she started looking for a more supportive sponsor. "I wanted to be with a company who respects women and wants us to do well in all facets of life," she says. She began negotiations with athletic brand Asics, and at first things looked promising. "They had a woman [in leadership] who was sitting in a head position to help make changes and listen to voices of women athletes. It was everything that I would want to be a part of," she says. She was even able to make room for pregnancy in her deal—or so she thought. "At that point, I didn't know to use the words 'pregnancy protection clause.' I was just like, I want to know I'm going to be supported," she says. Montaño was assured that she would be, she says, but to be sure, she negotiated extra time for recovery under her injury clause, hoping that would be enough to cover her.

By this point in her career, Montaño had a stacked list of accomplishments including three World Championship bronze medals and a fourth-place finish at the 2012 Olympics. "I was a freaking five-time national champion," she says. "I had all these accolades. It was like, now I *deserve* to have this baby." Still, when it came time to actually get pregnant, "I was terrified," she says. "What if everyone's word wasn't what they said it was?" Montaño got pregnant in 2013 and at first everything was great. She felt so supported by her sponsor she made the decision to champion birthing bodies at the now iconic 2014 race she ran at eight months pregnant. There was "no pressure" from Asics to compete, she says; she simply wanted to run to show the sports world what it looked like to be pregnant and a professional.

But after Montaño gave birth to her daughter Linnea in August, she says things changed. The woman on the team at Asics, Montaño's champion, left the company. "The first thing I got after she left was an email from two dudes that were basically like, 'Hey, you didn't compete enough last year. We're going to reduce [your pay],'" according to Montaño. No congratulations, just a pay cut. The way Montaño saw it, "because I was pregnant, I was being penalized." (A representative for Asics declined to comment on Montaño's experiences with the brand. In regard to their current maternity policy, they said, "It is Asics' policy to honor the contracts of female athletes, and they are paid in full during pregnancy and after childbirth.") The idea that pregnant and postpartum athletes were "throwaways" was so pervasive inside the sports community that "many women felt like they deserved to be penalized if they didn't perform during pregnancy," Montaño says. No one liked it, but with sponsors holding all the power, "people were afraid to have those conversations," she says. So she decided to start a conversation with the *New York Times*.

In 2019, Montaño made the treatment of pregnant athletes public in a viral video op-ed for the *Times*. She named names, parodying Nike's gritty girlpower "Dream Crazier" marketing campaign that the company had debuted earlier that year. "If we show emotion, we're called dramatic. If we want to play against men, we're nuts. If we dream of equal opportunity? Delusional. And if we want to be an athlete and a mother? Well that's just crazy," she said.[2] "The sports industry allows for men to have a full career. When a woman decides to have a baby, it pushes women out at their prime."

It was a watershed moment, turning a floodlight onto the dirty little secret that every sponsor knew but no athlete was supposed to talk about. "People were afraid to share too much because there's a gag order within your contract—you can't talk about what's in it, including the fact that there's no maternity clause or support for women athletes," she says now. Going public was terrifying—she knew she'd be moving forward in her career with a target on her back. That fear keeps many women (understandably) silent. It's a "crazy, vicious, insidious cycle" similar to discrimination in any workplace, Montaño says. "You're like, 'I still need my job.'"

~ ~ ~

MONTAÑO'S STORY MADE explicit an assumption that has been hiding in contracts and workplaces for decades: that a person's value plummets when they get pregnant. Athletes are a particularly good example of the pregnancy penalty—pregnancy impacts their work in a much more visceral and immediate way than, say, a lawyer who can theoretically be at her desk until the moment her water breaks—but they are certainly not the only ones to experience it. Being pregnant can currently get you fired in thirty-eight countries, according to the World Bank.[3] Even in countries with laws against pregnancy discrimination (including the US, which passed a law banning it in 1978), birthing and raising children still shapes women's professional lives in powerful ways.

Pregnancy is only the beginning of the "motherhood penalty," a multilayered stack of biases that disadvantage moms over dads and people without kids. Globally, the motherhood penalty is one of the biggest contributors to the gender pay gap. It's so strong, some experts even suggest it can affect women who don't have kids—a so-called assumed motherhood penalty that discounts women simply based on the possibility that they might one day become moms.[4] And because it is rooted in assumptions about birthing bodies in addition to the lifelong task of mothering, the motherhood penalty exists for people who become pregnant but don't identify as mothers (whether because they are transgender, nonbinary, or surrogates) as well as for non-birthing mothers. If you are associated with pregnancy, birth, or the gendered expectations of motherhood, you're getting hit.

Understanding why women face such a steep motherhood penalty starts with understanding how the market reacts when a body gets pregnant. When five-time Olympic runner Allyson Felix got pregnant with her daughter Camryn in 2017, she was so sure it would be a negative in the eyes of the industry that she hid it for as long as possible. Felix didn't post glowing bump pictures on Instagram, she didn't make public appearances, and she certainly didn't tell her sponsor, Nike. She had seen athletes get dropped by their sponsors after becoming moms and she didn't want to become one of them. "This is a time that should be celebrated but looking back, I often feel like I wasn't even pregnant. It's really sad," she says.

Instead of optimism and joy, that period of her life was often characterized by stress and anxiety. What would she do without the support of a sponsor? Would she still have the resources to compete? Was this it?

Felix was at a pivotal moment in her career. She was coming off her fourth Olympics, having added three more medals to her stash. She was at the top of her game and had no reason or desire to retire, but at thirty-one, she says her sponsor didn't see it that way. Her contract had recently expired, and when Felix and Nike started negotiating the renewal, she says the company offered her 70 percent less than what she had been making. She was "old" for an athlete, she concluded, so she was getting pushed out. "I wasn't being offered what I felt like I was valued—and that was even before they knew that I was pregnant," Felix says. "At that point I'm thinking, I'm coming off four Olympic games and I guess they're feeling like I'm at an age where I have no more to give. Now add mom? I've already seen what happens," she says.

Once she did share her pregnancy, "all the right things were said on the phone," Felix says. "It was negotiations that were the issue." She had reluctantly swallowed the fact that despite all of her victories, her value was drying up in the eyes of her sponsor. She still wanted to compete, and if that meant a radically reduced sponsorship deal, she was willing to accept it. She was not, however, willing to accept that her check would be reduced even further during her pregnancy. She refused to agree to the standard pregnancy-related performance reductions. "I had been seeing this going on since I was a teenager and here was an opportunity to try to do something about it," she says. "I actually thought maternity protections were an easy ask. Why would you not do this?" Her optimism was short-lived. "I was met with a no. They were willing to give me a period of time to get back to where I needed to be, but they weren't willing to tie it to maternity in any way," Felix says. In other words, "they weren't willing to put it in the contract, therefore setting the precedent for other women," she explains.

So she too went public. Ten days after Montaño's *New York Times* bombshell, Felix shared her own Nike pregnancy story in the *Times*. "If I, one of Nike's most widely marketed athletes, couldn't secure these protections, who could?" she wrote.[5]

Having this experience at a moment in her life that should have been filled with joy and excitement "spoke volumes to me," Felix says. "To me, [Nike] didn't believe in me anymore. It started to affect me internally. It was like, well, maybe I'm not what I think I am, maybe I can't do this, maybe I can't come back." Like Montaño, Felix felt that as a pregnant woman she no longer had value in the eyes of her sponsor. "It was just incredible to me that was the position that they were taking," she says.

≈ ≈ ≈

LACK OF PAID support for pregnant people isn't a problem unique to sports—at least, not in the world's largest economy. The United States remains one of just six countries globally—and the only industrialized country—that does not guarantee paid parental leave. As a result, one in four women returns to work within two weeks of giving birth. Globally, the average paid maternity leave is twenty-nine weeks and the average paid paternity leave is sixteen weeks. The US government does mandate that employers must offer twelve weeks of job-protected *unpaid* leave, but there are important caveats to that legislation that make even that available to only 60 percent of the workforce. Only 14 percent of women receive paid leave from their employer, according to Paid Leave for the U.S. And that number is actually *decreasing*. A report from the Society for Human Resource Management published in the *Wall Street Journal* in August 2022 found that, post-pandemic, many private companies were quietly shrinking their parental leave policies. In 2020, 50 percent of companies surveyed offered some paid maternity (beyond what is required by law); in 2022, that number was down to 35 percent. (Dads are even more likely to be losing paid leave—the same survey found that only 27 percent of companies offered paid paternity leave in 2022, compared to 44 percent in 2020.)[6]

This is a stats-heavy way of saying working moms in the US are largely on their own. In 2021, the House of Representatives passed a historic paid leave bill. If signed into law, it would expand paid leave to all Americans, but, as of this writing, the bill's political future remains uncertain—and at just four weeks, also completely unsatisfying.[7] "Most daycare chains won't even take a newborn baby at four weeks," says Lauren Smith Brody, who helps workplaces build gender equity through support for moms and caregivers as founder of the Fifth Trimester and cofounder of the nonprofit Chamber of Mothers. "What is this? People are still bleeding after four weeks."

Paid leave is also an incredibly important racial justice issue. The lack of support during this period is one of the many factors influencing the shocking maternal mortality rate in the United States—the worst among the world's wealthiest nations—an epidemic that is disproportionately killing Black women, who are three times more likely than white women to die from pregnancy-related complications.[8]

Felix might have been one of them. At thirty-two weeks pregnant, she went in for a routine prenatal checkup. "I thought everything was right on track, I thought I was healthy, I thought my daughter was healthy," she testified before the US House of Representatives. But her doctor sent her straight to the hospital where she was diagnosed with a severe case of preeclampsia, a condition that threatened the life of both Felix and her daughter. At thirty-two weeks, she was rushed in for an emergency C-section. "The next month was spent in the NICU and I learned that my story was not so uncommon, there were others like me—just like me. Black like me, healthy like me, doing their best—just like me. They faced death like me too," she testified.[9]

There are many causes for this epidemic—chiefly racial bias in the healthcare system and critical failures in healthcare resources available to marginalized communities. Stress—a well-documented driver of poor birth outcomes for both moms and babies—like the kind athletes experience worrying about whether they'll have a job to come back to, can also play a role. Further underscoring the importance of paid leave for all moms is the chilling fact that more than half of all maternal deaths in the US occur after the day of delivery—12 percent happen after six weeks postpartum (a figure higher than all other high-income countries). A report released by the CDC in 2022 found that 80 percent of pregnancy-related deaths in the US are preventable, suggesting that increased support during this period could be lifesaving.[10] Instead, many women are back at work just weeks after giving birth so that they can support their families. As Felix sat in the NICU with her daughter, she had to worry: Will I have a sponsor after this? Will I get paid? "It was just emotionally a lot," she tells me. "When all the negotiation stuff was happening and I knew that I needed to get back to work, being in the hospital shook everything up. It was just another layer of stress with everything else that was on my plate. It was one more thing that was adding to feeling emotionally and physically drained. It definitely took a lot out of me at a very crucial time."

~ ~ ~

A LACK OF understanding and empathy about birth and postpartum bodies has created a dangerous web of often conflicting assumptions: we expect too much from women after birth, impatiently waiting for them to get back to the grind while we simultaneously assume they'll be capable of far less. The tension forces women into a lot of terrible choices. Kara Goucher, a two-time Olympic runner and former Nike athlete, also spoke out in the *Times*, sharing her postpartum experience. Like Montaño and Felix, running is her livelihood, and after getting pregnant she found out that Nike would stop paying her until she was able to race again. Every body is different, but experts recommend waiting twelve weeks after giving birth to even start running in order to avoid serious injuries—the kind that could derail a professional runner's career, including hernias and muscle tears. Think about what this means for a professional runner: in order to give your body time to heal, thus preserving your career longevity, you would have to live without a paycheck nearly a year, including the months during late pregnancy where you couldn't compete, a three-month postpartum rest period, and then months of training to get back in the groove. Many women simply couldn't afford it—Goucher included. (Meanwhile, she made more than a dozen unpaid promotional appearances for Nike during her pregnancy, the *New York Times* reported.) She committed to running a half marathon just three months after she was due to give birth. Not only was that a risk for her recovery, it meant forgoing the option to breastfeed. (Goucher's doctor told her that she would have to choose between breastfeeding and her training regimen, which required her to run 120 miles a week to get ready for race day.) When her son got ill and ended up in the hospital, the pressure she felt to get back to competition—to get paid—meant choosing between running and being by his side. "I felt like I had to leave him in the hospital, just to get out there and run, instead of being with him like a normal mom would," she told reporter Lindsay Crouse at the *Times*. "I'll never forgive myself for that."[11]

Women shouldn't have to choose between having a family and having a career—or feel pressured to go to extremes to prove that they can do both. Despite the centuries-long campaign to paint pregnancy as the beginning of the end, women aren't damaged goods after they become mothers. "We have these stereotypes and these expectations around the birthing body based on the idea that postpartum, you're broken," says Molly Dickens, founding executive director of &Mother, an advocacy platform she cofounded with Montaño to help implement maternity protections in sports and beyond. "It's this myth that makes motherhood the career killer."

The truth is, given a healthy recovery period, many women come back from pregnancy stronger. Every pregnancy, every body, is of course different, but some exercise physiologists believe pregnancy has the potential to give elite women athletes clear physical advantages, at least theoretically: an expanded rib cage that makes postpartum breathing easier, dramatically increased blood volume and a turbocharged heart able to pump oxygenated blood to the muscles more efficiently, increased pain tolerance, and an increased capability to deal with the physiological effects of stress. Depending on the pregnancy, hormonal changes can also offer an energy boost. This isn't the story for every athlete, and these changes aren't necessarily long-term, but there is enough emerging evidence on postpartum performance to suggest that women athletes smashing assumptions after giving birth isn't some weird anomaly. In 2022, researchers in Canada published the findings of a small study of forty-two elite women runners (more than half of whom had competed in the World Championships and/or Olympics). Sixty percent of the runners intended to return to "equivalent performance levels" after giving birth. In examining their postpartum career trajectories, the researchers found that, contrary to what the industry standard for sponsorship contracts suggests, the running moms experienced no statistical decrease in performance in the one to three years post-pregnancy. Nearly half of those women—46 percent—actually got better.[12] This was the case with Montaño. "I ended up winning nationals at six months postpartum, I broke an American record, I won a World Championships gold medal with the 4×800 relay team, I ran the fastest on the team at eight months postpartum—while breastfeeding," Montaño says. Two months later, she clinched another national title and made the

World Championship team. "I mean, it was like this ridiculousness of proof points."

As more women begin to challenge postpartum assumptions, the proof points keep piling up. In 2022 Keira D'Amato and Sara Hall, both moms in their thirties, set new American records for the marathon and half marathon in the same weekend. After breaking the marathon record in a stunning comeback, D'Amato, a pro runner who retired in 2009 and started a family, told the *New York Times*, "I sat on the sidelines for a decade wondering what if—what if I would have done things differently? I lived with that for a decade, and then I finally found out," she said. Her victory, and Hall's, changed the narrative. "Two mothers in their late 30s just changed the history books in the same day," D'Amato said.[13]

It's not just Olympians and world-class athletes (who it's safe to assume are in a class all their own) who are challenging assumptions about postpartum performance. A more relatable example: there's evidence that motherhood makes women more productive workers. A study of ten thousand economists found that moms were more productive, as measured by the research they published over the span of their career, than women without children. Moms with two kids were the most professionally productive.[14] Moms are "less about the bullshit," says Smith Brody. "Moms need less transition time between tasks. It's a muscle that's been built in them by having to care for a baby—your baby doesn't give you time for a reset between tasks, you have to use every minute you have. That translates to the workplace."

Felix also came back from her traumatic birth experience better than ever. At the Tokyo Olympics in 2021, she won her tenth and eleventh medals, making her the most decorated American track-and-field athlete—of any gender—in history.[15] When she clinched the bronze medal in the 400-meter final, she did it in 49.46 seconds. It was her fastest time in six years, meaning Felix was officially faster as a thirty-five-year-old mom than she was when she took silver as a thirty-year-old at the Rio Olympics in 2016—back when her former sponsor thought she was worth 70 percent more. "Something my coach has always said to me is that, it's not that women aren't capable, in terms of age or becoming mothers, it's just that we haven't seen this happen because women haven't been supported long enough," says Felix. Most athletes don't have the platform to do what she did—"they have to go on to another job, or they start families and they step away," she says. "We're just now starting to see more and more women run for a longer time and we're seeing these amazing performances. If you support women holistically, this is what happens."

~ ~ ~

SUPPORT ISN'T JUST financial: workplace policies that cater to the specific needs of mothers are critical. Canadian basketball player Kim Gaucher didn't want to give up her career to become a mother either. A three-time Olympian and twenty-year veteran of the Canadian National Team, she and her husband tried to line up their pregnancy with "the right time frame"—i.e., not an Olympic or World Championship year. But after struggling with infertility, Gaucher ended up getting pregnant just over a year before the Tokyo Olympics were held in 2021. She was thrilled—and despite the tight timeline, determined to compete. "Some of the doctors and trainers were like, 'There's no chance. Why would you even try?'" she says. "As a high-performance athlete, you're used to putting your body in uncomfortable situations—you wouldn't get to the level of being an Olympian without being able to push yourself. And so I wasn't worried about that. I thrive on that."

Gaucher got herself ready, but the International Olympic Committee, it turned out, wasn't ready for her—or any moms. The day after her daughter Sophie was born, Olympic organizers announced that overseas spectators, including the families of athletes, would not be allowed to attend the games as a pandemic safety protocol. That would make it impossible for breastfeeding moms like Gaucher to compete unless they stopped breastfeeding (a logistically and emotionally complicated process) or shipped breast milk back home (an option Gaucher looked into at length, ultimately getting tangled in international shipping red tape). Gaucher snapped into problem-solving mode: *How do I start working with this? Who can I talk to?* She hit wall after wall in a seemingly endless maze of people who couldn't help her. "I was just getting so frustrated. Everybody that I spoke to was supportive—they were like, 'Well, yes, of course you should still be able to breastfeed. That should be allowed, I support you—but I can't do anything,'" she tells me.

Imagine that: you spend nine months growing a human, give birth, and get yourself into Olympic postpartum shape in just four months, only to be told that because a planning committee failed to consider moms, it would all be for nothing. So Gaucher did what many frustrated mothers do when they reach their breaking point: she took to social media. "Right now I'm being forced to decide between being a breastfeeding mom or an Olympic athlete—I can't have them both," she said in an Instagram video while breastfeeding Sophie. "It's 2021. Let's make working moms normal."[16] Other breastfeeding Olympic hopefuls spoke out and almost instantly, a viral movement was born. It turned out many women didn't have to imagine what it would feel like to be in these athletes' shoes. "I had so many messages that were like, 'When I told my work that I got pregnant, my pay was cut and I wasn't given the same kind of opportunities in my job.' 'Keep fighting.' 'This happened to me in the business world.' 'This happened to me in my organization.' 'I was let go because of this,'" Gaucher says. "It was really eye-opening." At first, she was intimidated by all the attention, but she quickly realized how important her experience was. "Clearly, I'm not the only one who has stories like this," she says.

Responding to the pressure, Olympic organizers ultimately made an exception for athletes with nursing children to be able to bring their children to the games "when necessary," though it came with a tough set of restrictions that some athletes still felt were unworkable.[17] Gaucher was able to travel to Tokyo with her daughter and compete, but some nursing athletes opted not to.

At thirty-seven, Gaucher doesn't get a tidy ending to her story. After competing in Tokyo (Team Canada was ultimately knocked out before the quarterfinals) her basketball future remained uncertain. "I am trying to get back to another club overseas and play, but obviously a thirty-seven-year-old new mother is a lot harder to sell," she says. "That's something that I'm grappling with now: Did I play my last game? I'm still fully capable, I'm still really strong. But once you add that 'mother' tag, there's a lot of people who don't want to take that on." Like a lot of the moms I spoke to, Gaucher feels like she's a stronger player after becoming a parent—she nevertheless lives with the threat of motherhood being a career killer. "I've done a lot with my career. I've had a lot of opportunities," she says. "Having to end it like this would be really unfortunate."

The point of sharing these stories is not to diminish the physical, mental, and emotional toll of pregnancy and birth—women do not need to run postpartum, get themselves into Olympic shape within weeks, or have their most productive year at the office to prove that they still have value. The point of sharing these stories is that, as we've discussed throughout this book, athletes have intense symbolic value—seeing women with global attention refuse to be cowed by expectations about what birthing people are capable of, particularly in ways that seem extreme to most of us, helps shift perceptions. The more women we see thrive as parents and professionals, the more their stories demand that we ask ourselves why we treat pregnant and postpartum people as incapable of being anything but that. "When every message fed to you in your career has signaled that 'mothers do not exist in this space,' at what point do you realize that mothers *can* exist in that space?" Dickens wrote in a 2021 Medium post titled "The Mothers Are Missing."[18]

"If you actually dug down below the surface," Dickens told me in an interview, "you would see all these different layers that set this woman up to fail or forced her to feel like she had to retire because of the image that's been projected."

~ ~ ~

NOTHING SETS MOMS up to fail quite like the criminal way almost every world economy treats care work, an unsexy term that describes everything it takes to keep our households running smoothly—the grocery shopping, the scheduling of doctor's appointments, the rounding up of rogue socks—and encompasses the mammoth time commitment of child-rearing. It's the biggest driver of the motherhood penalty. Even as women have increased their hours working in the paid labor economy, men have not closed the gap in who is responsible for the unpaid care work at home. Globally, women do three times the amount of unpaid care work as men, according to the United Nations, for a total of thirty-one unpaid hours per week, on average. As unpaid labor, it's economically invisible, going uncounted in the gross domestic product. But as every woman who has ever outsourced that work—an option that is disproportionately available to wealthy white women and disproportionately reliant on the low-wage labor of women of color—knows, being invisible doesn't make it free. A 2020 attempt to place a number on the value of that labor came up with an eye-popping $10.8 trillion globally—more than the total valuation of Apple, Amazon, Facebook, Google, and Microsoft combined.[19] That's real money women should have in their pockets, real economic value that should be formally recognized as such. "If you hire a house cleaning service, that service is counted in our gross domestic product, but if I decide to take over the cleaning of my house, that productivity vanishes," says Eve Rodsky, author of *Fair Play*. "Just poof, like a magic trick."

Both the perception and the reality of caregiving affect women's ability to get hired and receive equal pay, starting with the opportunity to get work in the first place. Mothers are less likely to get hired than women without children, an appalling fact we know thanks to a growing body of research on discriminatory hiring practices. One study, conducted by researchers at Cornell, asked participants to review resumes for college-educated workers applying for professional roles, which were identical except for subtle indicators of parenthood status (like, say, a mention of being a member of the Parent Teacher Association). No one wanted to hire moms; women with the scarlet letter M casting a shadow on their resume were consistently rated lower on perceived competence, commitment, and promotability and were less likely to be recommended for hire. Resumes tinged with the specter of fatherhood, meanwhile, faced no such penalty. The same bias exists in low-wage work. In 2021, sociologist Patrick Ishizuka sent fake applications to low-wage service job postings, submitting two similarly qualified candidates to each job. Again, one application subtly indicated that the applicant was a mom. Nearly 27 percent of the childless women got calls, compared to only 21.5 percent of moms, showing that "discrimination is not limited to women with college degrees in time-intensive professional occupations," Ishizuka said.[20] No matter their income or education, moms are seen as less attractive hires.

When they are hired, moms are paid less. When the reviewers in the Cornell study did recommend hiring mothers, they did so at a discount, recommending salary offers 7.9 percent lower than those that went to women without children and 8.6 percent less than fathers. Across the workforce, working moms make just 75 cents for every dollar working dads make, according to a 2021 analysis from the National Women's Law Center—a pay gap significantly wider than the one between men and women in general (which, as a refresher, was 17 cents in 2022). The financial penalty for being a mom increases with each kid. University of Massachusetts sociologist Michelle Budig found that on average women lose an additional 4 percent in lifetime earnings with each child. Low-wage women suffer the majority of those lost earnings. Similarly, when we remove white privilege from the equation, the numbers get worse. Women of color are slapped with an even more staggering financial penalty when they become mothers; for every dollar white, non-Hispanic dads bring home, Black mothers make 52 cents, Indigenous American mothers make 50 cents, and Latina mothers make just 46 cents.[21]

Becoming a dad (of course) actually pays. Budig's research found that men who become fathers receive a "daddy bonus"—a salary bump of over 6 percent, according to her analysis.[22] In other words, women, expected to be mothers, are ultimately penalized when they have children and continue working, whether by choice or necessity. But men, who are expected to be breadwinners, are financially rewarded when they choose to become a parent in addition to being earners.

These depressing data were all gathered *before* the pandemic—before droves of white-collar women were forced to "lean out" to pick up the new childcare demands created by COVID, before women were driven out of the workforce entirely at four times the rate of men, and before what economists have called a catastrophic generational setback to the progress of working mothers. In the thick of the domestic upheaval, women around the world took on three times as many additional hours of childcare—173 hours over the course of the year—as men.[23] That is an additional four weeks of full-time, unpaid labor. "Time is everything," says Rodsky. We treat women's time as being infinite, she says, "but we guard men's time as if it's finite."

The resulting systemic failure cost working moms $800 billion in lost income in just one year.[24] By this point, what happened to working moms over the course of the pandemic shouldn't be surprising, given the systemic disadvantages faced by women in the workplace. It was predictable, yes—but it wasn't inevitable, says Rodsky. In fact, "it was fucking *evitable*," she tells me. "Anybody who works in this space knew that something like this was going to come."

Women often take on care work because paying someone else to do it is too expensive: daycare costs $16,000 a year for the average American family in 2021, which was over 20 percent of the median household income. In the UK, full-time care runs between US$16,000 and US$30,000 per child; in Australia, it's around $9,000 for families who qualify for government subsidies and $20,000 for those who don't. "If I put [my son] in a daycare, that's my entire paycheck," Jessica McDonald, the only mom on the USWNT during the 2019 World Cup, said after winning the championship.[25] McDonald is one of the best soccer players on the planet, but for most of her career, she's made less than minimum wage. Her biggest professional challenge hasn't been overcoming injury or navigating a newly formed professional league. It's been finding childcare. "I got traded to six different teams in my first five years in the NWSL and had my son at the same time," she says. Six trades meant six periods of scrambling to find a new childcare setup, six periods of acute stress that took away from her game. "There were a lot of days where my son sat on the sideline in a stroller by himself while I was training. That was really tough—gut-wrenching—because it made me think, is my career worth it? That was probably the most frustrating part about trying to juggle motherhood and my career—just trying to find a support system," she tells me. "I've had a lot of friends who have retired at a very young age because they wanted to be moms and being in the NWSL wasn't bringing that possibility for them."

Male athletes almost never have to ask themselves these questions—fatherhood doesn't come as an existential threat to a dude's financial and professional dreams. "I don't ever see the struggle with male athletes trying to juggle parenting and doing what they do for a living," McDonald says. "First of all, they get paid more, so there would be no struggle to pay for childcare." But most male athletes aren't worrying about that anyway, she points out. "I don't think Steph Curry's children have ever traveled with him on the road to a game where it's just him and the kids." That's no shade to Steph—a vocal champion of gender equality—it's just the way the system is set up. Society, and by extension, our workplaces don't see caregiving as a responsibility that falls to men. If it did, every office would have a daycare center.

Nothing made this attitude more searingly clear than COVID-era sports bubbles. When the pandemic shut down in-person events, and sports leagues faced the gargantuan logistical challenge of figuring out how to keep the lights on, leagues couldn't escape the question of childcare. In basketball, the WNBA made specific accommodations for parents, rightly acknowledging that athletes with kids obviously couldn't just stop being parents for months to live and work on a closed campus. It was a huge move in support of working moms and an investment in the league's business—a nonnegotiable for WNBA commissioner Cathy Engelbert. "I'm a mom of two children. Here we were ready to tell all our players that we wanted them to come to a single site for ninety days—ninety-two if they made it to the championship—and we wanted them to feel as comfortable and supported as they possibly could," she says. Before becoming the first WNBA commissioner, Engelbert was the first woman CEO of consulting firm Deloitte, and the first woman to run a Big Four professional services company. Her kids were older by the time the league was tackling the logistics of creating a COVID-safe bubble, but she was extremely familiar with what it cost to juggle a demanding job and childcare in an environment not set up to support moms. She was not about to create one. "With an infectious disease, experts were saying to limit the number of people in the bubble as much as we could. But letting mothers bring their children? Nonnegotiable. Being a mom, I was like, yeah, we are going to do this."

The NWSL also made accommodations for moms to bring their kids when the league kicked off their 2020 season in a bubble. "It was like, really? Where has this support been my entire career?" McDonald told the *New York Times*.[26] That was the second time she'd experienced what a game changer employer support can be for moms. On the USWNT, "they bring a nanny in," she told me of her WNT experience. "They really take care of everything. It was just such a good feeling having that support. That part of it was really emotional. It was like, wow. No wonder this team succeeds."

The WNBA's and NWSL's brother leagues—the NBA and Major League Soccer—handled childcare during the pandemic season differently. In both bubbles, players' children and families were banned in an effort to minimize exposures. The assumptions behind the different strategies were searingly obvious: for men with kids, caregiving is optional (though asking men to choose between their careers and their kids is also terrible). But parenthood is obviously not just a woman's job. There are literally hundreds of fathers in the NBA and MLS and only around two dozen moms in the WNBA and NWSL.[27] When you look at the numbers, it's hard not to see how comparatively difficult it is for moms to make it as professional athletes—and how different the child-rearing expectations of dads.

~ ~ ~

WHEN WOMEN ARE forced to work around an economy designed for men, they pay. When they take time out of the full-time workforce, they pay then too, in three ways: the real-time earnings they lose during the period they're not working, the wage growth they would have earned during that time, and the retirement income they would have accrued. Taken together, the total cost of taking time off for caregiving responsibilities over the lifetime of a woman's career is three to four times greater than the real-time lost income during the months they weren't collecting a paycheck, according to the Center for American Progress (CAP). To help illustrate just how financially dire the consequences are of taking time off for care work, CAP even created a handy calculator. A twenty-eight-year-old teacher who makes $79,000 a year and takes three years off to give birth and care for a young child, for example, would have a lifetime income loss of $703,323. A thirty-two-year-old gig worker who brings home $150,000 a year but has no access to benefits like paid leave or 401k matching would forfeit nearly double her yearly income in lost earnings to take a single year off.[28]

Lost earnings are a powerful way to understand just how much women pay to balance the demands of a career with childbirth and caregiving. But they can never fully capture the emotional and mental toll it takes to navigate a system that penalizes pregnant people and caregivers of all genders. Ten months after Allyson Felix's emergency C-section, she broke a major record previously held by Usain Bolt, winning the most gold medals in track-and-field World Championships history.[29] It was an amazing victory for moms—the feminist headlines practically wrote themselves—but Felix doesn't want the gauntlet she went through to get lost in the glory of the moment. "I think it's amazing that it was able to happen and that I was able to get back to the World Championships, but at that time I still wasn't myself. I was still far from being at my best. I was still struggling with a lot of things," she says. "The real picture of it is that it was hard." And for most, unattainable. "Even though I went through a really rough period, I still had a lot of support from my family and from my coach. A lot of women don't necessarily have the support or the resources," she says.

The caregiver penalty might be easier to understand (though still deeply shitty) if moms who also work outside the home were an easily overlooked minority. But they're not. The vast majority of children in the US grow up in dual-income households, and in 41 percent of households, the mother is either the sole or cobreadwinner for her family. Women of color are significantly more likely to be their family's sole breadwinner: Sixty-one percent of Black mothers, 44 percent of Indigenous American mothers, and 31 percent of Latina mothers are their family's sole economic engine (as compared to 21 percent and 11 percent of white and Asian moms, respectively). And still, women take on the burden created by an economy that ignores half its workers, bootstrapping and funding their own support systems, rising to superhuman challenges that the majority of men in the workforce simply are not faced with. "We're bending around the workplace that has not been constructed for us and taking pay reductions that we put on ourselves to accommodate that," Dickens says, referring to the one in three women who considered reducing their paid professional hours in 2021 to meet the rising demands of care work. "This is an emergency for corporate America," the authors of McKinsey's 2021 "Women in the Workplace" report wrote. "Companies risk losing women in leadership—and future women leaders—and unwinding years of painstaking progress toward gender diversity."[30] As Dickens put it, "We've set ourselves up to take on pay reduction as a way to navigate our working world, but maybe the working world needs to be restructured."

~ ~ ~

ONE COULD BE forgiven for thinking that hanging moms out to dry must be a real cost-saving measure for businesses, or that not compensating care work must be saving the global economy big bucks. But it's not that simple. Take paid leave, for example. An economic analysis by the Time's Up Foundation published in 2021 found that a national paid family and medical leave plan of just twelve weeks—which would cover people of all genders and extend to all types of care work, not just childcare—would add $28.5 billion to the US GDP and create 162,000 new jobs. Not only would the leave-takers earn more money; their increased economic power would stimulate an additional $9.4 billion in growth as they would have more freedom to spend on things like takeout or a trip to the movies.[31]

Supporting working moms would also help prevent the costs of burnout, which has reached a record high: an alarming 42 percent of women report that they often or almost always feel burned out. That stat helps explain why so many women considered down-shifting in their career and why college-educated moms with access to remote work were the most likely to actually quit during the pandemic. This is a huge hit to the already challenged leadership pipeline. "When moms go missing from the workforce, that expertise, that training, that talent, all the things that these women would bring to the table goes with them," says Dickens. "And it's all because they were set up to fail." Providing childcare and implementing economic solutions designed to ease the motherhood penalty would, by some estimates, boost women's participation in the labor force by 2.2 percent and increase the GDP by $330 billion in the US alone.[32]

So, why continue to penalize working moms? "We have built our society on the backs of the unpaid labor of women," says Rodsky. That labor replaces a formal social safety net. For free. Counting what is currently the unpaid labor of care work in the global economy is the first step in changing that equation, she argues. "It is ultimately a reckoning around control and power. Controlling women is what we've done since the beginning of time. How we want women to act, behave, make their economic decisions," says Rodsky. "When I have as much time choice over how I use my day, then power structures will change."

≈ ≈ ≈

WHEN MONTAÑO, FELIX, and Gaucher spoke out in the *New York Times*, things did change. Facing intense public pressure—and congressional inquiries into whether male athletes received similar pay cuts after becoming fathers—Nike announced a major change to its maternity policy, guaranteeing an eighteen-month period surrounding pregnancy in which their pay and bonuses cannot be cut based on performance. The move standardized language that was first negotiated over a year prior by Lindsay Colas, the agent at Wasserman, on behalf of WNBA legend Maya Moore. When I asked her why she thought she was able to succeed in getting maternity protections into Moore's contract, who was then the biggest player in the league, when so many other athletes had faced resistance, she said simply, "What I'll say on the record is when you've got leverage, you've got leverage—and you have to use it." Other major sponsors Burton, Brooks, and Nuun followed suit.[33]

For Montaño and Felix, it isn't enough. Both women are working to rebuild the industry in a way that not only protects moms but respects and supports them. On the advocacy side, Montaño and her &Mother cofounder Dickens are hoping to make maternity protections the default in athlete contracts across the industry. For many brands, this still isn't standard practice, meaning women often have to ask for language to be added to their contracts, Dickens says, which can feel like putting a target on your own back. In 2021, &Mother partnered with activewear brand Oiselle to create publicly available standardized contract language, which covers pregnancy and postpartum recovery. They hope it will be a resource for any athlete, agent, or brand hoping to make change.[34]

After parting with Nike, Felix, you'll recall, became the first professional athlete to sign with Athleta—a partnership that not only accepted her identity as a mom but celebrated it. With Athleta's sponsorship strategy of championing the whole athlete (not just her performance), Felix does the usual things like compete in Athleta gear and appear in marketing campaigns, but that's far from the whole deal. By far the most impactful aspect of their partnership is the resources they've put behind supporting women and girls throughout their many life stages—including pregnancy and parenthood. Together with the Women's Sports Foundation, Athleta and Allyson launched the Power of She Fund in 2020, an ambitious multipronged grant program supporting women in sports and beyond. Since launching, as of Q1 2022, the fund has awarded over $1.45 million in grants for childcare (funding twenty-three mom athletes, including six who competed in Tokyo and two in Beijing) to movement-based organizations serving women and girls, and to WOC-founded organizations aiming to make wellness more inclusive and accessible in BIPOC communities.[35]

In 2022, Athleta and &Mother joined forces to provide free on-site childcare at the US National Track and Field Championships.[36] "Almost every woman we know who has children needs childcare help in some way, shape, or form," says Kyle Andrew, the former chief brand officer at Athleta. From their perspective, Athleta wanted to work with Felix as soon as they saw her op-ed in the *New York Times*, noting that their customer base is largely working moms. "There's something that's just so relatable about a mother—going through the different phases of life and the honesty of what that's like, of coming back and trying to be who you were, of being something different and that being okay," Felix says.

Why did brands overlook this part of the motherhood story for so long? Andrew won't speculate about what went on at other companies, but she says Athleta jumped at the chance to build a meaningful partnership with Felix for one reason: women in leadership positions who got it. "A lot of us are mothers. There's empathy there," Andrew says. There's also a shared understanding that their customers are facing many of the same challenges. "It's not that big a leap for us to say, 'Of course, women who work [outside the home]—whether you're an athlete, or you're sitting at a desk, or you're at a checkout counter—women who work and have children are under incredible pressure," Andrew says. "Of course it's resonating with our customers."

Elsewhere in sports, the women of the WNBA are also redefining what support for working moms looks like. When the players negotiated their groundbreaking 2020 CBA, they went in with motherhood protections as a top priority. It was a natural move, says Nneka Ogwumike, president of the WNBA Players Association at the time of the negotiations. "We are a league of women who use our bodies for our careers," she says. They scored big: fully paid maternity leave, a $5,000 childcare stipend, league-provided two-bedroom apartments for players living with their children, and up to $60,000 in family planning benefits to help cover the costs of adoption, surrogacy, egg freezing, or fertility treatments. That's miles ahead of maternity and family planning benefits available to most families in the US. "The deal represents moving forward both from a WNBA perspective, but also in general, for women in sports and society," Sue Bird, a member of the WNBA Players Association executive committee, told the *Seattle Times*. "When you look at things like what we're able to do with maternity leave and family planning . . . we're going to be looked at as—I think—pioneers in the sports world."[37]

~ ~ ~

ROLE MODELS PLAY a powerful part in moving women closer to parity (if you can see it, you can be it, or so the feminist mantra goes), and this is especially true with moms who face some of the biggest biases and institutional roadblocks. The more moms who make their stories visible, the more the penalties and biases around motherhood start to erode. Joann S. Lublin, the *Wall Street Journal*'s first career columnist and author of *Power Moms: How Executive Mothers Navigate Work and Life*, was in her twenties when she was offered a job as a bureau chief—a very big deal. It would have made her the first woman to run a bureau in *WSJ* history.

But Lublin turned the job down. "I didn't know any female managers with children in or outside of the *Wall Street Journal*. How could I think about taking a managerial role? I couldn't do that and possibly be a mother," she told me. "I think if I had female role models at that point in my career, I wouldn't have been so terrified about essentially stepping off of the diving board and not being sure whether there was water in the pool."

Lublin ultimately had (and still has) an extremely successful decades-long career as a journalist. But "for all my successes in my career, I never did become a bureau chief," she says. "Was it because I passed up the chance when I could have had it? Who's to know?" She did, however, become the working-mom role model she never had. "I'm often asked, Wasn't it scary being in the trailblazing generation? And I always say, our foremothers who were settling the frontier would have the same answer: It was exhilarating to be there, but it was also terrifying because you did not know what lay ahead or how you could succeed," she says.

The lack of women, and particularly mothers, in executive positions is still significant. But it's much rarer to hear a story like this today; to be up for a job and have literally zero mom role models to look to, thankfully, feels like a story from a different era. And in a very tangible way, it is. As Lublin found while interviewing eighty-six executive mothers for *Power Moms*, millennials approaching the challenge of combining parenthood and professional work were much less likely to doubt it could be done. "They had role models, had seen that it was possible, and in many cases had worked for women who had achieved the kinds of things that they were fantasizing about," Lublin says. That doesn't mean millennial working women live in a feminist utopia—instead of worrying *if* it is possible, they simply worry about how to be a mom in the workplace without losing their sanity—but things have undoubtedly improved. "They aren't uniformly in the dark ages, which often seemed the case in my generation," Lublin says about baby boomers like her.

Perhaps change will always require a sacrificial generation. Perhaps we as a culture need to see women like Montaño and Felix so offensively undervalued when they become moms that they spark viral internet outrage, or perhaps we need to witness a third of women in the workforce driven to their breaking point before we are eventually dragged into action. "Bringing these conversations forward is very vulnerable," says Ogwumike. "But it is also humanizing." This is where athletes have the most power—they face the same challenges as all working moms, but they do it on a much bigger stage.

"When our stories get out there and get told, it hits mainstream media in a way that lots of these other women haven't been able to have their stories told," says Gaucher—who ultimately did go on to play another season of professional basketball after the Olympics. When a lack of accommodations for breastfeeding prevented her from being able to do her job, it made global news, unlike the dozens of women who DM'd her whose best hope for an outlet was HR.

The more these women tell their stories, the better off we all are. The more Alysias (and Linneas) we see, the more normal it becomes to see pregnant bodies as capable of greatness. The more Allysons (and Camryns) out there, the faster the falsehood that women lose professional, revenue-driving value when they become mothers erodes. For every Kim (and Sophie), it gets easier to believe that support at home and at work is possible. "Seeing high-level athletes becoming mothers, having their story told, talking about the gender gap and pay inequality is going to raise awareness," Gaucher says. "So in the future, when my daughter Sophie is older, this won't be a thing."

PART II
POWER

I do not wish women to have power over men, but over themselves.

—MARY WOLLSTONECRAFT

CHAPTER 4

STRONGER TOGETHER

IN THE WEEKS LEADING UP TO THE 2017 WORLD CHAMPION-ships, the US Women's National Hockey Team found themselves at a crossroads. Despite medaling in every Olympics since the women's competition debuted at the games (two golds, four silvers, and one bronze, thank you very much), they were treated less like a global hockey superpower and more like an after-work rec league. While other women in sports were fighting for equal pay, these women had spent most of their careers fighting for *any* pay.

For the task of remaining one of the top teams in the world, USA Hockey paid them a pathetic stipend of $1,000 per month—just in the six months leading up to the Olympics. Otherwise, the players received "virtually nothing," according to their legal counsel. Without a sustainable professional hockey league where players could earn a living wage outside of their National Team work, many players felt they had no choice.[1] "We were forced to have another job while training full-time in order to be successful and win gold medals," says Kendall Coyne Schofield, a three-time Olympic

forward. Most women I know understand some version of this situation. One in which those with the power to write checks suggest
that we should merely be thankful when we're given bigger opportunities and responsibilities, not get greedy by asking to actually be
paid for our work too—that if women want equal treatment, they
should just hustle harder.

Meanwhile, the 2017 World Championships were just weeks
away and negotiations with USA Hockey were going . . . poorly.
"We just weren't taken seriously," says Hilary Knight, eight-time
world champion and four-time Olympian. "We had people from
the other side fall asleep at the table." If women in hockey were
ever going to get equal pay, let alone power and respect, the team
knew they had to raise the stakes.

So together, they threatened to quit.

For every top women's hockey player in the United States to
boycott the World Championships was a huge gamble. But frustrations with the lack of investment in women's hockey had been
simmering since before Coyne Schofield, Knight, and their teammates were old enough to hold a stick; they were sick of begging
for scraps. A boycott may have been a massive risk, but it was their
best chance to change the game. "This was the pinnacle of our
sport. For some players, this was their first opportunity [to play
for Team USA] and could have been their last," Coyne Schofield
says. But for all the individual reasons the women had for wanting to play, there were many more collective reasons not to. This
generation of players had grown up watching women stars dominate in sports—Mia Hamm, Venus and Serena Williams, Sheryl
Swoopes—and still be summarily dismissed. They'd watched
them break attendance records and still be denied raises. They'd
watched them crush stereotypes and still be called sexist names.
They'd watched over and over again as women in sports fought
for power. And they'd learned a lot: namely, that their strength as
a collective was much bigger than any individual ambition. "We

finally had the right women in the room and the right culture to be able to trust one another to really put it all on the line," says Knight. "I think we knew we had nothing to lose."

Those in power at USA Hockey did not take kindly to the team's show of united strength. Rather than meet the National Team at the bargaining table, they tried to replace them on the roster—first with Division I collegiate players, then with Division II and Division III. They even reached out to players still in high school. The National Team players thought that USA Hockey might do something like this in an effort to make the best women's hockey players on the planet feel replaceable. But to see it actually going down? Infuriating. Imagine being the objective best in the world at what you do and finding out that instead of paying you minimum wage, your boss would rather replace you with a high school intern.

USA Hockey had a history of treating its women players as replaceable. In 2000, the Women's National Team players sent their federation a letter making a case for greater investment in the women's game and asking for more resources. They were fresh off a victory in the first ever Olympics for women's hockey in 1998 and fired up by the Mia Hamm–era US Women's National Soccer Team, who had just begun their own fight for equal pay and investment. "We felt like our team had garnered enough respect after our gold-medal victory and U.S.A. Hockey would be ready to entertain the issues we raised," wrote Cammi Granato, the team captain during the late '90s, in an article for ESPN. It did not go over well. "They were furious. . . . I will never forget the call from my coach; he scolded me, telling me we betrayed them and broke a trust that could never be repaired," she wrote. "We had no support and no leverage." Instead of making positive change, asking for more had triggered a culture of fear in the players, Granato said—speak up and you might lose your spot. A few years later, the women's head coach did unceremoniously fire Granato, widely considered one of the best hockey players of all time and still at the top of her game, in a highly criticized decision called "classless," "cold," and "merciless." (His reasoning: "Like all players, if they choose to try to play forever, their number's liable to come up," then head coach Ben Smith told reporters during a conference call.)[2] "That's one of the things that we were all scared about," says Knight. "But we knew that if we stayed together, we were going to be fine."

The 2017 National Team had learned from their predecessors—a fact USA Hockey gravely underestimated. This was not an issue of twenty-three ungrateful women a powerful governing body could simply sweep aside. The battle for equitable support had exposed a culture of disrespect toward women in hockey so obvious to every woman and girl who played that it quickly turned into a movement. While USA Hockey was trying to recruit younger players to undermine its rogue athletes, the National Team players were making their own calls—"We had a phone tree. We went old school," says Knight—to high school and college hockey players. The players worked the phones constantly, sometimes skating with an AirPod in one ear during practice, explaining what they were fighting for—a sustainable future for all women in hockey—and why it was so important that they were unified.

Fair or not, the players knew that to pull this off they would have to stay in flawless form, ready to compete in the quickly approaching World Championships, in the event they were able to reach a deal with their federation. "The pressure was really on us to go win," says Knight. So they did it all—they trained, they talked to their lawyers about the negotiations, they fanned out to call every amateur player across North America they could possibly reach. "Women have this capacity to carry more because we have to. We don't have a choice," says Knight. "Whether we like it or not, our future lies in our hands—we have to create it."

By the time USA Hockey got to the amateur players, it was too late. One by one, they told USA Hockey to take their offer and stuff it—they were standing with the National Team. "That could have been their first and only chance to ever put on a Team USA jersey in their lives. It's what you're dreaming to accomplish from the time you're a young girl," Coyne Schofield says. "All of these players saying no to USA Hockey speaks to the fact that this boycott was about way more than the twenty-three players who were on the 2017 World Championship roster." But it wasn't just the amateur players who stood with the National Team. The WNBA stood with them. The USWNT stood with them. The NHL, the NFL, and the MLB all stood with them. Across sports, leagues issued statements in solidarity. Their collective action was so inspiring that twenty US senators even stood with them, writing a letter to USA Hockey in support of the players.[3] "When you rally the troops and you have your army of women and men wanting to change this game for the better," says Coyne Schofield, "it's scary and it's exciting."

Within two weeks of announcing their boycott, the united front of women's hockey players had a deal—a $24,000 yearly training stipend from the US Olympic and Paralympic Committee (still miles from a living wage but a significant move in the right direction), a pool of prize money and performance bonuses, travel provisions equal to the men's team, and the creation of a Women's High Performance Advisory Group tasked with growing investment in women's and girls' hockey.[4]

By coming together, by speaking with one voice, the women had ultimately clinched something even more consequential than a gold medal: power.

~ ~ ~

THE SINGLE MOST dominant force behind the progress made in narrowing the gender gap is the fact that women are organizing. They're crossing the borders between teams, between industries, and between countries to build a collective, closing the power gap one negotiation, one hashtag, one cultural reckoning at a time. "As women, we have had to be so competitive because there's always been only one seat at the table for one of us. But by being collaborative, they can't ignore us," Chiney Ogwumike, a forward for the WNBA's Los Angeles Sparks, told *Glamour*. "We're realizing that we can shake that whole table down."[5]

Women's participation in unions—in sports and other industries—is a game changer in closing the pay gap. An analysis of 2020 wages found unionized women made 88 cents to unionized men's dollar, while non-unionized women made 82 cents to the non-unionized male dollar. Latina workers receive the biggest benefit from collective action: unionized Latinas typically make 40 percent more per week than women from this group who aren't union members. It's no wonder women are "taking over" the modern labor movement, as one headline put it, unionizing in record numbers. Women still make up marginally less than half of all union members, but they're the fastest-growing group in the labor market—as much as 60 percent of all workers organizing over the past decade have been women. "It's such an exciting moment because people are awake," says Liz Shuler, president of the American Federation of Labor and Congress of Industrial Organizations (AFL-CIO)—the largest federation of unions in the United States, which is home to some of the most recognizable unions in the world, including the Screen Actors' Guild, American Federation of Teachers, and the NFL and NWSL Players Associations. Since 2020, the labor movement has seen several high-profile wins—from soccer players to Starbucks baristas, restaurant workers to Etsy sellers. Women led many of them.[6]

Women are born to revolutionize the workplace, says Shuler. "Women are naturally more collaborative, we are better listeners, we are problem solvers," she says. "And when you push us too far, watch out." But gender is only one part of the story. The majority of these modern labor movements are led by women of color—a fact wholly unsurprising to longtime organizers like Ai-jen Poo, president of the National Domestic Workers' Alliance, cofounder of SuperMajority, and executive director of Caring Across Generations. At the most basic level, women of color are disproportionately concentrated in underpaid, undervalued industries. "We basically considered them . . . well, we never really considered them at all," says Poo. But it's not just their proximity to the most fundamental challenges of the power gap that makes women of color the most important voices in closing it. To create change, you need to really understand power. You need to understand its ugliness, its oppression. Its potential. Poo describes experiencing multiple hierarchies of power and privilege like wearing 3D glasses—it gives you a multidimensional view of reality. "That means when women of color are designing strategy and solutions, we're seeing the world in relief, we're seeing the relations of power as they exist," she says. "If you have lived experience of how race and gender and class and disability and all these things work together, it gives you a different capacity to imagine solutions, to design them, and to push for them." Maybe women are inherently better at collective action—or maybe they've simply been forced to be.

What labor movements driven by women show again and again is that closing the power gap often starts with opting out of existing systems. This is what happened in 1975 when nearly all the women in Iceland collectively quit. At the time, Icelandic women were making less than 60 percent of what men in the country made for performing equal work. Not only did they opt out of showing up for their paid jobs, they refused to cook, take care of children, or perform any of the other dozens of unpaid functions so often labeled "women's work." The orderly hum of Icelandic life fell apart in precisely one day: businesses were forced to close, government offices ground to a halt, panicked hordes of men, unsure how to prepare dinner for their families, caused stores across the country to sell out of easy-to-boil hotdogs. It was madness.[7] Who could have known that women's labor was such a key factor preventing society from falling into chaos? (Women. Women knew that.)

Nearly fifty years later, Iceland's "Women's Day Off" remains a gold standard example of women's collective power. The gaping hole women left in the fabric of Icelandic society when they stopped contributing for just a single day led to lasting social and structural change. In the aftermath of the Women's Day Off, the Icelandic parliament passed a law banning wage discrimination. Five years after the strike, Vigdís Finnbogadottir, a divorced single mom, was elected as Iceland's president. She was the first democratically elected woman head of state in the world. Vigdís was among the crowd of twenty-five thousand women who gathered in Reykjavik's Downtown Square on that history-making day in 1975 and credited the Day Off as setting her on the path to the presidency, to which she was reelected three times before retiring. At the risk of overstating it, women in Iceland came together *and the world literally changed*. Iceland is now the most gender-equal country in the world—an accomplishment that in many ways can be traced back to that single day when women stood shoulder to shoulder.[8]

Lasting change requires these kinds of multidimensional shifts in power, says Poo. You need to change laws, but you also need to change hearts and minds. And athletes are particularly good at this. Over the last fifty years, the world of sports, both men's and women's, has been home to some of the most recognizable and successful demonstrations of the collective voice thanks to athletes' big personal platforms and news-making players' unions. With remarkable consistency, the women in these movements know exactly how their collective force can ignite change for women everywhere.

That legacy of power could reasonably be credited to Billie Jean King. Three years before she handed the world an updated understanding of women's power on a silver platter with her victory over

Bobby Riggs, King put together arguably the most consequential sports contract ever signed (if not one of the most important deals ever made by women in any industry) by getting women to stand together. King joined forces with eight other top tennis players— Rosie Casals, Nancy Richey, Julie Heldman, Valerie Ziegenfuss, Judy Dalton, Kerry Melville Reid, Peaches Bartkowicz, and Kristy Pigeon—to spearhead the formation of the first all-women's tennis tour. The Original 9, as they were dubbed, were sick of unequal treatment by the male-run US Lawn Tennis Association (now referred to simply as the US Tennis Association)—grossly unequal prize money, lack of investment, rampant sexism, you know the drill—so they broke with the governing body of the sport and signed symbolic $1 contracts to create their own tour. The Virginia Slims Tour was the immediate precursor to the creation of the Women's Tennis Association in 1973 and was so threatening to establishment tennis that the USLTA went so far as to suggest they would ban the top women in the sport from competing in their events. (The two Australian players in the O9—Dalton and Reid— were actually banned from some tournaments by the Lawn Tennis Association of Australia.)[9]

Opting out of the organization that governed their sport to form their own tour was a serious risk—the Original 9 gave up the establishment prestige and validation offered by the USLTA as well as all their resources and funding. They did it to build something that would be better for the women who came after them, a gamble that ultimately paid off. Their act of collective defiance grew into the greatest financial success story in women's sports; tennis players have dominated the top ten spots on Forbes's highest-paid women athletes list in the decades since.[10]

Fifty years later, when women come to King asking for her advice as they fight their own battles for equality, the first thing she asks is whether they are fighting as part of a united front. "This is the first thing you must do," she told the women's hockey players when they came to her for advice ahead of the 2017 World Championships. "You must get your very top players—all of them or else you cannot make this happen." In fact, she urged them to think even bigger, encouraging them to reach out to their biggest rivals: fellow hockey powerhouse Team Canada. If they wanted to see real change, they'd need to put their differences aside for the common goal of advancing the sport for women. "You can try to kill each other when you're playing for the gold or World Championship, but not when it comes to this. You've got to be absolutely connected," she recalls saying.

After their landmark victory in 2017, women's hockey still faced massive challenges. The fledgling National Women's Hockey League (NWHL), which rebranded as the Premiere Hockey Federation (PHF) in 2021, was on shaky ground—player salaries for the 2017–2018 season were between $5,000 and $7,000. Then in 2019, a bombshell: the more established (though still low-paying) Canadian Women's Hockey League (CWHL) ran out of funding and abruptly folded.[11] Suddenly, many of the best women's hockey players in the world had nowhere viable to play—and no choice but to unite. "When we are playing for our respective countries, there's a strong dislike for each other on the ice. You can see it," says Knight. But this was bigger than any rivalry. News of the CWHL shutdown reached the players just before they all arrived at the World Championships in Finland, where they were set to face off for gold yet again. Before they hit the ice, the Americans and the Canadians sat down in the hotel lobby to talk about teaming up. The result of that meeting was the Professional Women's Hockey Players Association (PWHPA), formed in 2019 as a joint effort between the two biggest rivals in hockey to advance the women's game.

Step one: organize their own tour, just as the Original 9 had done. "It was one of those things like, build it as you fly," Knight says. And they had to build *everything*. Where were they going to play? How would they create teams? Who would coach? Where could they order jerseys? Who would be in charge of hiring refs? Where could they secure a consistent locker room? How much should tickets cost? Oh, and how do you *run a business*?

Skates on, AirPods in, the players had to figure out the answers to every one of these questions while still training as professional athletes. "We had two hundred players at the time who were relying on us to provide training resources, games, and a bit of funding for everything in between to make it all work," Knight says. Even scheduling practice times presented a challenge: "How do we arrange ice time for practicing when, oh, by the way, half of our organization works a legitimate day job, and plays professional hockey part-time," Knight says. The result of their work was the six-city Dream Gap Tour, which included games at Madison Square Garden in New York City and the United Center in Chicago. These were venues so big and storied in hockey (the home ice of the New York Rangers and Chicago Blackhawks, respectively) that the women had always been told, "You guys couldn't even turn the lights on," Knight says. "Well, we did, and we did it ourselves."

Following the success of the dream the players built themselves, they announced another history-making collaboration: this time, with the King herself. In 2022, the PWHPA and Billie Jean King announced plans to launch a professional women's hockey league in which players will finally have the chance to make a living wage, with salaries starting at a reported $55,000.[12]

~ ~ ~

THE WOMEN OF the WNBA are also no strangers to the power of the collective voice; they know precisely how impactful it is to opt out and build something better for women. They formed the first professional labor union in women's sports in 1998 and began laying the groundwork for future generations of players to have the chance to one day make "LeBron money." But progress was slow; in 2018, over twenty years since the league was founded, the median player salary just barely qualified as a living wage. So the WNBA Players Association made a historic move: they opted out of their contract with the league, formally requesting the league meet them at the table to negotiate a new deal for players moving forward and putting the establishment on notice. The system wasn't working, and they, the 144 women of the WNBA, were taking it upon themselves to build a new one. "We're opting out because there's still a lot more work to be done. And we're betting on ourselves to do it," Nneka Ogwumike, president of the Players Association (and Chiney's older sister), wrote in an essay announcing the opt-out.[13]

Opting out of the deal they had with the league, the players knew, would almost certainly result in them being called "greedy," as women so routinely are, every time they dare to ask for more than the status quo. Even with a chasmic pay gap, the WNBA was by many standards still the most successful professional league in women's sports. The WNBA had been steadily rolling along since 1996, had grown to include franchises in twelve markets, and had even produced some household sports names like Sue Bird, Lisa Leslie, and Sheryl Swoopes. But they weren't here to please the "you should be grateful just to be here" crowd. In a profound statement, all 144 women—the majority of whom were Black women—said *No, thanks. We can do better.*

What the players had realized was that as long as they operated in a system designed by and for men, they were playing at a disadvantage. "There hadn't been advocates for women in that space, so we have to advocate for ourselves," Nneka says. The players focused on three areas: player compensation (the cash), player health and safety (mental health, maternity protections, and more), and player experience (standards of play covering everything from locker rooms to travel accommodations). They brainstormed on a league-wide group chat and compared notes with what was happening in soccer and hockey. "We had to know the business better than the business itself, so that when we asked for something and they said, 'Oh, that might be too much,' we could say, 'Actually we ran the models. It works,'" Chiney says. (A lack of information about who's making how much and how you can reasonably expect to measure up is a major barrier to pay equity: a report by the National Bureau of Economic Research found that laws requiring salary transparency for university faculty reduced the gender wage gap by up to 30 percent—particularly on campuses where faculty was unionized.)[14] They were negotiating a basketball contract, but throughout the year-and-a-half-long process, the players were acutely aware that their final agreement would resonate beyond sports. "It's exhausting, but this is why we prevail—we will go above and beyond, we will do our homework, we will over-deliver," Chiney says; examples of women turning their collective voice into collective power were still too few for them not to get this right.

Just days before the new collective bargaining agreement was set to be announced, the players had a crisis of confidence. Was this proposal really the best they could do? At the eleventh hour they asked for more, making a "huge change" in the economic model for their salary and compensation. It was terrifying to push the boundary one more time, and the players agonized over the ask, Chiney says. "I think that's a big, big issue for us as women—we are in our own heads a lot because we're existing in spaces that aren't built for us." But they stuck together, and the league accepted the change. When that version of the CBA was ultimately announced in 2020, it was hailed as a model for other leagues. The average player salary is now over $120,000 (with a league minimum of $57,000) and loops the players into a revenue-sharing model, which means they'll actually get a piece of all the value they're generating for the league.[15] "By thinking big, we found solutions that we thought weren't even possible," Chiney says.

~ ~ ~

ONE OF THE many beautiful things about women's collective power is that it's cumulative. Tennis, soccer, hockey, basketball— all these women in their separate sports have learned from each other, shared resources, helped build upon each other's victories. And the same is true outside of sports: when women in one industry, or one company, or one sport win, they raise the collective bar, "permeating the entire ecosystem," says Shuler. That happens very literally—when workers at one company secure better pay by unionizing, they drive wages up at other companies who need to stay competitive—but also helps to create broader cultural shifts. Every moment that women step into their shared strength to say "no" has a ripple effect. This is what professional labor organizers like Poo call a 360-degree narrative, "where we are populating the cultural environment with models for something different, something new," she explains. "You're starting to feel actual momentum in the cultural environment around a new story and the idea that you can build and create an alternative to the status quo." When we see a win by the USWNT, or the women's hockey players or the women of the WNBA, it expands what people understand to be possible, Poo says.

Look no further than the USWNT. When the team first went public with their fight for equality in 2016, the force of their collective voice shot through the world of soccer like the breaking of a dam. As they spent years deadlocked in negotiations with their own federation, their efforts shifted the landscape of the global soccer community. Immediately after the USWNT filed that first claim with the EEOC, women's soccer players in Ireland and Denmark threatened their federations with a strike. Australian players went all in, launching their own strike. Nigeria's women's national team took their fight for unpaid salaries and bonuses public, marching on parliament. And by 2017, Norway had signed an equal pay deal with its men's and women's players. After the US team won the 2019 World Cup to chants of "Equal Pay!" at least five other

countries followed through: Australia, England, Brazil, Sierra Le-
one, and Ireland all struck equal pay deals with their men's and
women's soccer teams (the latter of which involved the men's team
agreeing to a pay cut). The USWNT's influence helped women in
hockey and basketball step into their power and ultimately get paid.
Their story ignited the frustrations of women much like Billie Jean
King's fight for equity that had inspired a generation of women to
ask for raises. When Dawn Staley, coach of the legendary University of North Carolina women's basketball team, signed a historic
$22.4 million contract, making her the highest-paid Black coach in
women's college basketball, she gave credit to a documentary she'd
watched about the USWNT's legal battle. "I watched it, and they
gave me the strength that I needed to keep pushing," she said.[16]

uh...

But it's how the team's fight stirred something in women across
industries that shows the true power of collective force. "Everyone
is paying attention to equal pay because women's soccer players
are talking about it," says Shuler. "They've used their platform in a
way that was so effective and more compelling than we've seen in
decades; all these women in the seventies out there in the streets
paved the way for us, but for whatever reason, they didn't open
people's ears as much as women in sports are now." Sports is a context that most people understand—there are clear metrics of success with outcomes that tell you how good a given person or team
is at their job. In the case of the USWNT, "people were able to see
us working hard and winning [and not getting paid]," says Rapinoe.
"I think it was an easily distilled example on public display of what
happens so often behind closed doors."

That the team filed their lawsuit on March 8, 2019—International Women's Day—was no coincidence. They wanted people
across the world to make the connection between their fight and
the fight for all women. They wanted people to join them. And
they did. "Girls stepped up. It was like heck yeah, let's go," says
Jessica McDonald. "Coming together with all these other women

from different backgrounds, different careers, it's a beautiful thing. We're all fighting now."

~ ~ ~

MANY OF THE most highly publicized demonstrations of collective power result in some real rah-rah, feel-good, girlpower moments. And those are deeply important. But we can't understand collective power without talking about the ability it gives women to burn down abusive systems.

On August 4, 2016, Rachael Denhollander, a former gymnast, wrote an email that would start a revolution. The *Indianapolis Star* had just published a bombshell report detailing a decades-long culture of abuse within USA Gymnastics (USAG), the organization responsible for helping gymnasts across the country realize their Olympic dreams. According to the *IndyStar*'s investigation, USAG had routinely covered up dozens of allegations of sexual abuse by USAG-affiliated coaches, compiling "complaint dossiers" on over fifty coaches and filing them in a drawer, rather than reporting the child abuse to authorities. Within hours of their story going live, reporters at the *IndyStar* received Denhollander's email. "My experience may not be relevant to your investigation, but I am emailing to report an incident that may be. I was not molested by my coach, but I was molested by Dr. Larry Nassar, the team doctor for USAG," she wrote. In another email: "My hope with a story would be that it would give a voice to others who have also been victims, and encourage them to come forward as well. I know this will be a long road, if it goes anywhere at all."[17]

In September 2016, the *IndyStar* published Denhollander's story along with the testimony of a second anonymous gymnast, who later came forward as Olympian Jamie Dantzscher, and their voices lit a powder keg. Since Denhollander sent that initial email, at least 332 women have come forward as accusers. Nassar was ultimately sentenced to up to 175 years in prison by Judge Rosemarie

Aquilina, who proclaimed, "I just signed your death warrant," at his sentencing.[18]

The culture of silencing women in gymnastics—which allowed predators like Nassar and the coaches named in the *IndyStar*'s original investigation to continue their abuse—hadn't exactly been a secret. Individual whistleblowers had been coming forward, by the dozens, for decades. In addition to the individual reports of sexual abuse that had gone mostly ignored within USAG, by Nassar's employer Michigan State University, and even by the FBI, there had also been public reports on emotional and physical abuse in the organization. First, there was investigative journalist Joan Ryan's shocking book *Little Girls in Pretty Boxes: The Making and Breaking of Elite Gymnasts and Figure Skaters*, originally published in 1995, which exposed the "legal and even celebrated" mental and physical abuse of women and girls in gymnastics and a culture of coaching in gymnastics and figure skating that caused eating disorders, mental suffering, and, in at least two extreme cases, death. (A report in the highly respected *New England Journal of Medicine* published the following year echoed her findings.) Yet little changed. Over a decade later, Jennifer Sey, a former national gymnastics champion, sounded the alarm again in her memoir *Chalked Up*, detailing a culture where all the same abuses reported by Ryan still dictated the experience of many girls in the sport. She was painted as a sore loser who never made the cut for an Olympic team and was ostracized from the gymnastics community, she says. "I would say there were more than fifty credible accounts before anyone started to say, 'Okay, maybe we need to take this seriously.' Getting to fifty, those young women were just dismissed and discredited," says Sey. In 2020, she produced a documentary about another whistleblower who went ignored. *Athlete A* told the story of abuses in gymnastics through the experience of Maggie Nichols—the first athlete to report Nassar's abuse to USAG. The organization allegedly worked to make Nichols's claim disappear, according to her legal counsel.

(USAG called this accusation "baseless," saying in a 2018 statement, "Contrary to reported accusations, USA Gymnastics never attempted to hide Nassar's misconduct.") "I am haunted by the fact that even after I reported my abuse, so many women and girls had to needlessly suffer at the hands of Larry Nassar," she testified before the Senate Judiciary Committee in 2021 about the failure of another powerful organization—the FBI—to act on reports of systemic sexual abuse in the sport.[19]

Not only did they fail to protect their athlete, some suggested USAG allegedly retaliated against her for speaking up. Nichols was heavily favored to make the 2016 Olympic team before she and her parents reported her abuse to USAG. In the months prior to the Olympic trials, Nichols had made a stunning comeback from a knee injury, ultimately finishing sixth place, which should have been enough to guarantee her a spot. But despite her pre- and post-injury performance, Nichols was unceremoniously left off the team of eight gymnasts (five competitors and three alternates). Being left off that Olympic team was not only soul-crushing; it likely also cost Nichols hundreds of thousands of dollars in endorsement deals surrounding the games. (The team was chosen by Martha Karolyi—the team coordinator and one-half of the wife-and-husband duo accused of fostering a "culture of fear" in US gymnastics and at their famous training ranch where Nassar committed much of his abuse—who explained the Nichols decision by saying her scores in each event simply hadn't been high enough to meet the threshold for the best combined winning team.)[20]

All these women were speaking up, often alone, and nothing changed. The abuse continued; the people in power stayed there. It often feels like the plight of women has to reach a grotesque level for people to take it seriously. How many women do you know who have worked in a toxic culture? How many have said something? How much has actually changed? Speak up alone and you have no power—you're the problem. And so most women leave: a toxic workplace culture is ten times as likely to cause you to quit your job as low pay, according to findings from the *MIT Sloan Management Review.*[21]

When Denhollander, Dantzscher, and the dozens of women who followed came forward, something was finally different: this time, there were simply too many women to ignore. "It's not Larry Nassar who exposed the culture in gymnastics, it was the fact that this army of gymnasts stepped forward," says Joan Ryan. "If he had been put in jail but all these gymnasts hadn't publicly stepped forward and said, 'Me too, me too, me too,' nothing would've changed."

This all happened before the Me Too era, when the call to believe women wasn't so firmly stuck in our collective consciousness. As more and more gymnasts came forward throughout 2017, women in other industries were undoubtedly taking notice, watching carefully as the growing army of women and girls who had felt powerless for so long came together to share their stories. A firestorm of cultural accountability was coming that would leave no industry untouched. And in the months before a viral tweet would spark the beginning of the Me Too movement, the Sister Army of gymnasts laid the kindling.[22]

Within sports, their collective accomplished a lot: a $500 million settlement reached with Michigan State University (where Nassar had been employed as a team physician and associate professor) and a $380 million settlement reached with USAG and the United States Olympic and Paralympic Committee (USOPC) were among the largest in the history of sexual abuse cases. The movement also sparked the creation of the USOPC-affiliated United States Center for SafeSport and the survivor-run Army of Survivors nonprofit, both watchdog groups tasked with making sure women in sport are never silenced again. But their collective force also helped to change the culture far beyond their sport. Following the testimonies of so many highly visible women in the gymnastics case, the

Rape, Abuse, and Incest National Network reported a 46 percent increase in calls to the National Sexual Assault Hotline.[23] Inspired by the strength of their sisters, women were starting to tell their stories. The first domino of the Me Too movement had fallen.

~ ~ ~

IT IS RAGE-INDUCING that this is how change happens—that women must come forward by the hundreds to be heard and by the millions to shift the culture. It is infuriating that women have to start a global movement in order to convince their employers to pay them equally. It is frustrating that women have to break the system, to boycott, to opt out in order to secure an equitable status quo. There is power found in the collective voice, but it often comes at enormous cost. There is no reimbursement for the reliving of trauma, or worrying you'll be without a contract and won't get paid, or the time spent organizing in the fight for the most basic resources. "There's days I wake up and I'm exhausted and it's not from training, it's from fighting. It's from the constant phone calls and conversations about the lack of resources the girls and women's game has gone without for years. Conversations that we've been having for years about things that should have been done a long time ago," says Coyne Schofield. But here's the good news: "It's in these times of disruption when the status quo shakes loose and there are big opportunities to accelerate change for everyone," says Poo.

That's precisely what Simone Biles did. On the eve of Nassar's sentencing, the greatest gymnast of all time added her voice to the Sister Army. "I am not afraid to tell my story anymore," she tweeted with the hashtag #MeToo. Biles was the only Nassar victim still competing for USAG. Training for the 2020 Tokyo Olympics meant doing so with the organization that had failed her so horrifically. But she was determined to make it mean something, to compete on her own terms, and to deliberately bulldoze a path for other women in the sport to do the same. In true opting-out-of-abusive-systems fashion, Biles delivered a resounding "no thanks" to the traditional post-Olympics victory tour. The cross-country exhibition historically hosted by USAG every four years featured the men's and women's Olympic teams and reportedly made the organization millions. In 2019, Biles effectively announced that era was over—she'd be staging her own tour after the Olympics, which would have zero affiliation with USAG and put women in gymnastics unequivocally in the seat of power. The decision to center the joy and skill of women was a deliberate choice. "It's an all-girl tour for women's empowerment. It was a great year for women to speak out, and I think it's nice to keep the ball rolling on that and to have women feel happy, and find their love and passion for gymnastics again," Biles told *Glamour*. "I know the men were really upset, but it's my tour."[24]

CHAPTER 5

CHANGEMAKERS

Gwen Berry, an Olympic hammer thrower with a killer arm and a penchant for wearing bold lipstick during competition, didn't have the benefit of a collective when she spoke out against racial injustice. She stood alone in 2019 when, during the final bars of the US national anthem at the Pan American Games in Peru, she bowed her head and raised her fist from the podium. It was fifty years since John Carlos and Tommie Smith became the first athletes to make the peaceful sign of protest against racial injustice, but just as it had been perceived then, an athlete raising a fist on the podium still felt radical. (It would be another few months before the Black Lives Matter movement would reach a cultural tipping point—among white people, at least—and protests against racial injustice would become common, even perversely cool.) Berry wasn't the only athlete to defy the rule against protests at the games in Peru—white male fencer Race Imboden kneeled on the podium during his medal ceremony. But as a five-foot-ten Black woman wearing blue lipstick, Berry provoked a different reaction with her fist raised in the air for eleven seconds.

The backlash against Berry was immediate and absolute, and in the aftermath, she almost lost her career. Her $35,000 grant from the US Track and Field Foundation vanished. The $40,000 to $50,000 Berry typically made annually (based on performance bonuses, qualifying for championship teams, and salary) with Nike disappeared. An $8,000 yearly stipend from the New York Athletic Club she'd come to rely on evaporated too. "Nike gave me no reason. They just called me and said they wouldn't continue my contract. The USA Track and Field Foundation, they definitely explicitly said we will not support what you did on the podium. The New York Athletic Club explicitly said it was because of my protest," she says.* "I literally lost $88,000 because of one moment." That was nearly all of her income.[1]

Political action has long been unwelcome or outright barred in sports under the guise that the space is some kind of apolitical utopia where the problems that plague the societies in which athletes play suddenly disappear. Even in a post–Black Lives Matter world, the International Olympic Committee Athletes' Commission warned athletes against any "divisive disruption" like kneeling ahead of the Tokyo Olympics held in 2021.[2] But sports—an institution with a long history of banning people from participating because of the

---

* In response to cutting ties with Berry, Nike said in a statement provided to the *Washington Post*, "Nike has a long history of supporting causes important to athletes and in line with our values. We have a long-standing belief in the power of sport to move the world forward. We continue to support athletes across the sports community in their response to the issue of systemic racism experienced by the black community. We do not comment on athlete contracts, but we respect Gwen as an athlete and her efforts to elevate an issue and drive change in a very critical area of importance to society." The USATF Foundation also denied that Berry's protest impacted her funding. CEO Tom Jackovic provided documentation of payments made to Berry after her protest to the *Washington Post*, but also confirmed that she did not receive the foundation's largest grant following the Pan-Am Games. "Gwen's allegation that her stance from the podium at the Pan-Am Games adversely affected our grant-making decisions in 2020 is inaccurate," he said.

color of their skin, or their gender, or, most recently, the chromosomes they possess—have never been neutral. Sports are political
by nature. They provide an arena where we can digest and decide
how we feel about inequality. In sports, we routinely see harmful
stereotypes about who belongs upended. It's here where we get to
see the most marginalized among us step into their full power as
teammates on an equal playing field. And it's on this field where
progress on social justice issues often reaches a cultural tipping
point. Athletes like Althea Gibson and Jackie Robinson who broke
the color barrier in sports in the 1940s and 1950s, for example,
made a measurable impact in advancing civil rights and bringing
conversations about equality to every game they played. As much
as the "shut up and dribble" crowd may not like to hear it, athletes
are obvious political changemakers.

Berry grew up in Missouri, near Ferguson, the city where an
unarmed eighteen-year-old Black man named Michael Brown was
shot and killed by a white police officer in 2014. "He died on the
streets that I grew up around, a couple miles away from my son's
school," she says. "That could have been my child." As Berry took
the podium in 2019, she should have been thinking about her joy—
she had just won a gold medal. It was the peak of her career and she
deserved to revel in the moment of glory athletes spend thousands
of grueling hours chasing. But instead she was thinking about
Brown. "I'm thinking about police brutality and cycles of violence
and basically what it really costs to be Black in this country," she
recounted in an essay for the *Players' Tribune*. "And eventually, I just
think like, *You know what? This song doesn't speak for me. This anthem
doesn't represent me.*"[3]

In addition to the lost sponsorships and grants, Berry was put
on probation by the US Olympic and Paralympic Committee for a
full year (as was Imboden).[4] "I felt betrayed because I knew that I
was doing something right, something necessary, something that
needed to be done, even though it made people feel uncomfortable,"

she says now. At that point, the USOPC's long-standing policy around athlete protests of any kind was still in effect. Berry had known the risks when she raised her fist. But, the way she sees it, the rule, and the system that enforced it, blamed athletes for speaking about hard truths America didn't want to face. "I truly never had a problem with putting USA across my chest until I educated myself. Until I really dug deep into understanding that systematically and economically the world has not gotten better for Black people in America," she says. "We are still marginalized. We are still underprivileged. We are still underserved."

Had Berry staged her protest just a few months later, after the reckoning provoked by the murders of George Floyd and Breonna Taylor in 2020, her sponsors' reactions likely would have looked much different. Once racial justice caught hold of the white American consciousness, brands began falling all over themselves to align with outspoken athletes leaning into their activism. In 2019, standing up alone had cost her nearly everything. "Anytime you can single out a specific athlete and make a martyr out of them, it's an easy opportunity for people in power," she says.

With her sponsorship money gone, she was no longer able to afford her own place and moved in with family members. "Mind you, I'm a single Black mother still trying to live and work and qualify for championship teams," she says. Broke and essentially powerless, she considered quitting the sport. It was John Carlos, the Olympian who helped usher in a new era of athlete activism in the '60s, and one of Berry's mentors, who encouraged her to stay in the game. "He was like, 'You got to continue because your platform is where people are seeing you the most,'" she says. And he was right. Berry's continued presence at track-and-field events and activism on social media helped change the face of athlete protests. In March 2021, the USOPC released an open letter stating they would allow athletes to exercise their right to peacefully protest at the upcoming US Olympic Trials and also apologized to Berry for the way they'd responded to her protest a year earlier. (The International Olympic Committee still bans any demonstration of "political, religious, or racial propaganda" at the games themselves, vaguely stating that athletes who protest will be subject to some form of disciplinary action.[5])

"This moment really made me realize that athletes are only supported when they are being who other people want them to be," Berry says. "When they stand for what other people want them to stand for." And that's not good enough.

~ ~ ~

BERRY IS PART of a global sisterhood of women athletes who have used their platform to fight for change, often at great cost. Though routinely overlooked, women activists have been some of the most powerful changemakers in history, who often get shit done not just for themselves but for other marginalized groups. "You don't know what inclusion means until you've been excluded," says Billie Jean King. "Women know what that feels like. We have empathy."

In sports, no one is creating more inclusive change than the women of the WNBA—a league comprising roughly 80 percent women of color. Women's basketball was the first sport to bring the Black Lives Matter movement into the arena when, in 2014, college basketball player Ariyana Smith raised her fist during the national anthem and then lay on the court for four minutes to symbolize the four hours Michael Brown's body was left uncovered in the street after he was shot by police. Her protest received little attention nationally—as a collegiate women's basketball player, she didn't receive nearly the same coverage as NFL player Colin Kaepernick would when he knelt during the anthem two years later—but she still faced career-defining consequences. Smith was suspended from the team. The decision was reversed shortly after, but the damage had been done—Smith elected not to return to the team, citing an environment that was "not conducive to [her] growth."[6]

At the time, the news of Smith's protest quickly blew over, but her activism had set something in motion within women's basketball. The WNBA was beginning to mobilize. In July 2016, the Minnesota Lynx took the court in black warm-up shirts bearing the phrases "Black Lives Matter," "Change Starts with Us," and "Justice and Accountability" along with the names of Philando Castile and Alton Sterling, Black men who had both been killed by police in separate shootings that month. The shirts also bore the Dallas Police shield, in honor of five officers who had been killed in a shooting. The following day, players from the New York Liberty followed suit, showing up in warm-up shirts reading #BlackLivesMatter and #Dallas5, and were soon joined by players from the Phoenix Mercury and Indiana Fever. The league, still under the impression it could silence the players to uphold the existing power structures, issued fines—$5,000 per team and $500 per player for uniform violations. (The fines were later rescinded, and the league has since come under new leadership that is much more supportive of player activism.) Far from being deterred, the movement spread; players across the league refused to answer postgame press questions unless they pertained to Black Lives Matter and criticized the league for supporting activism around breast cancer awareness or PRIDE but not racism, which impacted the majority of its players.[7] All of this happened before Colin Kaepernick took a knee.

The women of the WNBA have mastered the practice of standing together, making space for their many intersectional identities, and using that power to build better systems for all women. It's in the league's DNA as a "collection of strong, fierce, unapologetic, Black women," says Chiney Ogwumike. Since the WNBA was founded, its players have been on the ground, making the sacrifices, doing the work. Aiding in their effectiveness is that they often get to do it on TV. "Our platforms are big," says Nneka Ogwumike, president of the Players Association. "If we can use our platform to bring [these issues] forward just by being

ourselves, then that's really where the intention lies. Our existence is the resistance."

That the WNBA's activism is intersectional to its core is notable
because so many activist movements led by women have not been.
For all women activists have accomplished, there's an oppressive
dark side in the history of the fight for women's equality—often
led by white women. It was powerful women activists who tried to
suppress the Black vote while advocating for women's suffrage; it
was white women who led the charge to bring more girlbosses into
the C-suite while staying largely silent about the overwhelming
whiteness, cis-ness, and able-bodied-ness of corporate leadership;
and "advocates" for women in sports who are currently leading the
fight against the inclusion of trans women and girls. All of these
harmful discriminatory movements have happened under the ban-
ner of a certain brand of white "feminism" with a toxic history
that's played a significant role in shaping who has power and our
ideas of who belongs.

The WNBA's activism in 2016 was just the beginning. The experience of negotiating their groundbreaking collective bargaining
agreement in 2018 and 2019 only deepened the players' commitment to social justice. "This is a league that is 75 to 80 percent Black
women and we were doing this [negotiating] at a time where we
were in the middle of social unrest," says Chiney. "Value—not just
when it comes to my job but as a human being—was something
that came front and center." This is what makes the women of the
WNBA such important activists—in fighting for the most marginalized, they lift us all. Unlike white feminism, which aspires not to
dismantle the power structures that create inequality but to climb
to the top of them, intersectional feminist movements build new
systems, centering the voices of the most marginalized. Intersectional feminism understands that there is no closing the gender
pay gap without closing the racial pay gap. There is no power for
women without power for trans women. There is no equal standing

for one without equal respect for all.[8] All systems of inequality are connected, so "if you address just one, you might get a temporary victory but you're not going to win the war," says Delia Douglas, the professor who studies race and gender in sport. One of the most obvious and pressing intersections of inequality is race and gender—"Through the experiences of Black women, you will see a way to address multiple systems of power," Douglas says, yet Black women are the most likely to be ignored by social justice movements.* That makes the examples of intersectional activism led by Black women all the more important. It's no coincidence that they often happen to be some of the most powerful, culture-defining movements in history: Tarana Burke founded the Me Too movement; Alicia Garza, Patrisse Cullors, and Opal Tometi created the Black Lives Matter movement; Stacey Abrams founded Fair Fight Action, which brought national attention to voter suppression.

The following WNBA season in 2020 was unlike any other—logistically, because of the coronavirus pandemic, and in purpose, because of the deaths of George Floyd and Breonna Taylor. By this point, athlete activism had become more common, with athletes across sports protesting in support of racial justice and igniting a national debate. Women athletes quickly emerged as the loudest voices, appearing on panels and prime-time news. "They could speak in ways that people connected with that were bold and smart and informed. And they weren't afraid to ask hard questions—they could carry this moment," says Lindsay Kagawa Colas, the activist agent of many of the top WNBA players. "We've always had a movement," adds Nneka. The moment had finally caught up.

---

* In a phenomenon dubbed "intersectional invisibility," researchers at the University of Michigan found that Black women simultaneously suffer from racist stereotypes and are less often associated with the concept of a "prototypical woman." In practice, that means they're often overlooked in both feminist and antiracist movements, which instead, respectively, center the experiences of white women and Black men.

Before the season began, the Minnesota Lynx and Seattle Storm stood on the court in the WNBA's bubble in Bradenton, Florida, which had been painted with "Black Lives Matter" in bold letters. Layshia Clarendon, a guard for the Minnesota Lynx and former first vice president of the Women's National Basketball Players Association (WNBPA) took the mic on behalf of the entire league. "We are dedicating this season to Breonna Taylor, an outstanding EMT who was murdered over 130 days ago in her home," they said. "We are also dedicating this season to the Say Her Name Campaign, a campaign committed to saying the names and fighting for justice for Black women. Black women who are so often forgotten in this fight for justice, who do not have people marching in the streets for them."[9] When the players turned their backs to the television cameras to observe a moment of silence, they revealed twenty-eight jerseys bearing Taylor's name. "Their activism really is an expression of Black love—love of self and love of community," says Douglas. "It was an affirmation that we matter, and we know we're stronger together."

The women and nonbinary athletes of the WNBA were about to prove exactly how strong, destabilizing one of the most old-school power structures in the country: electoral politics.

As the league prepared for its groundbreaking season, Commissioner Cathy Engelbert, who joined the WNBA in 2019 and helped set a new tone in the league's response to player activism, received a letter from a team owner expressing her "adamant" opposition to the "Black Lives Matter political movement." Kelly Loeffler was at the time both a co-owner of the WNBA's Atlanta Dream franchise and a Republican senator who was credited as the "single biggest supporter of President Donald Trump's agenda" during her time in office. She blamed the movement for promoting "violence and destruction across the country," and wrote that rather than put Breonna Taylor's name on player jerseys, the league should emblazon them with an American flag to "ensure we reflect the values of freedom and equality for all."[10]

Here was a conservative, wealthy, white woman who "owns" a team mostly made up of Black women, trying to censor their voices. It was a "slap in the face," says Elizabeth Williams, then a forward for the Atlanta Dream and member of the WNBPA's executive committee. So the players did what they have come to do best, the thing that makes them the leaders of a new generation of athlete activists: they joined together and, collectively, took action.

When news of Loeffler's letter spread, the players of the Dream were in quarantine. Play hadn't even begun yet and already the season's historic dedication to Taylor was being undermined by someone in a position of power over the players. The Dream immediately got on a Zoom call. "The biggest issue was, this is still our owner, she still cuts our checks," recalls Williams. There was no question that the team would speak out, but they "tussled" with how best to respond. After an initial team-wide Instagram post condemning Loeffler's letter and affirming the dedication to Black Lives Matter as a "statement of humanity," they began talking about a bigger league-wide response. Something that would shift the balance of power.[11] So the 144 women of the WNBA came together. They talked. They listened. They consulted advisors. And then calmly, thoughtfully, and decisively, they mobilized. Rather than attack Loeffler personally, only giving her more attention and airtime, the players stopped saying her name altogether and instead focused their efforts on dismantling the very platform from which she spoke.

Acting on the advice of Stacey Abrams, a member of the WNBPA's board of advocates, they asked for a meeting with Reverend Raphael Warnock—Loeffler's Democratic opponent in the upcoming Georgia (US) Senate race—and simultaneously launched a plan to get her the hell out of the Dream's ownership group.

Warnock wasn't just the guy who could unseat Loeffler; he deeply embodied the values of the league, championing voting rights, criminal justice reform, and reproductive rights, and they threw their full support behind his campaign. They showed up to nationally televised games wearing "Vote Warnock" T-shirts and, having done their homework, spoke convincingly about their reasons for supporting him in the press. Within days Warnock's campaign saw an influx of donations, and his poll numbers surged. An analysis by the *Washington Post* found that the WNBA's T-shirts alone accounted for a 20 percent boost in campaign donations for the underdog candidate.[12] After a runoff election, Loeffler lost her Senate seat to Warnock, and after all the pressure from the players, she sold her stake in the Dream. The women of the WNBA had won.

This kind of activism in sports was unprecedented. These women didn't do things the old way, shutting up and dribbling while their owner worked against everything they stood for. They didn't remain content with symbolic protests against racism. Nor did they heed the myth that sports shouldn't be political. They used their influence, turning the precious moments of media attention they receive as women athletes away from themselves and toward a cause that would impact more marginalized groups. They built a new system with intersectionality at its core instead of playing by the rules of the old one; and in doing so, they set a completely new standard for what activism in sports can look like.

I asked Williams and Nneka why the WNBA is so good at advocating for this type of system-wide change. Their answers were both practical and profound. The players, remember, had just come off the experience of negotiating the league's groundbreaking CBA. In advocating for themselves, the league had learned to work as a unit, to account for each other's individual differences, and to work toward solutions that would impact the collective good. It gave them a crash course in "understanding what it's like to have difficult conversations with people with a lot of different viewpoints" and to ultimately find a balance, Williams says. "The best reason I can give you is we listen to each other, we provide space to be heard,"

Nneka adds. "Leading by listening is what I think we do best. And it works."

~ ~ ~

EVEN IF THE women of the WNBA hadn't used their platform to explicitly fight for racial justice and gender equality, they would still be worthy of recognition. Every time a woman athlete steps into the public arena, she challenges the norms around what women "should" look like, "should" act like, and "should" be able to achieve. The very act of existence in a space created for and designed to uphold ideals of masculinity and heteronormativity is an act of resistance.

Visibility in sports as a form of activism has been particularly important in the fight for LGBTQ+ rights. Some of the highest-profile queer women in history have been athletes—Billie Jean King, Sheryl Swoopes, Abby Wambach, Megan Rapinoe, Sue Bird—all of them publicly out during their playing careers. Today women's sports have so many queer icons that it's almost strange to think being an out woman in sports was, in the very near past, a radical act. King, now one of the most famous LGBTQ+ activists in history, didn't come out voluntarily—she was outed in 1981 and lost every single one of her sponsors within twenty-four hours. A mere forty years later, Megan Rapinoe and her fiancée Sue Bird are gracing lists of the "Most Iconic Power Couples in Sports" and appearing in a naked embrace on the cover of two of the most historically heteronormative publications in media: ESPN and GQ. (Out men in sports are significantly rarer—in the 103-year history of the NFL, for example, only one active player has come out as gay, and that wasn't until 2021.)[13] One explanation for this is that women in sports are "already fighting against so many systems," says Alex Schmider, director of transgender representation at GLAAD, an LGBTQ media advocacy organization, that adding one more fight in the right to show up in their full humanity isn't as likely to faze them.

For transgender women and girls, being visible in sports is still a much riskier form of activism. "Every single day when I wake up and put on my sports bra, the first thing I think about is that I could go onto the track and somebody could just take me out," says CeCé Telfer, a NCAA Division II champion runner. Telfer is transgender (the first out trans woman to win an NCAA track-and-field title), a fact that became relevant to her running career when she began medically transitioning in 2017 and made her first appearance in competition as herself in 2018. Telfer just wanted to run, to do the thing that made her feel free and allowed her to explore her potential, but she found herself the subject of intense internet hate after Donald Trump Jr., then son to the president of the United States, tweeted an article referring to her as a "biological male" and claiming her success was a "grave injustice to so many young women."[14] The tweet instantly made Telfer a global target. "I know that society hates me," she says. That thought terrifies her every time she steps out on the track. "The thought that keeps me going is that now that I am able to be myself, I cannot hold back no matter how hard it is and no matter the fear in my heart. I have to live my life," she says. "Because representation matters."

The phrase "representation matters" has been so overused it's in danger of becoming a commodified husk of a once powerful idea à la "girlpower" or "empowerment." But hearing CeCé talk about why representation matters for her shows us why it's still such a vitally necessary form of activism, and why sports is such an important platform for it. "I need to not back down because there is a little girl out there that is confused about who she is and not sure if she should continue living her life because there's nobody else out here that looks like her," she says. "This journey is more than just myself. I have to do it for the little CeCés out there who are struggling with themselves, regardless of whether they're trans."

The potential of trans representation in sports is so powerful that it's become a wedge issue for opponents of transgender rights who've turned competitions from after-school sports all the way up to the Olympics into forums for heated debate about what it means to be a woman and who gets to make that decision. (Because, of course, women aren't given the respect of being able to decide that for themselves.) At least thirty-four states have introduced bills aiming to ban transgender youth from sports; they've already been enacted in at least eighteen states. Bills like this throw the full weight of the law behind policing women's bodies, keeping trans women and girls from receiving the mental, physical, and social benefits of sports participation, and ultimately denying all transgender people their humanity. Perversely, many of them attempt to use Title IX—the law that opened the doors to women in sports—to do it, cloaking some truly dark shit in the mantle of "feminism." In June 2022, Republican lawmakers in Ohio passed the "Save Women's Sports Act," a bill that bans the participation of transgender girls in sports and would require any girl "accused" or "suspected" of being transgender to undergo an examination of her genitals. An early version of Florida's "Fairness in Women's Sports Act," enacted in 2021, also gave schools the authority to make teen girls submit to genital exams as a means of enforcement (though it thankfully did not make it into the final law).[15] Everything about this is deeply unsettling, but perhaps the most concerning is the fact that a law giving schools the right to indiscriminately examine girls' genitals is being billed as a means of *protecting* girls.

Make no mistake: these lawmakers are not concerned with "protecting" women or ensuring fair competition; they are about policing women's bodies. And that goes for all women's bodies. "What does a trans woman look like? Can you see her transness? Because if you can't, then every woman on this planet is a threat to women's sport," says Telfer. Any girl seen to be too strong, or too tall, or too good at her sport can be violated on the suspicion that she might be transgender. "The notion that you can say well we're just talking about transgender women athletes and just draw a line around that? Don't kid yourself," says Ellen J. Staurowsky, the professor of sports media. "We are talking about women and women's place in this society and these laws are an example of just how vulnerable those boundaries are."

Perhaps the biggest tell is that many of these bills don't even mention the participation of transgender men and boys.[16] Boys' bodies will not be violated. Boys will not be subject to a witch hunt. These bills subtly reinforce the idea that what men do with their bodies is their business while what women do with their bodies is a threat, and that makes it the state's business. "If I could find a bright side in all this," Schmider adds, "it's that we are finally having a real dialogue about how resistance to trans people's equality is rooted in resistance to women and people of color's full equality."

~ ~ ~

A LOT OF people are uncomfortable with the issue of trans girls in sports. Even some of the most otherwise liberal people I've talked to, those who vocally support transgender rights in other areas, get a flash of panic in their eyes when the topic of trans women and sports comes up. They don't want to sound transphobic, they say, voices lowered. But . . . *Isn't allowing trans women and girls to play against cisgender women and girls giving them an unfair advantage?* they ask. In 2021, 62 percent of Americans said they believed athletes should compete in sports according to their "birth gender," whatever that means, including a full 41 percent of Democrats.[17] It's not prejudice, I've heard many otherwise inclusive people insist, it's just *science*.

So, let's talk about the science. "People have really strong beliefs about what bodies assigned male at birth can do versus bodies assigned female at birth," says Anne Lieberman, director of policy and programs for Athlete Ally, an advocacy organization that works to end homophobia and transphobia in sports. Namely, that men will always be bigger, faster, and stronger than women. Trans women athletes get lumped in with the former category, dubbed "biological males," and persecuted for their supposed biological superiority over "biological females." The debate generally boils down to testosterone levels. Incorrectly labeled the "male sex hormone," testosterone has for decades been credited as being the secret sauce behind strength, speed, aggression, and dominance.[18] If trans women have higher levels of testosterone, then they have an unfair advantage over cisgender women, opponents argue. Not prejudice, science.

The first problem with this understanding of the science is that testosterone is not "male"; the hormone is found in people of all genders and is necessary for healthy functioning in all bodies. "Testosterone is important and fascinating but it's far too simplistic to say that testosterone is the single most important determinant of athleticism," Rebecca M. Jordan-Young, PhD, and Katrina Karkazis, PhD, write in *Testosterone: An Unauthorized Biography*. This might come as a surprise, given that exogenous testosterone—the kind taken as a supplement—is considered a performance-enhancing drug. This form of testosterone has consistently been proven to measurably improve athletic performance by building skeletal muscle mass and influencing strength and endurance, which is why it's banned in sports—including for trans men (unless granted an exception for therapeutic use). Although it seems logical to infer that naturally occurring levels of testosterone would offer athletes a similar edge, the science doesn't bear this out.[19] Endogenous testosterone interacts with the body differently than the injectable kind, and researchers frankly don't know much about how it shapes the body and ultimately impacts athletic performance. Jordan-Young and Karkazis's review of research continues,

> Studies of T levels among athletes fail to show consistent relationships between T and performance. Some studies do show clear correlation between higher baseline (endogenous) T levels and either speed or "explosive" power, but many other studies

show weak or no links between baseline T and performance. Quite a few studies even find a negative correlation, meaning that higher baseline T is associated with worse performance.[20]

Those who oppose letting trans women and girls play rely on the supposed athletic advantage testosterone provides anyway. It is the "scientific" permission slip to go after not only trans athletes but women who are seen to be too muscular, too fast, *too good* to really be women. But if testosterone is not a "male" hormone, how can it be used to decide who counts as a woman? And more importantly, if there is no scientific basis to the idea that testosterone is the secret sauce of superathletes, how can it be used as a litmus test for who belongs?

Despite the lack of definitive science, testosterone levels remain the primary way transgender athletes in sports are policed. Rules for trans athlete participation vary from sport to sport, as determined by each individual governing federation, but most require trans women like CeCé to undergo hormone therapy designed to suppress endogenous testosterone levels for a certain period of time—typically a year—before competing according to their gender identity (which, it should be noted, many trans women want to do as part of their transition). What happens next is complicated. When Telfer began testosterone suppression as part of her medical transition, her athletic performance suffered—her coach noted that her muscle mass decreased, she slowed down, and she lost some of the explosive power she'd experienced on the track before her transition. But some research indicates that trans women may still retain an athletic edge over their cisgender peers after a year of gender-affirming hormone therapy. In an attempt to introduce some clarity into our imprecise understanding of the way testosterone impacts athletic performance, the International Olympic Committee released a "framework on fairness" in 2021. It officially hands the authority to set rules about competition eligibility to each sport and its governing body and condemns the practice of pressuring athletes to undergo "medically unnecessary" treatments and genital exams, saying no athlete should be prevented from competing because of "unverified, alleged, or perceived unfair competitive advantage" due to their gender identity or physical traits.[21] So far, not much has changed. Through rules like this, governing bodies in sports are, right or not, already controlling for "fairness," but trans women who meet eligibility requirements are still demonized. "We follow these rules to compete in the sport that we love, regardless of how aggressive the rules are and the toll it takes on our mental and physical health," says Telfer.

In addition to policing some women's bodies in the name of protecting others, advocates of banning trans women from sports also miss a fundamental truth about athletic competition. Sports are inherently unfair—and that's kind of the whole point. Every athlete shows up with a unique set of traits that makes them competitive. Some athletes are taller, some have better coaches, some have access to better training facilities, some spend more time on recovery, some simply want it more. And some have biological advantages. An analysis of Michael Phelps's physique—the one that earned him global adoration and countless medals—found that the biological variations that allowed him to be the greatest swimmer who has ever lived also made him a "biomechanical freak of nature." Phelps has a litany of natural advantages: double-jointed ankles, which allow him to create a more powerful flipper-like kick; a freakishly long wingspan and double-jointed chest, which give him a condor-like ability to create thrust in the water; a disproportionately large torso, which gives him a structural advantage in how his body sits in the water compared to his teammates. Most significantly, "Phelps has been scientifically proven to produce less than half of the lactic acid of his rivals," meaning he is biologically wired to recover faster. Why is a man like Phelps celebrated for his biological advantages when he wins but a woman like CeCé is targeted?

"When we start breaking that down, it becomes very clear that perceived differences are only an issue when women or gender minorities are succeeding," says Schmider. If we truly cared about an equal playing field, Michael Phelps would have been yanked out of the pool. Trans athletes are held to a completely different standard, wrote Olympic silver medalist Erica Sullivan in support of fellow swimmer Lia Thomas—a swimmer at the University of Pennsylvania and the first out trans woman to win a Division I NCAA title. "Like anyone else in this sport, Lia doesn't win every time," Sullivan wrote in her op-ed for *Newsweek*. "And when she does, she deserves, like anyone else in this sport, to be celebrated for her hard-won success, not labeled a cheater simply because of her identity."[22]

Overwhelmingly dominant athletes like Lia are rare in any gender. That's why there's only one Michael Phelps, even though there are dozens of tall dudes with large wingspans in the pool during every Olympic race. Like the vast majority of athletes in any sport, trans women and girls experience a lot of losses. In the same meet that Telfer earned the NCAA Division II title in the 400-meter race—which led to calls to ban "biological males" from competing—she got smashed in the 100-meter. Telfer came in fifth, which meant four cisgender women handily beat her, she pointed out.[23] But there were no headlines about her loss.

"When the saturation of headlines and legislation are about trans people's domination in sports, despite there being no numbers to actually support that claim, it reinforces this false notion that there is a superiority," says Schmider. "It is so important to see those athletes excel at the levels they do. And at the same time, there is such value in seeing stories of trans people who are just existing in sports—they don't need to excel to have value." To date, only one transgender athlete has won an Olympic medal, and Lia Thomas is the only trans woman to win an NCAA Division I title, despite the fact that many trans athletes compete at that level. "The NCAA rules regarding trans women competing in women's sports have been around for 10-plus years. And we haven't seen any massive wave of trans women dominating," Thomas told ESPN.[24]

The idea that girls' and women's sports are being overrun with trans athletes is another myth. When Ohio lawmakers passed their ban on trans youth participating in school sports, there was only one openly transgender athlete competing in the entire state. In fact, as of 2022, there were more laws banning trans girls from sports than there were out trans girls actually competing. More to the point, there is absolutely no evidence that the participation of any number of transgender girls in sports harms cisgender girls or reduces their likelihood of participating in sports, according to a report by the Center for American Progress. States that had fully trans-inclusive policies in place between 2011 and 2019 saw no change in participation in girls' sports, while states with trans-exclusive policies or outright bans saw girls' participation drop off.[25]

When you actually talk to a trans athlete, watch them play, listen to their stories about why they compete, the generalizations so often used to talk about trans women in sports seem obviously absurd. They're as varied and individual as any athlete. But as long as there are so many barriers to trans representation in society, every trans athlete who fights to be seen pushes culture forward. To be a game-changing advocate, Telfer doesn't have to raise a fist or influence an election; just showing up, knowing her very existence will be harshly debated in national media, is the kind of activism that has the power to shape public perceptions of who belongs. When I spoke to her in 2022, she was throwing absolutely every ounce of herself into getting to the 2024 Olympics. It is a chance to not only reach her full potential in the sport that she loves, but also show the next generation of trans athletes that there is a place for them. "That's the purpose of being a pioneer," she says. "Hoping that the next generation will have it better."

～～～

SPEAKING UP, OF course, comes at a price. Often, a literal one. For athletes like Gwen Berry who don't have seven-figure contracts, there's often no cushion if a sponsor or two decide to stop supporting you—there are no millions in the bank, no eight-figure deal around the corner. Speaking out or taking time off from playing to devote to social justice work means risking it all. Natasha Cloud, a WNBA player for the Washington Mystics, joined a handful of players in opting out of the 2020 WNBA season to devote all of her time to the Black Lives Matter movement. Cloud forfeited her $117,000 salary for the season, but even more at risk was the endorsement deal she'd just signed with Converse as the first woman athlete the brand had ever sponsored. "I was really scared of that because I worked my ass off for five years to put myself in this position to finally get a sponsorship," she told journalist Brittney Oliver. (In a huge show of support, Converse ultimately stepped up to cover her lost salary.) Khris Middleton, a Black athlete for the NBA's Milwaukee Bucks, also sat out in support of Black Lives Matter during the 2020 season. But whether his sponsors supported him or not wouldn't impact his ability to pay rent; he had just finished banking a $70 million contract.[26]

This isn't to say the activist work of men is less important than the activist work of women in sports. It's not. But speaking up always carries different risks and costs for women and marginalized groups than it does for white, cisgender men. The more axes of marginalization, the greater the risk that financial or reputational penalties could be career-ending. But increasingly, women are also paying for their activism in a more insidious way. Women are twice as likely to take on diversity, equity, and inclusion (DEI) initiatives at work—which most do for free, according to McKinsey and LeanIn.org's 2021 "Women in the Workplace" report. Despite the fact that this work is "very or extremely critical" to nearly 70 percent of companies, according to their analysis, fewer than a quarter of bosses seriously consider DEI work as part of an employee's performance evaluation.[27]

Over and over again, in sports and elsewhere, it's the least supported and the most impacted who wind up doing this critical activist work. It takes time, energy, and capital. And as if that wasn't enough, they are also tasked with leading the conversation on the mental and emotional toll all of this takes. Within two months of each other in 2021, two of the greatest athletes of our time quit, citing mental health concerns. Simone Biles and Naomi Osaka, both young Black women, had spent most of their careers fighting to thrive in a white male–dominated industry. Where others gave 100 percent, they gave 120. And they did so while using their platforms for activism: Biles built a resume as the most accomplished gymnast of all time while fighting to stop abuse in sport; Osaka became the highest-paid woman athlete in history while using her time on the court to call attention to racial justice. But their most powerful act of protest was to stop. In May 2021, Osaka dropped out of the French Open, revealing she was struggling with depression; in July, Biles delivered the most shocking Olympic twist ever when she walked off the floor at the team finals.[28] In quitting while so many eyes were trained on them, each woman made the loudest statement of her career—she was done giving, she was prioritizing herself. "Their willingness to show themselves—and by that I mean all of themselves, prioritizing their well-being—was an affirmation of their humanness," says Douglas.

By saying no in such spectacular fashion while at the peak of their professional success, Osaka and Biles ignited a global conversation on the power and importance of Black women's rest. They became icons for an entirely new reason. When Atlanta mayor Keisha Lance Bottoms—who also had been at a professional pinnacle, with national acclaim and enough clout to be on the shortlist of names for vice president in the 2020 election—announced she would be stepping down after just one term in office, she credited

Osaka and Biles with setting an example of how to prioritize your own well-being in a culture where succeeding as a Black woman is its own form of activism. "My assessment has not been any different than Simone Biles's or Naomi Osaka's," she told *New York* magazine during her last weeks in office. She was putting her emotional and mental health first.[29]

When Simone and Naomi pulled out of their respective events, something else remarkable happened: they didn't lose any sponsors. Granted, their message wasn't as overtly "political" as Gwen Berry's or the WNBA's (though there was more than enough backlash and negative press surrounding each woman's decision for her lifetime), but their sponsors' reactions still marked a change in the way they were seeing an athlete's value. As we've seen, sponsors have traditionally backed athletes because they are going to appear at as many highly televised competitions and win as many shiny things as possible, giving those sponsors plenty of opportunities to wrap them in their logo and blast out content on social media. But both Osaka and Biles had opened the door for a new model. "Marketing is just connection," says Colas. "It's about being aspirational, but also I think we've evolved to a place where some of that is about someone having the courage to be real and vulnerable." When Biles pulled out of competition, her sponsor Athleta didn't hesitate in supporting her, and immediately saw the value in the conversation her courage and vulnerability would start with their customers. "Simone being so raw and so human on a world stage is so brave, but it's also something that we're all facing on smaller stages every single day," says Whitney Standring-Trueblood, former head of PR at Athleta. "That really resonates with our customers because that is who they are too."

~ ~ ~

WOMEN ARE OFTEN activists because they have to be—staying silent often means continuing to be subjugated. "I really do believe that it's innate in women to be seekers of change because we want things to be better for ourselves," says Nneka.

It's a beautiful bit of irony that the very systems of power that uphold inequality are what so often galvanize the women who are taking them down. The sports economy, with its laundry list of ways for making women feel less than, is a particularly fertile training ground. Molly Dreher (pronouns: she/they), the Division I runner from California, got her first feminist wakeup call as an athlete. (Remember the coach who demanded Dreher's soccer team share their fundraising spoils in the name of "equal pay"?) "Fighting for women's equality in high school was just like running into a brick wall over and over again," she says. She remembers telling her mom she was joining her school's feminist club because she felt the need to do more. "She was like, 'people aren't going to like you, if you do something like that,'" Dreher says. "And she wasn't wrong." Hearing that from her own mother, who had gone through so many of the same experiences Molly was facing now, lit a fire in her. "They've been beaten down and they're telling you to submit too," she says. In that moment, an activist was born. Her freshman year of college, Dreher started fighting sexism in sports on the national level, joining a student advocate program started by Stef Strack, founder of VOICEINSPORT. The program, which trains student athletes on how to evaluate inequality in their school sports programs, is only really about sports on the surface. Strack hopes it will turn the feeling of disenfranchisement that so many girls in sports experience into a sense of power—which is exactly what Dreher felt when her work as a VIS advocate gave her the chance to address members of Congress on legislation she helped draft to close loopholes in Title IX enforcement. "They were actually listening to me," Dreher says. "Imagine this army of incredible leaders we're creating," Strack says. "These women have so much power. They don't even know it yet."

CHAPTER 6

PUT HER IN

I T STARTED WITH AN OFFHAND COMMENT: WOMEN TALK TOO
much. That was the justification of Yoshiro Mori—a former
Japanese prime minister, who was then the head of the Japanese
Olympic Committee—for why his planning team didn't include
more women in leadership positions. Lots of countries have a big
gender gap when it comes to representation at senior levels in cor-
porations and the government, but Japan's is particularly notable.
Countrywide, women held just 14.7 percent of senior and managerial positions and less than 10 percent of political offices in 2020.
Women held 20 percent of the positions on the Olympic committee. But this was still, apparently, too much for Mori. "On boards
with a lot of women, the board meetings take so much time," he
said when discussing a suggestion to include more women on his
executive team. "When you increase the number of female executive members, if their speaking time isn't restricted to a certain
extent, they have difficulty finishing, which is annoying," he said,
according to a translation.[1]

Gender was supposed to take center stage at the Tokyo Olympics—but not like this. The games were being promoted as the most gender-equal Olympics in history, with nearly equal numbers of men and women competing. It was a chance for countries to promote their women athletes and earn applause for their support of gender equality—especially the host. Mori's comments were not exactly sending the right message. The backlash against Prime Minister Mori was swift, and despite calling the uproar "pathetic," he was forced to resign after condemnation from the International Olympic Committee. (Mori delivered an apology with his resignation, though he appeared to have learned nothing from it; a few months later, he was again derided in the press for referring to a political staffer as "too old to call a woman."[2])

Mori's comments about women's "annoying" proclivity for chattiness were not just sexist, they were empirically wrong. The former prime minister's quip inspired Adam Grant, an organizational psychologist at the Wharton School of Business, to do what he does best: look at the data. Grant analyzes behavior in groups, digging into evidence (or lack thereof) behind stereotypes like "women talk too much." In this case, "the pattern is clear and consistent: It's usually men who won't shut up," he wrote in the *Washington Post*. "Especially powerful men."[3]

Citing studies examining dynamics among US senators, Supreme Court justices, and other arenas of politics and society, Grant confirmed that it is in fact men who are more likely to take up space with their incessant yammering. Or, as he put it, more likely to "manalogue." Take this troubling finding: in a group of five decision-makers that includes one woman, she speaks 40 percent less than each of the men in the room. When a majority of women make up the group—three out of five—each woman still speaks 36 percent less than the two men. It takes four women—an 80 percent majority—to reach verbal parity. Only then will each woman speak as much as the one lone manaloguer.[4] Which, to put it succinctly, is pretty annoying.

With Mori gone, Seiko Hashimoto—Japan's minister for gender equity and a seven-time Olympian herself—was promoted to run Tokyo's Olympic Organizing Committee. Under her rule, the committee added twelve women to its executive board (which meant the group tasked with organizing the most gender-equal Olympics in history was now composed of 42 percent women) and established a gender equity team run by Mikako Kotani, an Olympic synchronized swimmer who became the first woman flag bearer for Japan in 1988. In one respect, Mori was right: having women in positions of power did in fact change the committee's effectiveness. Under Hashimoto and Kotani, the Tokyo committee steered focus back to the games, overseeing an Olympics with a record 49 percent women athletes competing, despite the many challenges of an ongoing pandemic. For the first time, nearly every country was represented by a woman flag bearer at the opening ceremony; Naomi Osaka had the honor of lighting the Olympic cauldron; and notably, 60 percent of the volunteers running the most important event in sports were women—an intentional move the woman-led committee hoped would be a blueprint for future games. The gender equity team led by Kotani also pushed Olympic sponsors to publicly declare their own gender equality and diversity goals. Together, the committed organizers hoped their gender equity efforts would mark a "turning point" for the Olympics.[5]

~ ~ ~

PUTTING WOMEN IN leadership positions is about more than symbolic change. As with the Tokyo committee, women leaders often have an outsized impact in closing the gender gap, enacting policies, and making calls that prioritize gender diversity at every level. But there are still very few women—and fewer women of color—

in positions of power, particularly in sports. You can count the total number of women coaches of men's pro-league teams using your fingers—and none of them are head coaches. Basketball, baseball, football, hockey—of the hundreds of head coaches who have ever reigned in the history of the $308 billion market of Big Four US sports leagues, not a single one has ever been a woman as of this writing. At the collegiate level, fewer than 20 percent of athletic directors at Division I schools are women and fewer than 2 percent are women of color. For women's collegiate teams, women hold only 40 percent of head coaching jobs and only 4 percent are women of color. Even in the NWSL, the home league of some of the biggest feminist champions in sports history, the majority of head coaches are men. Women sports CEOs and presidents are even more scarce; fewer than 10 percent of sports institutions are led by women. The International Olympic Committee and FIFA, two of the most powerful sporting institutions on the planet, have never seen a woman in charge.[6]

This is yet another way sports are a microcosm of society at large. The abysmal number of women in leadership positions in sports—even in spaces like women's soccer—mirrors the equally abysmal numbers of women in leadership positions across industries. Women hold just 21 percent of government offices globally and just over a third of managerial roles at Fortune 500 companies.[7]

The leadership gap isn't for a lack of qualified women ready to step up and deliver. Becky Hammon, the first woman to hold an assistant coaching position in the NBA, was up for the job as head coach of the league's Portland Trail Blazers in 2021. So was Dawn Staley, a WNBA legend who went on to have an extremely successful coaching career in women's college basketball and for Team USA. If either woman had gotten the job, she would have been the first to serve as head coach in US major league men's sports history. Both women's records are stunning. Hammon became the first woman hired as a full-time assistant coach in NBA history when she joined the Spurs in 2014. She's served as head coach of the franchise's Summer League three times, including for the team's 2015 championship win. In the regular season, she's helped the team maintain a 62 percent win rate. In 2020, she became the first woman to serve as head coach of a regular season NBA game when her boss was thrown out for arguing with a referee and handed the reins to her. Staley, meanwhile, got her first head coaching job in 2000, when she took over the women's basketball program at Temple University. In eight seasons, she took the team to six NCAA tournaments before moving to the top job for the South Carolina Gamecocks. Under her leadership, the team boasted a 76 percent career win rate, five SEC Championship titles, four NCAA Final Four appearances, and two national championships. She also served as head coach of the US Women's National Basketball Team for the Tokyo Olympics, where she led the team to a dynasty-making seventh consecutive gold medal in 2020.

The Trail Blazers didn't hire either of these women. They ultimately went with a less experienced man. Chauncey Billups is a former NBA player—who had less than a year of coaching experience, having spent eight months as an assistant coach for the Los Angeles Clippers.

The decision was particularly frustrating for fans of Hammon, who by this point had interviewed for several head coaching positions in the NBA and was long expected to be the one to finally shatter the glass ceiling in the major leagues. After being passed up for the top job at the Trail Blazers, she changed course; in 2022 the WNBA's Las Vegas Aces announced they'd hired Hammon (and made her the highest-paid head coach in the league). Reflecting on the whole experience, she said, "I sat in head coaching interviews [in the NBA] and people said two things: 'You've only been in San Antonio and you've never been a head coach,'" as justifications for not hiring her. (Billups, it would appear, was not held to the same standards.) "Half the world's population hasn't been tapped for their mind and ability and skill sets in the sports world," she said in an interview after Billups was hired. "It's something that needs to change."[8]

It sounds familiar, doesn't it? Extremely qualified woman is passed over for a less qualified man. This is a challenge women face at every step on the path to power. The old boys' club bias is so strong that it often prevails even when organizations deliberately try to be diverse. The Bank of England made headlines in 2021 when their shortlist of candidates for chief economist was made public. Of nine candidates considered, five had been women—a huge milestone in an industry notoriously devoid of women. The bank, which issues currency and oversees monetary policy for the United Kingdom, has never had a woman serve as governor or chief economist, and just three officials on the nine-person mone- tary policy committee are women. It's notable that the institution went out of its way to change this—reportedly hiring a recruit- ing firm that specializes in championing diversity, paying them $59,000 for the search, and receiving a list of majority women can- didates—and, after all that, still hired a white man.[9]

Hiring a white man to run things isn't inherently problematic (and recent history is certainly not short on examples of women who have created toxic environments from the corner office). Per- haps Huw Pill, whom the bank ultimately hired as chief econo- mist, was indeed the best person for the job. The problem isn't the individual hires but the system-wide lack of change. Leaders are human, and like all humans, they're wired to work in service of their own best interests; when power lies concentrated so firmly with one gender, one race, one type of experience, it's likely to stay there unless there's a concerted, collective effort to make systemic change.

Most women never even make it to the shortlist for the top job—again, not for lack of drive, skill, or capability, but for a glaring gender gap in the leadership pipeline. Women aren't groomed for the top jobs, they're not mentored with the same intention, they have fewer role models in which to see themselves. And at every step of a woman's career, she faces deeply internalized biases shaping the way we appraise women and keep the ranks of power decidedly male.

There's a vast body of research that explores the many ways in which managers disparage a woman who negotiates for herself (Selfish! Aggressive! Threatening!), but women's leadership potential is unfairly judged even when they're not explicitly trying to advance. Women at work uniquely face what *Fortune* coined the "abrasiveness trap." Writer and tech CEO Kieran Snyder reviewed 248 performance reviews from people working in the tech industry and found while most reviews were positive overall, about 71 percent contained some sort of critical feedback. Those critiques, however, were not delivered equally. Nearly 88 percent of women received critical feedback as compared to just 59 percent of men. There was also gender bias within the feedback itself. Of the women who'd been given critiques, 76 percent of those comments were classified as "negative" feedback as opposed to being considered constructive. For men only 2 percent got explicitly negative feedback. Snyder cited several examples of what this looks like. One man was told, "Take time to slow down and listen. You would achieve even more." Here's how a woman was given feedback on her communication skills: "You can come across as abrasive sometimes. I know you don't mean to, but you need to pay attention to your tone."[10] The difference feels particularly grating: for men, feedback is a constructive tool to help them climb the leadership ladder successfully; for women, it's a reminder not to sound so shrill.

It's comments like this that encourage women to stop speaking up in meetings—a particularly pernicious problem considering that, in most professions, airtime is power. The more a person can control the narrative, the more they are able to dominate. But when women do earn enough power to get the mic, the claws really come out. In politics, the few women who have risen to the highest echelons of leadership face daily abuse meant to tear them off their hard-won perch. In the 2016 presidential primaries, what do you think was the word most commonly associated with critiques of Hillary Clinton? Untrustworthy? Emails? Pantsuit? An analysis of critical social media posts in the US, UK, and Australia compared words most commonly used to describe two political opponents—one woman, one man. In the case of Clinton vs. Democratic senator Bernie Sanders, the most frequently used negative words to describe Senator Sanders were "idiot," "moron," and "fuck." For Clinton, a former first lady, senator, secretary of state, and democratic presidential nominee, among the words most commonly used were "bitch," "whore," and "cunt."[11]

Let that sink in.

Attacking a politician's character is practically an international sport—people in democratic countries the world over love hurling insults at their elected leaders (often including the ones they voted for). The study reflected this global penchant for name-calling; no matter their political ideologies, male politicians in the study of the US, Australia, and the UK were often subject to insults like "idiot" and "moron." Australian prime minister Kevin Rudd was often called a "wanker," New Jersey governor Chris Christie an "asshole." These comments aren't nice—maybe they're not even fair. But they do represent a baseline for political character criticism. Calling someone a "moron" is not the same as calling someone a "cunt." Women who dare to lead face a measurably different level of abuse; Clinton and Australian prime minister Julia Gillard were subject to twice as many abusive tweets as their male counterparts, the content of which was often deeply misogynistic, if not downright violent—slurs that had absolutely nothing to do with their qualifications or competence.

This is one of the darkest manifestations of men and women being judged differently as leaders. Research tells us what you probably already know in your bones: when men exhibit "power-seeking" behaviors they face no negative consequences and are often lauded for it—voted into office or given a promotion with a fat raise. But when women exhibit the same traits, they become unlikable power-seeking sea witches who should be harpooned. One case in point is Alexandria Ocasio-Cortez, the congressional representative from New York who rose to power quickly, gaining political and cultural clout for her outspoken and unapologetic progressivism. Whether you like her or think she sucks, she's a politician with strong opinions, so it's not shocking that she's often deemed polarizing. But in her time in office, she's faced a steady stream of hate and abuse of a different class than the usual political name-calling. Nothing sums up this tactic so chillingly as an anime video posted by Republican representative Paul Gosar on Twitter, which depicted a cartoon version of him slashing AOC's neck. The message was clear: pay attention, ladies, we don't want you here, and if you don't play by our rules, there will be consequences. To some degree that message works: a study of US senators found that women in leadership roles, such as those who serve on committees, often self-censor, assuming—correctly—that if they talk more than others on the floor, they'll face backlash.[12]

Ocasio-Cortez's ethnicity undoubtedly plays a role in the viciousness of the attacks she receives; women of color are 34 percent more likely to be on the receiving end of abusive tweets, according to a study of online abuse from Amnesty International.[13] The way Ocasio-Cortez came to power likely plays a role too—she didn't temper her voice, send stiff press-release-style tweets, and spend years learning how to shrink and shape herself around likability landmines. She didn't, in other words, play by the rules for women that establishment men have deemed acceptable. Instead, she refused to stop being herself, sharing cooking videos and lipstick recommendations on social media, attending the Met Gala, and becoming one of the loudest and most influential voices in US government in her freshman term.

The specter of hostility toward women in power often subtly shapes how women lead in everyday interactions. Put simply, "When we look at a woman leader, we expect different things than when we look at a male leader," says Muffet McGraw. McGraw is a basketball legend, a titan of the NCAA who reigned over the Notre Dame women's basketball dynasty for thirty-three years, ultimately becoming one of the highest-paid women in coaching. She took Notre Dame to nine Final Fours, seven championship appearances, and two National Championship titles. Through all of it, she knew her leadership style would be held to a different standard than her male counterparts'. "We expect that women are going to be compassionate and empathetic and all these touchy, feely kinds of things. When they're not, we're not ready for that," she says. "We have to walk that tightrope of trying to lead while being a woman and knowing how people see us." Over the course of McGraw's career, "people" included outside critics, media, referees, even her own players, all of whom had different expectations of how she should act as a coach based on implicit beliefs about gender. "I can't talk to my team the way that male coaches talk to their women's teams," she says. People were more likely to excuse a male coach for a bombastic coaching style, but coaching as a woman required more finesse. "We're seen as hysterical, emotional, hormonal, neurotic—all these words that describe women that you just don't use for men," she says. "Men are frustrated, they're arguing, they're passionate. They're allowed to be those things. And we're not."

~ ~ ~

DESPITE ALL THE barriers—the smaller paychecks, the investment gap, the gendered judgments of women in power—women are rising. In Europe, women now hold 37 percent of board seats; in Australia, they hold 34 percent (the US lags behind at 30 percent). In 2021, forty-one Fortune 500 companies were run by women—an all-time high. It was also the first time the list included two Black women, Roz Brewer of Walgreens Boots Alliance and Thasunda Brown Duckett of TIAA. Kamala Harris became the first woman to ascend to the White House. In sports, Jeanie Buss became the first woman owner of an NBA team to win a championship. Bianca Smith became the first Black woman to coach professional baseball, and Kim Ng became the first woman (and woman of color) to serve as a GM in the sport. After being passed up for the head coaching job for the Portland Trail Blazers, Dawn Staley signed a historic seven-year $22.4 million pay deal with the South Carolina Gamecocks.[14]

The problem? Eight-figure deals like Staley's are a rare exception. Most women rising to leadership positions are not getting paid like their male counterparts. Having more women in positions of power is great, but the #girlboss headlines often distract from a disturbing historical trend: as women start to gain more power in an industry, the pay and prestige associated with the job start to decline. Decades of data show that when women enter high-status, high-paying jobs en masse, they're met with a systemic devaluation. When women flooded into the workforce during World War II, for example, they rarely earned more than half of what men in those industries had made. When the gender balance of teachers slowly shifted from being dominated by men to women over the course of the twentieth century, its prestige waned and wages stagnated. "We're not beyond having a cultural devaluation of women's work . . . if a job is done primarily by women, people tend to believe it has less value," Philip N. Cohen, a sociologist at the University of Maryland, told the *New York Times*.[15] Women, in other words, aren't choosing low-paid work (as pay gap apologists love to argue). Low-paid work is choosing women.

On the flip side, the more prestigious a job becomes, the more forcefully women are pushed out to make room for men. Take coding, for example. Women were the original "computers," playing a vital (and deliberately forgotten) role in developing the precursor to the all-knowing device currently in your pocket. Women dominated the field of computer programming at its inception in the 1950s and '60s, when it was a low-paid gig. As it became understood that coding was not a low-skilled secretarial job—i.e., the type women are suited for—and that it actually required advanced problem-solving skills—the type women couldn't possibly be capable of, despite the fact that they pioneered them—industry leaders started intentionally training and recruiting men. Up went the pay and prestige; out went the women.[16]

This has also been true in sports, where the number of women leading women's teams has sharply declined since the 1970s. Before the passage of Title IX, over 90 percent of women's collegiate teams were, not surprisingly, coached by women. But the legislation—and the sudden influx of cash that it made available to women's sports programs—made those coaching jobs newly prestigious. Today, women hold just 41 percent of coaching jobs for women's teams, according to the 2020 Gender Report Card published by the Institute for Diversity and Ethics in Sport (TIDES) at the University of Central Florida. "The coaching statistics in women's college sport remain the worst statistics reported by TIDES in all of the Report Cards we publish each year," the authors noted. These women are also—you guessed it—paid less. "You want to do your job. You don't want to be worried about what the guys have and how do I compare myself to this?" says Coach McGraw. At the end of her tenure, she was one of the few women coaches making more than her male counterpart. In the 2018–2019 season, she made over $2 million—about $400,000 more than the head coach of the Notre Dame men's team. She more than earned that status—that season, her thirty-second with the Fighting Irish, she led the team to a 35–4 record vs. men's coach Mike Bray, with a 14–19 record in his nineteenth year leading the team. But even among women coaches with a higher win rate, McGraw is an outlier. USWNT coach Jill Ellis, only the second coach in history to win back-to-back World Cups, brought home just over $700,000 the year she coached the women to their iconic victory in France, according to tax documents released by the US Soccer Federation. That made her the highest-paid women's national team coach in the world—and yet, that was barely half of what the US Men's National Team coach Gregg Berhalter made during his first full year on the job in 2019.[17]

These numbers sound (and are) big. In the grand scheme, few people would complain about a $700,000 paycheck. It's the pattern that matters—even women at the highest levels of power aren't immune to the biases and norms that keep women systemically underpaid. At the CEO level, the gender pay gap is around 15 percent (compared to the global gender wage gap of 17 percent). For startup CEOs, the gap is actually widening; a 2022 analysis found that the gender wage gap among this set of CEOs nearly quadrupled between 2019 and 2022. The pandemic helps explain why: male startup CEO salaries rose 2 percent in 2020, while women CEOs took a 30 percent pay cut—a self-sacrificial move in which women prioritized company cash flow over their own economic security. It's likely to have long-term effects on the pay gap in the startup world; the same analysis found that when salaries started to bounce back as the economic effects of the pandemic began to wane, women CEOs didn't regain the same footing they'd had with their male-identifying counterparts in 2019. Among the over 250 startups analyzed, the gender pay gap between CEOs had been just 4 percent in 2019. In 2022, women CEO's salaries lagged 14 percent behind the men's.[18]

Women in leadership roles aren't just getting paid less to do the same jobs—there's a rich cache of data that shows women are more effective leaders on several important measures. Especially the one that matters the most to a capitalist society: profits.

Companies with more women in executive positions and on boards make more money—a fact that is not news to the business world. A decade-old report from growth equity firm Catalyst found that companies with three or more women board members outperformed those with a low representation of women by an 84 percent return on sales, 60 percent return on invested capital, and 46 percent return on equity. That truth holds globally, according to McKinsey, which found companies in the top quartile for number of women in leadership positions performed undeniably better when pitted against companies with zero women on the executive committee. In Asia, the former out-earned the latter by a whopping 117 percent. Credit Suisse published similar research findings aptly titled "Higher Returns with Women in Decision-Making Positions." They looked at earnings for over three thousand companies around the world and concluded that the presence of women in leadership roles led to increased profits, revenue growth, and a boosted share price.[19]

The data are even more promising for younger companies, where women-founded ventures are outperforming companies founded by men. In an analysis of 2021 exits, market data company Pitch-Book found that the value of woman-founded firms rose nearly 50 percent more than the market average. Women-led startups were also first to exit—industry-speak for the lucrative cash-out that comes with selling your company or taking it public—averaging a payday for investors a full year sooner than the average for the overall VC market. The numbers prove "superior business performance for companies with women in leadership positions."[20]

Women's superior performance as leaders shone even during the economic crisis triggered by the pandemic in 2020. Among the many headlines about the generational setback for the millions of working women forced out of the workforce as they juggled the epic challenge of pandemic caregiving duties emerged another important story: companies with a higher proportion of women in leadership positions fared better through the economic turmoil. In 2020, companies on the S&P 500 that had more than 30 percent of board seats held by women were more likely to see revenue growth. (The same was true for companies with more racially diverse boards.) An analysis by BoardReady found that the 194 companies with the highest gender diversity had a combined income growth of $58 billion (1.2 percent during the worst of the pandemic), while companies with lower gender diversity saw a combined loss of $283 billion (3.9 percent). European companies saw similar results: a pandemic analysis of the FTSE 350 (an index of the top 350 companies listed on the London Stock Exchange) found that, again, companies with more women on top performed better throughout the turmoil. The report found that companies led by gender-equal boards saw a profit margin of over 21 percent during the pandemic. Companies with all-male executive committees, meanwhile, saw a nearly 18 percent drop in profits.[21]

~ ~ ~

THE NUMBERS DON'T lie. So *why* do women in leadership positions lead to better economic outcomes? And how might their leadership help move the needle on gender equity?

The research on women in leadership roles is, perhaps unsurprisingly, scant—there haven't historically been a lot of data to work with, after all. The research that does exist has produced a few theories, including some fascinating ruminations on gendered personality traits. Research has found women as a group are more likely to display key traits linked to better leadership outcomes, such as emotional intelligence, self-control, honesty and humility, and a tendency to be "equalitarian." "Female leaders are better suited for leadership than men," declared a study from the BI Norwegian Business School, which explored the "five factor model"—a set of five personality traits that are widely accepted as indicators of leadership skills (including emotional stability, extraversion, openness, agreeableness, and conscientiousness). When researchers analyzed personality survey data from over 2,900 managers (900 of whom were women), they found in regard to personality "women are better suited for leadership than their male colleagues when it comes to clarity, innovation, support and targeted meticulousness." Another qualitative study that examined gender differences in the language used by CFOs on quarterly earnings calls found that, contrary to stereotypes, "female executives are more concise and less optimistic, are clearer, use fewer idioms or clichés, and provide more numbers," which in turn is correlated with better stock returns and future firm performance.[22]

Maybe women are biologically wired (or perhaps more likely, socialized) to be better leaders. But the most likely explanation for why women are more successful leaders is the most obvious one: women are better leaders because they have to be. Tram Nguyen is the cofounder and co–executive director of the New Virginia Majority, a community-based political organization. For over a decade, she's been leading the organization in the fight for everything from economic justice to fair housing laws in Virginia, working with dozens of legislators along the way. In all those conversations, she's developed an expert's pulse on how these politicians lead, not just publicly but behind the scenes. When she works with male legislators to try to implement policy, it typically goes something like this: "They're carrying a bill and it's like, 'Okay, if it doesn't pass, that's fine. We'll try again next year.' And they move on to the next thing," she says. With women legislators, it's a different story— strategy sessions, persistence, creative thinking—they reach for any tool that might help get their agenda passed. "They work the bills more," Nguyen says. "Maybe it's because it's often more personal, but they just do not give up. There is a tenacity. And that is what we need if we're going to actually change things for people."

~ ~ ~

SIMPLY INSTALLING WOMEN at the head of the teams, institutions, and economies that have created and sustained the inequalities we are wrestling with won't solve all the world's problems. But there is an argument to be made that having more women at the top does more than just produce better stats on corporate leadership reports and make companies more money. When women have access to power, they're more likely to share it. As McGraw points out, "People hire people who look like them." Historically, that's been the problem. But McGraw made it a solution when, struck by the overwhelming number of men controlling women's basketball in the Big East Conference, she committed to hiring only women on her coaching staff. "I just remember looking around the room and seeing so many male head coaches and athletic directors—a room full of men. And then the conference commissioner came in and it was a man. It just suddenly hit me: this is *women's* basketball and we're surrounded by men. Why is that?" she tells me.

Before that epiphany, McGraw had always gone out of her way to hire a token male coach on her staff. "In basketball, a lot of the scouting services are male dominated and I thought I needed a guy to be in with that network," she says. She's worked with some fantastic male coaches, she stresses, but when the lone male assistant coach on her team left in 2012 and a woman named Beth Cunningham applied for the job, McGraw thought, "Well, that's an easy hire." Cunningham was more than qualified, having already served as a Division I head coach and having played for McGraw as an undergrad, where she was Notre Dame's all-time leading scorer. McGraw hesitated briefly, wondering if she really needed to have at least one male coach on the team. "I looked at myself and thought, I'm preaching about hiring women and then I'm the one that's actually looking to hire a man," she says. Once she committed to having a team of all women, she never looked back. "It was so wonderful. The chemistry was great. It was just such a family," says McGraw. More importantly, "The success of the program was unparalleled to any other tenure of any other coaches. In every way it was a huge success."

McGraw is no outlier in her mission to hire women. Once women are in positions of power, research shows that they help other women rise. Promotions—a significant factor in the gender pay gap—largely happen across gender lines; male bosses are more likely to promote men, women in charge are more likely to elevate other women. When Jill Ellis, the World Cup–winning coach of the USWNT, was named the president of the NWSL's newest franchise in San Diego, she made her priorities clear: "Now I get to go hire a female GM and hire a female head coach and provide opportunities for others . . . There's a ripple effect from there," she said. "Being able to open doors for others, that's just a really good space to be in to help them pursue their dreams, and in doing so, provide role models for the next generation." And this certainly isn't just a sports thing: Ava DuVernay hired only women directors (most of whom were women of color) for every episode of her show *Queen Sugar*; Issa Rae's hit HBO series *Insecure* (also directed by a woman) featured a groundbreaking episode in which every single item of clothing used for costumes was designed by a Black woman; when Stacey Abrams got her "first real access to power" as Atlanta's deputy city attorney, one of her first initiatives was to petition the city to create a paralegal training program for the department's underpaid and undervalued majority women secretaries who had previously been ineligible for raises and advancement. In Boston's historic 2021 mayoral race, Michelle Wu became the first woman and person of color elected to run the city. The victory was an exciting win for diversity, but even more exciting was that Wu's opponent was also a woman of color, Annissa Essaibi George—both were city council members and alums of Emerge, a national organization that offers leadership training and mentorship to Democratic women. US representative Ayanna Pressley—the first woman of color to be elected to Boston's city council in 2009—founded the Boston chapter, creating a pipeline for more women to follow in her footsteps.[23] These women exemplify a simple but powerful truth: women in charge have the power to help lift other women up.

For the women in leadership roles I spoke to, this was no coincidence—they made elevating women an explicit priority. Missy Park—the little girl who watched Billie Jean King win in the Battle of the Sexes—became a Title IX athlete at Yale and ultimately founded her own women's sportswear company. She's made hiring women part of her mission as a CEO and has committed to spending resources to find and even train the right women for the top jobs. She felt particularly passionately that the CTO and CFO of her company Title Nine should be women. When she couldn't find the right hires—finance and IT roles are overwhelmingly dominated by men—she made it a mission to bring in interim leaders to mentor and develop women within the company who will eventually take on those roles. "I realized, wow, we're going to have to grow our own here because I want women to lead every aspect of the business," Park says. Putting a woman in charge of Title Nine's finances is particularly important, she says. "I realized over the course of two decades, it's the CFO that holds the power." So why not make sure it lies with a woman?

With few women in positions to control capital, the investment gap persists. Take venture capital, the industry responsible for the appalling fact that only 0.27 percent of the billions of dollars in total venture funding goes to Black women founders. That number becomes less befuddling when you consider women are only 12 percent of decision-makers at US VC funds and Black investors hold just 2 percent of senior positions, per the *Harvard Business Review*.[24] And just like hiring, history shows people invest in people who look like them.

In sports, some of the most significant equal pay wins have happened when women are on both sides of the table. The USWNT finally won equal pay in 2022, after the US Soccer Federation elected a woman president—former WNT player Cindy Parlow Cone. This was by no means an instant fix—getting to a resolution still took time and tense negotiations, says Becca Roux, head of the USWNT players' union—but the change in leadership came with a significant shift in tone that for the first time allowed all sides to agree to work toward equality. Chiney Ogwumike felt similarly about the WNBA players' historic negotiations with the league, which has been led by Cathy Engelbert since 2019 after she left her role as the CEO of Deloitte. "The fact that we were negotiating with a woman who had done groundbreaking deals in corporate America, she was rooting for us," Ogwumike says. "We'd suggest something like paid maternity leave and she was like 'Yeah, I'm not fighting you on that.' Being across the table from another woman that has been a trailblazer, it just made it a harmonious situation."

A similar scenario unfolded in the World Surf League in 2018, when Sophie Goldschmidt, the newly minted CEO, made a major announcement: the WSL would become the first US-based global sports league to require equal prize money for men and women (progress that followed pressure from the Commission for Equity in Surfing, a group founded by women surfers, for the WSL to address its history of gender discrimination).[25] "It was a pretty transformative moment for surfing, which to be honest is pretty chauvinistic," Goldschmidt tells me. "When we announced equal prize money, it was a high-profile way to get attention, to show that we were taking it seriously, and, quite frankly, that we wanted to accelerate the change because the women's side of the sport had been held back for decades."

For Goldschmidt to be the CEO who finally made equal pay a priority isn't surprising given her background. Prior to the WSL, she worked for the Women's Tennis Association, learning from

Billie Jean King. Goldschmidt was there when women won equal pay across all Grand Slam tournaments (making tennis one of the first sports to offer equal prize money across all major events). And before she left, she'd brokered an $88 million sponsorship deal between the WTA and Sony—the biggest such investment in the history of women's sports up to that point.[26] When she got the chance to run the show at the WSL, equal investment in women—from prize money to sponsorship dollars—was naturally top of mind. Equal pay was number one on her list. "It's the most high-profile thing you can do," she says, adding, "but it's not a silver bullet." The investment in women surfers would have to run much deeper: promoting fan engagement through increased and equitable media attention, getting more sponsors on board, creating development pathways for girls in the sport. "We wanted to make sure that this was about changing female surfing holistically," Goldschmidt says. "We believed that it would pay off commercially in return—and it did."

Aside from profits and the impact on the leadership pipeline, there's symbolic value in watching women make it up the ladder despite all the many (many) obstacles thrown in their way. Over and over again, the women I spoke to emphasized the real change that's sprung from the old cliché: if she can see it, she can be it. "When I was coming up, I was looking out and it was all men coaching," says McGraw. "But then I played for three female coaches in college and I thought, 'Maybe that's a career option for me.'" After Carolyn Peck became the first Black coach to lead a team to an NCAA women's basketball championship in 1999, she cut down the historic net, eventually passing a piece of it to Dawn Staley, asking her to return it once she won her own championship and pay it forward to another promising young coach. Staley did her one better, sending a piece of her own championship net to every Black woman coach in the league. "It's a constant reminder of what's possible," said University of Denver coach Doshia Woods, after receiving a piece of the net.[27]

Seeing women in leadership roles doesn't just impact women's ideas of what's possible; it changes entire institutions. At General Motors, a company of nearly one hundred thousand employees, the appointment of Mary Barra, the first woman CEO in GM's century-long history, did more than add a feminine face to the company's C-suite. An analysis of corporate filings found that having a woman in the corner office changed the way the company appraised women throughout its ranks, associating active leadership qualities such as decisiveness with women across levels in a way it hadn't before. (The change was not the result of a broader cultural shift in attitudes toward women—filings from Ford Motors, which has not yet had a woman as CEO, showed a weakening association between women and leadership qualities over the same period.) The same pattern was true for many companies in which a woman CEO succeeded a male-identifying chief executive. Researchers at the Wharton School of Business analyzed over forty-three thousand corporate filings and transcripts from investor calls and found that the mere presence of a woman CEO had a halo effect for women throughout the organization, offering women a path out of the double bind discussed earlier in this chapter: women could be seen as capable, independent, and confident without being labeled aggressive or shrill. "Our findings suggest that female representation is not merely an end," the authors wrote, "but also a means to systemically change insidious gender stereotypes and overcome the trade-off between women being perceived as either competent or likable."[28]

~ ~ ~

THERE IS NO magic wand that will remove the systemic barriers to women's leadership in one swish or instantly improve the experience and paychecks of the women who do rise to power. But we do have something convincingly close: sports participation.

As we've heard throughout this book, sports provide an arena for girls and women to test the boundaries of their capabilities, making them the perfect training ground for future leaders. This is not my personal hypothesis, or even the result of a few dozen interviews. Nearly all C-suite women—94 percent, in fact—share a stunning commonality: they all played sports.[29]

The fact that an athletic background is correlated to leadership skills makes sense. But the extent to which it has influenced nearly every woman in a position of power in the business world is staggering. Even Nancy Altobello, who led the research at the consulting firm EY, was surprised. They expected the most powerful commonalities among C-suite women to be the usual suspects: Ivy League schools or top-tier MBA programs. Not a background in youth sports. "We were surprised by it, but then once we absorbed it, we were like, *of course,*" Altobello told me. Many women who played sports in college before conquering the business world did do so at top schools (another benefit of Title IX), but Altobello and her team knew there was something special about sports besides being a pathway to education. "The research said to us, there's something there," she recalled. "What is it?"

"In sports, we learn to physically overcome by sheer grit," says Lindsey Vonn, the greatest woman skier of all time.[30] It's one of the only places you can learn that skill—where you can fail safely, train harder, learn to persist. "Most of the time, the most successful people aren't the people with the most talent, or the most skill," Vonn says. "They are the people that refuse to give up and will outwork everybody."

"The other thing is pressure," adds Stef Strack, who prior to founding VOICEINSPORT was the CEO of Rag & Bone, a senior executive at Nike, and a competitive athlete. "When you are part of a marginalized group you can walk into a room and feel pretty uncomfortable," she says. The pressure of competing as an elite skier "going 60 miles an hour on two short little skis" as a girl taught her how to summon a calm sense of control. Sports taught her where her weaknesses are, when to accept them, and when to put your all into improving. They taught her where her strengths are, and how to use them to her advantage outside of competition. "I absolutely think it is a major part of how I accelerated in my career and just felt more confident while doing it," she says.

In the interviews I did with women athletes who went on to run their own corners of the world, another theme kept coming up: the idea that sports are a common currency that women on the rise can share with male gatekeepers. As Missy Park put it, sports experience gave her the ability to speak men's language as she was building a business in the 1980s. "I remember my dad saying when I decided I wanted to go into business—and he was a very traditional old, white Southern male—he said, 'I suppose one thing you have in your court is that you do understand the value of a good sports metaphor,'" Park remembers. Skill with a soccer ball literally came in handy for Strack during her days as a product manager in Nike's soccer division. As a petite blonde woman with an elfin face, she knew exactly what male execs and athletes from the best football clubs in Europe would be thinking when they saw her. She started making it a point to have a ball around; before meetings, which often took place on a pitch or in training rooms, she would start juggling, showing off her skills. It was instant cred, she says. "It's unfortunate that I felt like I had to do that," she says. "But because of sport, I was able to have the confidence to stick around, to speak up in a room, and to really try to shift the bias that inherently exists."

EY's interest in women athletes started ahead of the Rio Olympics in 2016, when the company was named the professional service provider of the games, "which meant we were doing a lot of work to get Rio ready from a data and cyber service perspective," Altobello explains. Riding the wave of Olympic spirit, the company decided to hire women athletes who'd announced they planned to retire after the games as a way to "give something back." Hiring these women could have easily just been a PR stunt—a way for the establishment firm to score a few points for "investing" in women. In actuality, hiring those women athletes ended up completely changing the way the $45 billion company does business. Athletes' ability to bounce back from failure and improve their performance in real time relies on getting immediate feedback—something that rarely happens in a business world beholden to sluggish annual reviews. Altobello, who was at the time EY's global vice chair of talent, realized how inefficient this was when she was talking with a former pro golfer she had hired. "She was like, 'Okay, so my feedback in July is going to be, Last December you didn't bring your swing back far enough? What is that going to do for me?'" Altobello recalls. "That caused us to completely change our performance management system at EY," she says, explaining that because of the insight from the women athletes they'd hired, the entire firm moved to a more agile and immediate feedback system.

They started to wonder what else they could learn from women athletes. "What we found, and what I observed directly, was that they are very committed," she says. "They are really fearless." This may also explain another finding of EY's research: women who played sports make more money. Across levels, the wages of former women athletes are 7 percent higher on average than salaries of women who didn't play sports. "I think it's because they're better advocates for themselves," says Altobello. "When their performance is good, they know it and they're confident in it. Many women are not confident in their performance—they don't realize how good they are or they don't realize they need to express it. Athletes, they stand by what they did."

Once they launched the study and the data came in, "we had a real soul search," Altobello recalls. They had identified athletes, both women and men, as a golden pipeline for leadership talent but "our business is so technical—would it be easier to hire people who have the technical background and teach them leadership skills or hire people with tremendous leadership and preparation skills and teach them the technical piece?" Ultimately, EY decided they needed both and began hiring former athletes to work in lockstep with more technical hires, betting that it would make the resulting teams stronger. "It has been very successful," she says.

Cathy Engelbert, a former athlete, former CEO, and current commissioner of the most powerful league in women's sports, understands the connection between sports, women, and power better than most. She knows the women in her league are the future "not just in sports, but in society," she tells me. "These are the women that we want leading our country, because they're role models—it's in their DNA." Their power doesn't come from any board or promotion; it comes from the deep well of experience they've had as women athletes, learning to succeed authentically and without compromise in a system that tells them they don't belong. "We want powerful women to lead," Engelbert says. Championing them, lifting them up, getting them the resources they deserve is bigger than sports. It's a proven way to change the face of who calls the shots.

CHAPTER 7

OWNING YOUR WORTH

Renee Montgomery was a point guard for the Atlanta Dream when the turmoil of 2020 hit. Like a handful of other players, Montgomery opted out of playing the 2020 season to prioritize social justice issues full-time. Montgomery's focus was voter turnout and she joined with her Dream teammates to help find the most effective way for their voices to be heard. The experience was transformational for Montgomery—the muscle the team had built by coming together was empowering, and got her thinking about power in a new way. Who takes ownership—and the diversity of perspective they bring to the table—matters in ways she understood in her bones. It's the owners who are the real shot callers, Montgomery realized, the owners who have the most tools to create change. With former owner Kelly Loeffler gone, someone new would be taking over, assuming the power to either amplify the Dream's work as women and activists, or to insist that they keep their politics out of sports. Montgomery's wife posed a simple question: Why not you?

At first the idea seemed ludicrous. "I was so stuck in what's normal," Montgomery tells me, which is ownership positions held by people who are (mostly) white, (mostly) men, and (mostly) rich. Even in the WNBA, one of the most progressive leagues in sports, only one team (the Seattle Storm) has an all-woman ownership group. And no one had made the jump from player to owner and executive. But the more Montgomery thought about it, the more she thought, *why not her*—largely thanks to a powerful group of women in Atlanta climbing the ranks in other highly visible industries. "Being in Atlanta, the city is very used to having women in positions of power," she says, referring to former mayor Keisha Lance Bottoms and gubernatorial candidate and political activist Stacey Abrams. "Whenever I started thinking about becoming a part owner of the Atlanta Dream, it didn't seem as wild as it could because of our city." Inspired by their leadership, she felt capable of upping the ante. The following winter, Montgomery retired from the WNBA and formed an ownership group of investors to buy the Dream.[1]

~ ~ ~

WOMEN ARE NOT just less likely to own sports teams. They are also less likely to own homes, land, cars, and businesses. Just 20 percent of all small businesses with employees in the United States are owned by women, who are in turn much less likely to receive small-business loans. A landmark report from the US Senate Committee on Small Business and Entrepreneurship found that 95 percent of all small-business loans—22 out of every 23 loan dollars—went to men.[2]

Even women in the highest executive positions of S&P 500 companies own fewer shares of the companies they run. Women account for around 25 percent of top executives but control just 1 percent of executive-owned shares, according to findings from Swedish gender-data company ExecuShe. In an analysis of 2020 shareholdings, researchers found male executives owned $770 billion in shares—a key part of executive compensation—while all top executive women combined controlled just $9 billion. When researchers removed company founders (more likely to be men with more control) and super outliers like Elon Musk from the executive group, they still came back with a "giant gender power gap."[3]

Even when women create the company, they don't always own it. In exchange for the venture capital dollars needed to grow a business, founders give up a portion of the ownership of the company, or equity, to investors. This is true for founders of all genders—it's the price they pay for getting access to cash— but research shows women are often pushed into giving up a bigger share. A 2020 analysis found that investors "intended to take a significantly higher percentage of equity from the ventures led by female as opposed to male founding CEOs," leaving women founders with an ownership gap of around 7 percent. For women who found companies in male-dominated industries—say they've developed an app used to help train high-performance athletes instead of a more stereotypically "female" product like a period tracker—the equity gap gets even bigger. Men CEOs in male-dominated industries retained an average of 76 percent equity in their companies while women CEOs in the same spaces retained just 64 percent ownership—a total gap of 12 percent.[4]

"When I look at a headline and see that a woman got some massive amount of money for her startup, all I can think is 'Damn, she probably gave up a disproportionate amount of equity and has little to no control over her company anymore. Once you know how the sausage gets made and who actually owns what, things land differently," says Nathalie Molina Niño, an impact investor who is cofounder and chief strategy officer of Known Holdings, a Black-, Indigenous-, Asian American-, and Latinx-led growth platform that provides capital and development for BIPOC-owned companies. Securing funding has become shorthand for success, she says, but the reality is that it only serves the interests of people in power. "If I'm a venture capitalist, I want people to believe in the mythology. I want people to believe investing in someone is a win for everyone," Molina Niño says. When in fact, as the numbers go, it may not be.

It's easy to cheer *any* investment in women or support any effort that helps women inch closer to parity through incremental gains in pay or power. We need all the progress we can get. But investments, promotions, and raises aren't good enough on their own. "We are lulled into complacency thinking that some progress is being made but it's not really in a sticky way," Molina Niño says. More important than women fighting for greater equity in the system is women taking control of the whole damn thing. "Women need to own and control the machinery of the economy," she says. "The only progress that's sticky is ownership."

As long as any marginalized group is reliant on others to give them power, they'll be vulnerable to having it snatched away. Take women CEOs, for example, who are more likely to be forced out of their roles and serve an average of 3.3 fewer years in their positions than men.[5] "I don't believe in 'empowering' women," says Missy Park. "I hate that effing word. I believe in women *in power*. Because if someone can empower me, they can easily disempower me." That's core to the way she runs Title Nine, which remains a privately held business three decades after its founding because she too believes "women need to control the levers of capital." Park balks anytime someone suggests she sell or when they offer to put her in touch with investment bankers who could take the company public. "You think I did this thing for my whole life to just hand it over to those guys that I was fighting with for basketball court time forty years ago? Oh hell no."

Stef Strack, the former Nike executive who founded VOICEINSPORT, understands the difference between the power you hold as a leader and the power you hold as an owner better than most. As someone who's held both roles, the former is definitely more challenging, she says. "It is harder to go into an existing system and try to drive change where you don't have all the control," she says. For many women, an exciting promotion ends up turning into an infuriating exercise in patience and compromise. "Depending on how the board is set up, the investors, the structure of the company, you might not actually be able to shift the system where you want it to go." It's important, she says, to be realistic.

Most women never get the opportunity to say no like Park or take total control like Strack. The ability to do that generally comes at an extremely high price—literally—which means for most women to get the power of ownership, they have to first get really fucking rich. "Twenty-five-year-old Nathalie might have had these ideas about ownership but couldn't have done anything about them—you need people in positions where they have capital, influence, and power," Molina Niño says.* That's been Cindy Eckert's mission since she sold her company Sprout Pharmaceuticals (which created a libido drug the media dubbed "the female Viagra") for a cool $1 billion in cash in 2015. Once the company she'd sold it to allegedly failed to market the drug adequately per the terms of the sale, Eckert successfully fought to regain control.[6] Ever since then, she's made it her life's work to get more women the funds to be able to retain all the control in their lives that they want. "Ownership always represented freedom to me. The freedom to make my own choices and to retain as much financial value as I was willing to put in the hard work to create," she says. She became an entrepreneur to "escape the pattern of creating value for others that I did not participate in beyond a paycheck," Eckert explains. "Money isn't

---

* To buy the Atlanta Dream, for example, Montgomery had to pool her resources with two other investors to form an ownership group. Her WNBA salary certainly wasn't going to cut it—while the details of the Dream sale weren't made public, one estimate calculated the value of the average WNBA franchise at $17 to $35 million.

the actual mission—never has been—but the impact that can come from it definitely is."

After selling Sprout, she founded an early-stage investment fund called the Pink Ceiling aimed at "fueling an army of women owners" by helping women build, and retain control of, their companies. "If my pot of gold can help her create her pot of gold, and her pot of gold can help another woman create hers, I will have accomplished my goal," she says.

~ ~ ~

WE'RE ABOUT TO see a lot more examples of women in ownership positions and the power that has to create lasting parity, thanks to an NCAA decision about the right of college athletes to own something extremely valuable: their own talent.

For decades, as colleges and universities made millions promoting them, college athletes were barred from any type of sponsorship opportunity—no partnerships with brands, no endorsements, no paid social media posts. The NCAA rule preventing athletes from owning their own name, image, and likeness (NIL) even prevented college athletes from receiving a check from a hometown small business wanting to help them pay for books. (It also prevented many of the world's greatest athletes, like Simone Biles, from competing in college at all. With limited time to monetize their careers, many opt to go pro ASAP.) For women athletes, many of whom have influencer-worthy social media followings, the rules prevented them from potentially making millions. "It's just crazy," Hailey Van Lith, a star guard for the Louisville Cardinals, told Just Women's Sports. "We have so much potential to grow the game and allow ourselves to be successful, but the rules have kept us held back." In 2021, athlete marketing firm Opendorse released an analysis of the most followed college basketball players in the Elite Eight, including an estimate of how much money they could make if they were able to monetize their followings. Eight of the ten most followed athletes were women, representing a combined $2 million in potential income. Van Lith alone stood to earn nearly $1 million a year, Opendorse estimated, if she were able to take ownership of her NIL rights.[7]

Women control an estimated 84 percent of the $16 billion influencer economy, which may be due in part to the idea that "women are better at establishing relationships with their online followers," Lee McGinnis, professor of marketing and director of the integrated marketing communications master's program at Stonehill College in Massachusetts, told the *Washington Post*.[8] "You don't need [as] huge [an] audience as traditional media in order to be profitable because you're able to engage your audience members in a much more interactive way. That's extremely powerful."

Under pressure from state and federal lawmakers, the NCAA finally agreed to give college athletes NIL rights, opening the floodgates to a new era of athlete ownership.[9] The change was especially powerful for women athletes, blowing open an entirely new revenue stream for athletes who will likely get paid significantly less over the course of their careers (regardless of whether they eventually turn pro). Sedona Prince—the Oregon basketball star whose viral TikTok helped shine a light on disparities between the men's and women's March Madness bubbles—was one of the first to cash in. Three months after the NCAA NIL rules changed, Prince launched her own clothing line, to the delight of her three million TikTok followers. "She's doing over half a million in partnerships revenue since NIL started," Lindsay Kagawa Colas, Prince's agent, told me. She could be doing more deals, Colas says, but they're "picky" about which brands they agree to partner with. "Ownership is very much centered in the business that we're building with Sedona," she says. "Control is really important."

NIL deals show that once gatekeepers are removed, the traditional system that has kept women down becomes less relevant, and women have the potential to realize more of their value. During March Madness 2022, Opendorse again analyzed the social media value of the women's and men's top players. Paolo Banchero—who became the NBA's number one draft pick after graduating, inking a deal for $9 million in his first season—had the most social media earning potential of all the men's players in the Final Four. Opendorse estimated he could earn $10,000 per post. Pretty good, but unimpressive compared to Paige Bueckers, the top-ranked woman basketball player. Opendorse estimated Bueckers stood to make $63,000 per post—which, if she turns pro after graduation, is likely close to the salary she would make in an entire year in the WN-BA.[10] This is of course an apples-to-oranges comparison: follower count doesn't necessarily translate to league revenue. But it reveals some of the assumptions we make about the value of men vs. women athletes. The traditional marketplace assumes Bueckers is worth a fraction of Banchero (partly based on each athlete's ability to draw audiences), but in a marketplace where women get more control over their image, their message, and whom they do business with, those assumptions prove wrong. That's great for the Sedona Princes and Paige Bueckerses of the world who are suddenly able to monetize the communities of fans they've built. But it's also great for all women, because it shows the world that women taking ownership unleashes a new stream of value—value that was previously unrecognized, because those running the show refused to see or nurture it.

The USWNT players are a powerful proof point. While the fight for equal pay in soccer raged, the women of the USWNT scored their own important victory for athlete ownership. One major win in their 2017 collective bargaining agreement was the securing of group NIL rights. For the first time, players had "complete control" over their monetization, says Roux. This was a top priority for Roux when she came on as head of the Players Association in 2017, after doing some pro bono consulting work for the team. "It was right after they won the World Cup for the third time in 2015 and players, Meghan Klingenberg especially, were like 'Why are we not feeling the windfall [from post–World Cup hype] here? What's happening?'" Roux recalls. Their win had triggered a media frenzy, but that wasn't translating to revenue via merch sales because there weren't really any products available. "You couldn't buy anything," Roux says. In her research prior to joining the Players Association, Roux realized group NIL rights were generating millions of dollars for players in men's sports, helping them fund the operations of their players' unions and putting money directly into players' pockets.

US Soccer didn't see the value in the women's NIL rights, Roux says. "They hadn't been able to make money off of them and they asked, 'Why do you think you'll be able to?'" she says. "They were like, 'Fine, you take them. They're not worth anything to us anyways.'" (In a statement to the *Wall Street Journal* in 2022, US Soccer's former outside counsel denied this characterization of the negotiations, saying, "We always believed the USWNT players' [name, image, and likeness] rights would become more valuable over time due to their continued success and U.S. Soccer's commitment to growing women's soccer.")[11]

The ownership gave the players power in three significant ways. Most obviously, it meant they got money. Within a year, the players had signed deals with over thirty licensees, creating a new marketplace for merch that actually benefited the women helping to sell it. From 2019 to 2021, player NIL rights reportedly generated $2 million in royalties. But the team doesn't just benefit at the point of sale. "Ultimately what consumer products are is marketing. You see someone walking around in an Alex Morgan T-shirt and it's another way of raising awareness," says Roux. After the USWNT won the 2019 World Cup in France, demand for jerseys exploded. But Nike hadn't anticipated such enthusiasm, reportedly only initially producing a thousand four-star jerseys—to represent four World Cup wins—to sell following the tournament. They sold out immediately and repeatedly, scrambling to keep up with demand.[12] Think about how much more the profile of the USWNT might have been raised if suppliers had simply anticipated the women would sell a lot of jerseys. But most importantly, taking control of their group NIL rights "gave us a seat at the table," says Roux. Because the women took ownership, US Soccer can no longer make merchandising deals without involvement from the Players Association. "If US Soccer wasn't going to invite us in on those conversations, we were able to force our way into the opportunity," Roux says.

The opportunities NIL deals offer women are significant. But it's not all good news: because the NIL landscape is evolving in a culture that still views women as less than, it's inevitable that there will be a gender gap here too. In fact, one is already emerging. An Opendorse analysis of all NIL deals through July 2022 found that women were getting just 37 percent of NIL opportunities and that men's sports—led by football and basketball—were consuming two-thirds of the total compensation, most of which came from paid social media posts.[13] It's "another fundamental example of an inequity in a system that we won't be able to change overnight," says Strack. The hope is that creating more opportunities for women's ownership will structurally change this system. Colas hopes NIL deals in particular will "inform women athletes in college from an earlier point about what it means to understand and advocate for your value—that is a muscle that has to be developed," she says. "The sooner folks who are at the top of the market do it, the more it helps everybody else."

~ ~ ~

As WOMEN GET more ownership, they get more power in other spaces too. For athletes, that means getting to operate as equals in an ecosystem that has historically given all the power to agents, brands, and media, and exercise control in new ways, even when they're making money for someone else. The biggest shift caused by the rapidly evolving NIL landscape and decentralizing influence of social media, says Strack, is the leaching of power from companies like Nike and Adidas. They may still have the largest checks to write, she says, but they know they're facing a new landscape where athletes have the option to do things on their own if the deal isn't sweet enough or if a brand's values don't feel like the right fit. With multiple ways to monetize, Strack says, "athletes are making different decisions now, and those decisions are led more by their own personal values."

That new landscape is changing how brands operate from the outside in, forcing the industry to shift away from a model where they own the athlete to one where the athlete has the power. Allyson Felix's relationship with Athleta may well be the new paradigm. After Felix left Nike for Athleta in 2019, she was still without a shoe sponsor—pretty vital for a runner. (Athleta, an apparel company, doesn't make shoes.) So, she became her own sponsor, launching Saysh, a shoe company that makes sneakers specifically designed for the anatomy of a woman's foot. Instead of "begging for companies to see [her] worth," creating her own company gave Felix the opportunity to set the terms not just for herself, but for other women. "Please be clear. I used my voice and built this company for you. So that you never have to train at 4:30am while you're 5 months pregnant to hide your pregnancy from your sponsor. So that you won't have to fight someone so much bigger than you for a right that should be basic," she wrote on Instagram when she launched her brand.[14]

As Felix's sponsor, Athleta could easily have said, "Great idea—we'll make sneakers for women and you can promote them." But that's not how things work anymore. Rather than try to take ownership, Athleta backed Felix, coaching her through the launch of her own retail company and leading an $8 million Series A investment in Saysh.[15] "Anything we can help her do to grow it, manage it, and run it," Andrew says. "We're there."

~ ~ ~

OWNERSHIP MIGHT BE the most effective tool we have for closing the pay gap—and, ultimately, the power gap. "Most every solution we discuss will only change women's financial status incrementally," says Eckert. "We talk about negotiating raises and asking for promotions when what we should be talking about is getting skin in the game." Ownership, she says, is the quickest path to transformational wealth—for individuals, and to a lesser but still significant degree, for women everywhere. As we know, women who own businesses are more likely to hire and to promote women and invest in systems, companies, and solutions designed by and for women.[16] "I call it underdog unification," says Eckert. "It's my experience that most people who have played the game on an uneven playing field and managed to succeed become highly motivated to turn around and level it."

The money, in other words, is really about power. What you do with your "chunk of the machinery of the economy" is up to you, Molina Niño says, but until you clear the "ownership hurdle," the conversation can't even begin. "Once we are all at the table and 50 percent of everything is controlled by women and 70 percent of everything is controlled by people of color—what we represent in the population—then you can have debates about how to run things," she says. "But until you control your fair share of the machine, you don't get to have an opinion about how it runs."

There are still so few examples of what it can look like to have diverse voices in ownership positions creating real, sticky change. In sports, there were practically none. Then came a revolution in the National Women's Soccer League.

After years of struggling to sustain a stable professional league, women's pro soccer was finally on stable ground following the 2019

World Cup. The NWSL had been growing slowly but steadily since it was founded in 2012, but even though it was the home league of the World Cup–winning, movement-building, equal-pay heroes of the National Team, the NWSL somehow wasn't getting the buzzy cultural hype the USWNT enjoyed. Pay was pathetic, attendance was mediocre, and player reports of abusive coaching practices were starting to surface. This league was packed with potential. But something wasn't working.

As was the case in US Soccer, the sports industry, and really the whole world, positions of power in the NWSL were overwhelmingly filled by men who were clearly missing the mark. Prior to 2021, there were almost no women in ownership positions across the league's ten teams. To unleash the value of the women in the league, something needed to change. "There's a full top-down approach that I think needed to happen," Roux says. "You have to get people in power, that have money, that are willing and that can see the light. . . . And that's where Angel City comes in."

In 2022, the NWSL welcomed Angel City FC—a majority-woman-owned Los Angeles–based team that was attempting to write the future of sport by building something fundamentally different. The team was birthed out of the Time's Up movement, so the story goes. Like millions of people around the world, actor Natalie Portman (a founding member of Time's Up) was glued to the USWNT's fight for equal pay, but what really got her thinking was her son's hero-worship of the team. "Watching my son idolize players like Megan Rapinoe and Alex Morgan the same way he did Lionel Messi or Karim Benzema, I realized that amplifying female athletes could rapidly shift culture," Portman told the *Guardian* in a 2022 interview. She'd never played sports, and certainly hadn't run a sports team, but she realized there was an opportunity there to create something profound for women. She shared the idea with fellow Time's Up member and venture capitalist Kara Northman, and the idea began to grow. Within months, they'd built an ownership group one hundred strong—two-thirds of whom were women—that reads like an Oscars after-party guest list. In addition to Portman, the team is owned by Uzo Aduba, Christina Aguilera, Sophia Bush, Jessica Chastain, Glennon Doyle, America Ferrera, Becky G, Jennifer Garner, Eva Longoria, Lilly Singh, and Gabrielle Union (and her daughter Kaavia Wade). Not to mention the athletes—ACFC's owners also include greats like Mia Hamm, Candace Parker (and her daughter Lailaa), Lindsey Vonn, Abby Wambach, Billie Jean King, and Serena Williams (and her daughter Olympia).[17]

A majority-woman ownership group was nonnegotiable from the start (there are male owners too—Alexis Ohanian, Serena's husband, owns the majority stake in the team) and remains a core pillar of the team, according to Kari Fleischauer, Angel City's chief of staff and VP of strategy in charge of building the ownership group as the team continues to grow. The idea was to "try it a different way," creating a team and business for women, by women, Fleischauer says, that allowed women to dictate their own value. Their strategy was audacious—Angel City's founders went out to potential investors with a valuation "more than what the league thought the team was worth," says Fleischauer. "This was April 2021—we had no players, no brand, no colors, had sold no tickets," she says. "It took a lot of faith." It paid off; Fleischauer is currently turning potential investors away. "We're really selective. Our strategy is getting good people who genuinely care," she says, people who see this as a "long-term investment—something to pass down to their daughters."

Fleischauer has the ability to be picky about the ownership group because the team has been so commercially successful since launching in early 2022, thanks in large part to Jessica Smith, Angel City's head of revenue. She came to ACFC after a twenty-year career in sports—an industry she was always fighting to fit into. "This industry is not made for a mom—the hours are ruthless, you work on holidays. I did a lot of personal questioning around who I was making money for," she says. She stayed because she so deeply believed in the power of sports as a cultural force, but she felt like the industry wasn't capitalizing on its ability to create real systemic change. Angel City "seemed idealistic at the time," she says, but her gut told her she had to be a part of it. "To be able to pour the same energy into something with purpose that wasn't afraid to tackle all of society's issues under the umbrella of equity through sports brought me here," Smith says.

Her first task was to sell jersey sponsorships—the logos you see on the front, back, and sleeve of pro sport jerseys around the world. What these sponsorship spaces sell for sets the tone for brand investment in the team, serving as a microcosm of a team's valuation—top-tier men's soccer teams can sell jersey sponsorships for tens of millions.[18] "I'll never forget the first [league] call I was on," Smith tells me. After the perfunctory welcome to the NWSL, they asked what she planned to charge for ACFC's front of jersey. She named a figure more than twice what would have been considered aggressive for the league. "And I'm not exaggerating, multiple people laughed. They laughed out loud in the meeting," she says.

Smith had been selling jersey sponsorships her entire career. Even when teams are well established and have sky-high viewership numbers, it's hard. "There's only so many qualified companies who can hold a line item for millions of dollars a year," she points out. Smith didn't want to sell the team short by bowing to the pressure of precedent. "I remember having this fire. I was kind of like, *Oh, you have no fucking idea what we're capable of.*" If things were going to change for the league, someone had to push. "I quite literally said no," she recalls. Backed by the majority-woman ownership group, Smith was able to see a different way to value the jersey. "The traditional valuation process skews a way that doesn't understand what women's sports is today—it doesn't measure empathy, it just measures impressions on ESPN," she says. "But that's not what this is." This jersey was not just going to be seen by a few thousand fans every week—it was going to be one of the coolest items of clothing you could own. Natalie Portman was going to be wearing this jersey, Christina Aguilera, Becky G—"She has thirty-two million Instagram followers alone," Smith says.

She sold that spot—along with the two other jersey sponsorship spaces—within two months. The club now has well over $5 million in total jersey partnerships, which ACFC believes makes it the highest-grossing kit "of any women's team in the US," according to club cofounder and president Julie Uhrman.[19] "The market proved it was worth that," Smith tells me, "but someone had to come in and have the confidence to question the valuation, increase the valuation, and go out and get it done."

When women own, things change. Before the team had even begun playing, ACFC had sold merchandise in all fifty states and thirty-eight countries. Their opening game sold out a stadium of twenty-two thousand fans—more than the average attendance for many NBA teams.[20] And they are already pioneering a best-in-class player experience for women athletes, including breaking ground on a state-of-the-art practice facility designed to support women and their families (think: on-site daycare for athlete moms). And most importantly, ACFC granted their players the right to own a piece of the team's success, coming up with a creative way to boost players' salaries by cutting them in on a share of ticket revenues and paying them for the use of their image and likeness.

Smith was "a mess" on ACFC's opening night where Angel City defeated the North Carolina Courage 2–1, scoring their first goal less than 150 seconds into their NWSL tenure in front of a sold-out crowd.[21] Fans roared. Jennifer Garner shimmied along with the pregame marching band. And the women behind ACFC knew it was all just beginning. "I'm looking around at twenty-two thousand fans that believed in us enough to buy tickets, I'm looking at our ownership group at the after-party that showed up in their jerseys with their friends and family. I'm looking at the twenty-four corporate partners that people didn't think were possible, who paid us fair sponsorship dollars and didn't undercut our value. It was overwhelming," she says. "We have so much more to do. But I don't want to lose sight of that moment of success."

PART III
RESPECT

Culture does not make people. People make culture.
—Chimamanda Ngozi Adichie

CHAPTER 8

SEX SELLS, WOMEN PAY

L INDSEY VONN BUILT A CAREER ROCKETING DOWN A MOUN-
tain at speeds up to ninety-five miles an hour, smashing the
records of all but one other person to ever strap on skis, with nothing but spandex and two small pieces of fiberglass between her and
the icy slopes.* She was a supernova of skill, a once-in-a-generation
athlete who left jaws on the floor every time she competed. But
with every medal came cringe-worthy comments, "praise" that
undermined her competence as an athlete. "She is without question one of the most famous athletes in the world. Part of that is
her unparalleled success on the mountain," read a 2018 ESPN profile of Vonn. "Part of that is her runway model looks."[1]

---

* When Vonn retired in 2019, she was four World Cup wins short of Swedish skier
Ingemar Stenmark's record of eighty-six. But some ski buffs debate whether that's
really the best metric. Vonn won titles in every World Cup discipline, demonstrating a total mastery of technical skill and speed, while Stenmark only ever won in
two disciplines. Vonn held the title of the winningest woman on skis until Mikaela
Shiffrin broke her record in 2023.

Vonn was the best woman in the history of an entire sport, but comments about her appearance followed her throughout her career: "I felt like more people thought I was good-looking than thought I was a great ski racer," she tells me. It should go without saying that ski racing is a profession in which looks are irrelevant, but that never stopped commenters from picking over Vonn's body, questioning her legacy, or attributing her success to her sex appeal rather than her hard-earned skill. In 2010, Vonn landed the cover of *Sports Illustrated*'s Winter Olympics issue—a big deal considering fewer than 5 percent of *SI* covers at the time featured women.[2] She was at the peak of her game, and this was the moment for an icon-status shoot—the kind *SI* is so good at. For men, at least. The previous Winter Olympics issue featured four male members of the US Ski Team standing like mountain gods, skis jammed dominantly in the snow. Bode Miller and company looked as epic and towering as the menacing peak rising behind them. "FEARLESS" appeared in big bold letters above their names.

When Vonn's Olympic cover dropped four years later, it elicited a very different word: sexist. In the image, Vonn is in a downhill tuck—which, for non-ski fans roughly translates to bent over with her butt in the air. It created an immediate controversy, dividing the internet into two camps arguing over whether the image was overtly sexist—the result of a misogynistic magazine deliberately creating a provocative image to sell issues—or simply an accurate representation of a skier, who also happened to be an attractive woman, in an authentic ski pose. No one asked Lindsey what she thought. And in this rare moment when a woman in sports got a big spotlight to show off her accomplishments, all anyone wanted to talk about was her ass.

~ ~ ~

THE WAY WE talk about women in sports matters. Even with equal pay and equal opportunity, equality you can sink your teeth into doesn't exist without equal respect. This is why Vonn's *Sports Illustrated* cover touched a nerve. Here was a chance to talk about the raw power and skill of one of the most competent sportswomen in history—to respect her game—and instead people were objectifying her.

Perhaps the pose was the problem: "If you only see women in sports in sexualized poses," says Mary Jo Kane, the director emerita of the Tucker Center for Research on Girls and Women in Sport at the University of Minnesota, "it doesn't in any way upend, challenge, undermine, or destabilize all of the ways in which we think about women and their physical, biological and emotional capacities." There is a vast body of research that supports this idea. "Sexualized women are viewed as lacking in both mental and moral capacity," found one analysis published in the prestigious journal *PLoS One* in 2019. "As a result, they are seen as less competent and less human."[3] When the conversation became about Vonn's sex appeal, it meant it wasn't about her strength or speed or dominance or control. It wasn't about her competence; it was about her body.

This is often the narrative that follows women in the public eye. From 2012 to 2016 women appeared on only 10 percent of *Sports Illustrated* and *ESPN the Magazine* covers, according to a 2017 study—spicily titled "Sacrificing Dignity for Publicity"—conducted by Cynthia Frisby, professor emerita at the University of Missouri, who researches bias in media coverage. When women athletes did get the spotlight, the images featured "sexually objectifying poses, seductive eye gazes, scantily clad clothing, and sexy/inviting body poses," Frisby found. Male athletes, unsurprisingly, "are often seen in their team uniforms depicted in active, game playing athletic motions associated or related to his sport."[4]

Vonn's controversial cover straddles the line between those two categories. It was meant to be a re-creation of a famous *Sports Illustrated* cover from 1992, in which US Ski and Snowboard Hall of Famer A. J. Kitt also appeared in a downhill tuck with his spandex-clad butt in the air. There are a lot of similarities between the two images: same magazine, same sport, same downhill tuck. But there are also many subtle but powerful differences: Kitt's cover feels much more like an action shot, his helmet is on, his focus is on the slopes. He is presented, unambiguously, as a competitor, a faceless master of the mountain. On Vonn's cover, she's clearly posed in a studio, rocking a smokey eye and glossy blonde hair, and staring straight at the viewer with a smile. Those differences are important. But so is this: we have a tendency to view women as sex objects no matter what they're doing, or wearing, or how their hair is styled. "That never crossed my mind when I saw the image, but because I am a woman, it was somehow sexualized," Vonn says now. "It was like this obscene thing. All of a sudden everyone was talking about it—I was like 'Why is Bill O'Reilly commenting on my downhill position?' Why is it even a conversation?"

Women athletes can't avoid their bodies being subjects of conversation. Actions and poses that make men seem respected, brave, and competent often translate to slutty, dramatic, and incompetent when they're done by a woman. "Male athletes get to just be the athlete, and they can portray themselves however they wish to portray themselves," says David Berri, the sports economist. Case in point: when Tom Brady made his *Sports Illustrated* cover debut posed coyly without a shirt in 2002 (it's worth a google), no one let his sex appeal distract from talking about his competence as an athlete. When people discuss LeBron James's legacy, no one presumes his "runway model looks" have anything to do with it. But for women, the scrutiny of the male gaze is constant and strategic: when the conversation is about whether a magazine cover is sexual, it's not about the skill of the woman on it.

Despite all the gains women athletes have made in recent years, women still receive just 5 percent of sports media coverage. The tiny fraction of coverage they do receive is often objectifying, infantilizing, insulting, or some head-spinning combination of the three. Given how little women are covered, each story that does appear in a major media outlet has outsized impact on the way they are viewed.

No one knows this better than Lolo Jones, an Olympic hurdler and bobsledder, who was the subject of particularly misogynistic media coverage from the *New York Times* in 2012. While she was fighting on the track in London to realize her dream of winning an Olympic medal, the *Times* published a story about Jones—in the irony of all ironies—about the sexist way the media tends to cover women athletes. For this, male sportswriter Jeré Longman blamed Jones. The media attention she received, Longman wrote, was "based not on achievement but on her exotic beauty."* He accused Jones of "[playing] into the persistent, demeaning notion that women are worthy as athletes only if they have sex appeal." He shamed her for posing nude in ESPN's "Bodies We Want" issue, which included several male athletes, none of whom Longman shamed or called exotic, and for wearing a bathing suit on the cover of *Outside*. "Jones has decided she will be whatever anyone wants her to be—vixen, virgin, victim—to draw attention to herself," Longman wrote. "If there is a box to check off, Jones has checked it. Except for the small part about actually achieving Olympic success."[5]

This isn't just fringe internet trash or the work of a few out-of-touch assholes—it's the bedrock of public perception of women. Longman wrote these things in a globally respected publication, as a supposed *defense* of women in sports. Men in sports don't face the same slut-shaming or doubts about their credibility. When the *New*

---

* Jones is biracial. That makes her a mixed-race person who identifies as both white and Black—like 20.5 percent of the US non-Hispanic multiracial population—not an "exotic" beauty as defined by a white male.

York Times covered Lamont Marcell Jacobs—another mixed-race Olympic runner who also felt no shame in showing off his body—after he became the fastest man alive at the Tokyo Olympics, the story noted his seven hundred thousand Instagram followers, his "ripped torso," and his proclivity for looking "model-serious" in "risqué Jacuzzi shots" with his fiancée. But nowhere did the writer imply that any of this had anything to do with his success or the press coverage he received at the Olympics.[6]

Let's acknowledge something: athletes are hot. Ours is a culture that lusts over ripped abs, tight glutes, and razor-sharp triceps, and there is no denying that athletes' bodies—of any gender—are part of their appeal. It's sexual, to be sure, but it's also more primal than that. Athletes represent the peak of human performance—the result of the tens of thousands of hours of discipline and drive that turn the earthly human body into an elegant machine. Athletes' bodies are their instruments, and it's fair that we talk about them when we talk about their achievement and power to inspire. But when we talk about men in sports, we don't confuse their physical accomplishments with their physical attractiveness. We don't suggest that they are winners because they're dreamy. And we typically don't congratulate them for winning championships by making creepy comments about their bods the way a fifty-two-year-old David Letterman did by "constantly" referring to the history-making 1999 US Women's National Team squad as "babe city."[7]

Major magazine covers like Lindsey Vonn's and overtly sexist stories like the one about Lolo Jones get the most attention, but sexism is as ingrained in our media coverage as it is in our daily lives. Danica Patrick—the most successful woman driver in American racing and the first woman to win an IndyCar Series race—made her debut in the Sprint Cup Series (now the NASCAR Cup Series) in 2012. Patrick was already a racing icon, the most visible woman in the history of a sport that thrives on toxic masculinity. A local San Diego Fox station covered the barrier-breaking moment. Here's how the full segment went:[8]

"Danica Patrick is such a pretty girl. And she makes a lot of money in sponsorships because of it. But what's not attractive is that she's sexy and she knows it," anchor Ross Shimabuku says in pitch-perfect "this is a fact" news anchor cadence. As if to offer proof, the segment cuts to a clip of an interview with Patrick. "I don't quite understand why when you're referring to a girl, a female athlete in particular, that you have to use the word 'sexy.' Is there any other word that you can use to describe me?" she says. The words "I'm sexy and I know it!" are added under her name by the station. "Oh I've got a few words. Starts with a 'B' and it's not 'beautiful,'" Shimabuku says, before going on to announce the details of the race, as if his commentary was just another part of the news.

In a moment that should have been all about Patrick's power and achievement, the man in charge of covering the news used his platform to undermine her value—to distract from her skill by talking about her sex appeal—and to suggest her accomplishment shouldn't be taken seriously because she's a bitch. This guy was not only seeing her as an object, he was getting annoyed that she refused to act like one. "When it comes to men sexualizing women, we have thousands of years of evidence that says many men subsequently cannot think of women in any other way," says Berri. So when Patrick is painted not as a racecar driver but as a woman who is "sexy and knows it," it's harder to see her value—and all the things that come with it, including high-profile racing contracts and lucrative endorsement deals—as a dominant competitor who is as good as, if not better than, many of the men on the track.

The impulse to objectify women is not really about sex. These conversations "are much more about power," says Caroline Heldman, dual department chair of Critical Theory and Social Justice, and Gender, Women, and Sexuality Studies at Occidental College, and executive director of the Representation Project. "It is a constant reminder of women's lesser status in our society." Men get to be sexual subjects, she explains, in the driver's seat of desire. Women, meanwhile, are treated as sexual *objects*, playthings to be acted upon. They're judged for being too sexy and judged for not being sexy enough to reach their full athletic potential. See sportswriter Jason Whitlock's appraisal of Serena Williams in a column for Fox Sports in which he flaunts his "right to rip her":

> Serena is arguably pushing 175 pounds, content playing hard only in the major tournaments, happy to be photographed on dates with pro athletes and proud to serve as a role model for women with oversized back packs. . . . I'm only knocking Serena's back pack because it's preventing her from reaching her full potential as an athletic icon. I am not fundamentally opposed to junk in the trunk, although my preference is a stuffed onion over an oozing pumpkin.[9]

For women of color, objectification becomes exponentially worse, and racism and sexism become impossible to disentangle. "Anyone who falls outside of 'normal femininity,' which essentially means delicate white Western femininity, will be policed," says Anne Lieberman, the director of policy and programs at Athlete Ally. Frisby's research found as much when she examined the compound effects of gender and race by comparing news coverage of Angelique Kerber, a white tennis player ranked number one at the time of the study, and Serena Williams (then ranked number two). Despite the fact that they were both top-ranked women athletes, Williams experienced a higher frequency of sexist microaggressions and "racialized, sexualized, and dehumanizing comments," Frisby wrote. Even "positive" coverage of

Williams was loaded with microaggressions, grounded in "stereotypes about black people, and black women specifically (masculine, unattractive, and overly sexual)."[10] Here's a sampling of the ways mainstream media publications have talked about Serena Williams's body over the years:[11]

> Generally, I'm all for chunky sports stars. . . . But tennis requires a mobility Serena cannot hope to achieve while lugging around breasts that are registered to vote in a different US state from the rest of her.
> —MATTHEW NORMAN, *THE TELEGRAPH*, 2006

> On some women [the catsuit] might look good. Unfortunately, some women aren't wearing it. On Serena, it only serves to accentuate a superstructure that is already bordering on the digitally enhanced and a rear end that I will attempt to sum up as discreetly as possible by simply referring to it as "formidable."
> —OTIS GIBSON, *SUNDAY TELEGRAPH*, 2002

> [Maria] Sharapova is tall, white and blond, and, because of that, makes more money in endorsements than Serena, who is black, beautiful and built like one of those monster trucks that crushes Volkswagens at sports arenas.
> —STEPHEN RODERICK, *ROLLING STONE*, 2013

This misogynoir isn't just present in the way we talk about Black women's bodies, but in the way we treat them. Weeks before the Tokyo Olympics in 2021, Black sprinter Sha'Carri Richardson was banned from competition after testing positive for marijuana. As many activists were quick to point out, the ban on THC (the psychoactive compound in marijuana) is controversial since it's not known to enhance performance. More importantly, the rigidity with which the ban was enforced for Richardson felt like a racist double standard. A year later, when it came to light that white Russian figure skater Kamila Valieva had tested positive for a drug known to improve cardio function, she was still allowed to compete in the Beijing Olympics while the doping was investigated.[12] "It's very dangerous to support and uphold rigid norms and ideas that are rooted in white Western femininity because it's upholding deeply racist, sexist structures of power," says Lieberman. "Structures we ultimately want to dismantle if we want to have the most equitable world of sports for all."

~ ~ ~

FEMININITY IS COMPLICATED for women in sports. While danger lies in being too feminine, as Vonn experienced, there's a similarly perilous fate for women who aren't feminine enough. The long and complicated tradition of homophobia and transphobia in women's sports is very much alive in the way we talk about athletes' bodies today.

For much of this history, the call has come from inside the house. As journalists, commentators, and trolls have waged the campaign to paint women athletes as a bunch of butch lesbians (Hide your daughters!), leaders in women's sports have, at various times, tried to distance themselves from "controversial" stereotypes by forcing women athletes into caricatures of white Western feminine sex appeal. In preparation for early galas for the Women's Sports Foundation (founded by Billie Jean King, who, you'll remember, lost every single one of her sponsors when she was outed in 1981), women athletes were often given hair and makeup advice, Susan Ware reported in *Game, Set, Match: Billie Jean King and the Revolution in Women's Sports*. Sports activist Pat Griffin recalled the vibe: "Female athletes in their natural state are not acceptable or attractive and therefore must be fixed and 'femmed up' to compensate for their athleticism."[13]

That idea stuck around for a long time. As recently as 2016, WNBA rookies were given hair and makeup classes—in 2008, a third of the orientation for new players was dedicated to styling tips, sportswriter and activist Frankie de la Cretaz reported in the

New York Times. That was tame compared to a 2003 promo for the league that featured a sexed-up Sue Bird staring seductively into the camera and proclaiming, "I'm not as sweet as you think I am."

The women of the WNBA, it should be noted, have completely changed this narrative—the league has become increasingly influential in fashion, not because they've "femmed up" but because they've helped promote an authentic androgyny that pearl-clutching fashion consultants would never have allowed. "The range from masculine to feminine and everything in between and on the periphery is a thing of beauty," Nefertiti A. Walker, professor and vice chancellor at the University of Massachusetts Amherst, wrote on Twitter after the 2022 WNBA Draft red carpet. "The W is one of the few sports leagues where people can be their whole selves and it shows." But a fear of the unfeminine lesbian still casts a shadow over sports, where over half of LGBTQ-identifying adults in a recent study reported experiencing discrimination, insults, bullying, and abuse while playing, watching, or talking about sports.[14]

Cisgender women athletes are also routinely compared to men as a means of belittling them (which is . . . ironic). Shamil Tarpischev, head of the Russian Tennis Federation and a member of the IOC, referred to Venus and Serena Williams as the "Williams brothers" in a national TV appearance, adding, "It's frightening when you look at them." This is the lowest type of schoolyard insult—the same uncreative misogyny responsible for the "gender reveal" signs held by fans of a high school hockey team in Pennsylvania in 2020 when a seventeen-year-old girl from the opposing team took the ice.[15] But the baseness of these taunts belies their seriousness. When a woman or a girl is in fact good enough to play right alongside the boys—when her existence proves they are not superior—she will often be attacked, temporarily "regendered," says Kane. In this way, "women" never succeed—every time a woman surpasses the expectations associated with her gender, she is masculinized. "By doing that, you've reinforced the notion that any sort of physical superiority belongs to men and simultaneously deny women's physical capabilities," says Kane. She will have her very identity questioned. She might even be banned from playing entirely.

Caster Semenya, a cisgender woman runner from South Africa, is the unwilling poster woman for this. Semenya started her career as one of the most promising runners in history, earning two Olympic gold medals and three World Championship titles. For succeeding in her sport, she was rewarded with an incredibly invasive and public investigation of her sex. "They thought I had a dick, probably," Semenya said in a 2022 interview.[16] "I told them: 'It's fine. I'm a female, I don't care. If you want to see I'm a woman, I will show you my vagina.'"

The practice of "sex testing," like the process Semenya was subjected to, and like the gender identity verifications being proposed by those opposed to transgender women competing in sports, seems like it's about fairness. It's not. It's about transphobia. Opponents of trans women use the idea that mobs of "biological males" are going to storm women's sports to stoke fear, positioning gender tests as a way to protect "real" women. It's a deeply racist, sexist, humiliating practice that for decades has been "intrinsically discriminatory" against women, according to a 2020 report from the Human Rights Watch. For decades, both the International Olympic Committee and World Athletics tenaciously persecuted elite women athletes, requiring them to "prove" they were women, via a mortifying battery of tests. Beginning in the 1960s, women athletes in the Olympics were required to submit to gender verification via "nude parades" that literally involved athletes parading naked in front of physicians tasked with visually confirming their female genitalia. As recently as 2014, World Athletics's sex testing protocol involved measuring testosterone levels in the blood, "measuring and palpating the clitoris, vagina and labia, as well as evaluating breast size and pubic hair scored on an illustrated five-grade scale," according to a report in the *New York Times Magazine*. This was the fate for any woman seen to be too muscular, too fast, *too good* to really be a woman. Once formal sex testing at the Olympics ended in the 1990s, "governing bodies moved to what's called a 'suspicion-based model,' which is exactly what it sounds like," says Lieberman.[17] "Essentially, if we don't think that you're a woman we're going to test you. And so who gets tested? Primarily Black and brown athletes from global south countries. It gets to the point where an athlete can essentially compete themselves out of the female category because they're just too talented [to be seen as a woman]."

The reasoning that organizations like the IOC and World Athletics gave for this violation of women's rights was to catch men masquerading as women looking to win titles. Not once, in the history of sex testing, did they find one. Not one. The practice did, however, out intersex athletes like Semenya, who has a condition known as hyperandrogenism, which causes her body to produce higher levels of testosterone than the level considered "normal" for a woman.* As a result of the gender testing, Semenya was banned from competing in 2011 unless she took medication to lower her natural levels of testosterone—a process she described as "taking the soul out of my body"—in the name of fair competition.[18]

If this is what straight, cisgender women get, what's it like for those who aren't? A racist, transphobic attack has a different impact when it's leveled at Serena Williams versus at CeCé Telfer, the transgender NCAA champion. On one hand, Telfer feels comments like this come with the territory of being a Black woman: "We get

---

* While intersex people and trans people face similar forms of discrimination, the terms mean very different things. "Intersex" is an umbrella term for bodies that fall outside of the typical male/female binary and can include naturally occurring variations in a person's chromosomes, genitalia, or internal reproductive organs, whereas "transgender" refers to anyone who identifies with a different gender than the one they were assigned at birth.

scrutinized for our bodies all the time because of how strong looking we are and how we are built—they always like to compare us
to men." For cis athletes, Telfer sees a way to own those comments.
She admires Williams's ability to take pride in her strength. "She
embraces it, almost like 'if you think my body looks like a man's
then listen, that just means I'm doing the thing, I'm where I need
to be athletically.'" As a transgender woman, finding a way to own
or brush aside these comments is a much bigger burden. "It's hard
for me to think like that because I don't want to be associated with
that human category [of a man] at all," she says. It's an isolating
experience. When the head of the Russian Tennis Federation made
a transphobic remark about Venus and Serena, he was fined and
met with a global feminist outrage trans women often don't benefit
from. "When somebody comes at me," Telfer says, "I just have to
take a deep breath in. It is what it is."

~ ~ ~

WOMEN IN SPORTS are always women first, athletes second. As
they publicly endure body shaming and the slimy creep of the male
gaze, the rest of us watch. We internalize it. We get comfortable,
whether we realize it or not, with the idea that women's bodies are
always fair game.

Not even maternity leave spared Michelle Wie West, one of
the most famous golfers of all time, from being dragged back into
the public discourse as part of a sexist anecdote told by none other
than Rudy Giuliani. While appearing on Steve Bannon's podcast,
Giuliani asked if he could share a story about conservative com-
menter Rush Limbaugh, who had recently died. When playing a
charity round of golf with the "gorgeous" Wie West, the pair apparently joked about photographers being around purely to photograph her "panties" as she bent over to putt. "What this person
should have remembered from that day was the fact that I shot 64
and beat every male golfer in the field leading our team to victory,"

Wie West wrote on Twitter. "I shudder thinking he was smiling to my face and complimenting my game while objectifying me and referencing my 'panties' behind my back all day. What should be discussed is the elite skill level that women play at, not what we wear or look like."[19]

For the record, Wie West's "panties" weren't showing. "Nike makes skirts with shorts built in underneath for this exact reason . . . so that women can feel confident and comfortable playing a game we love," Wie West clarified on Twitter. But many uniforms for women in sports do feel like they've been tailor-made for the male gaze. At the 2021 Olympics, women received a record amount of prime-time coverage: 59.1 percent of screen time, according to the analysis from the Representation Project. That's an important benchmark that shouldn't be overlooked, but Heldman says it's not the feminist dream it looks like at first glance. "This is not popular to say, but I think that the way that they have achieved gender equality in coverage is profoundly sexist. What we found is that women basically appear in something akin to a swimsuit for most of their coverage, whereas men have a great variety in the outfits they're wearing," she explains. In Tokyo, over two-thirds of women athletes were shown in revealing uniforms compared to just half of male athletes, according to their report, and it was ten times more likely for a camera to pan a woman athlete's body "and/or focus on specific body parts in a sexualizing way."[20] "There was one scene where we just sort of gasped," says Rebecca Cooper, director of research at the Representation Project. "There was a runner who was stretching and the camera just stayed on her rear end, and it was zooming in slowly. It was wild. It was like, are we watching HBO?"

The tendency for women's uniforms to be more revealing makes the opportunities for objectification all the more plentiful. A look through Getty Images' Olympic volleyball archives will quickly turn up dozens of women's butt cheeks and tightly cropped bikini shots. There are hardly any equivalent shots for men, who play in loose-fitting shorts and tank tops. The male body is a tool—a vehicle for action and power—while women's uniforms often remind us that a woman's body is an object meant to please. Asserting otherwise can cost you. That was the case with the Norwegian beach handball team, who were fined by the European Handball Association for daring to wear thigh-skimming biker shorts rather than regulation bikini bottoms in a 2021 tournament. When the players petitioned before the tournament began, asking to wear the shorts they trained in, they were threatened with disqualification. In their bronze medal match, they took a stand in shorts anyway and literally paid for it, proving we live in a world where we slut-shame women for showing their bodies and also fine them for covering up.[21]

Add this to the list of things women in sports have to deal with that male athletes simply do not—they don't worry that what they wear might undermine their performance, or, at the very least, that their genitals might accidentally slip out of their teeny tiny uniforms at the most important moment of their career. "In competition, we glue our leotards to our butts so they don't show," says Kim Bui, a three-time Olympic gymnast from Germany. "Imagine if a leotard slips during one of our splits, a photographer accidentally takes a picture, and this picture ends up on the internet," Bui says. This is why Bui and her teammates on the German Olympic team opted to wear unitards at the Tokyo Olympics, a move that was seen as a powerful stand against sexualization in the sport. "It should be a gymnast's choice to wear what she (or he) feels comfortable with," Bui wrote on Instagram.[22]

But choice isn't granted equally. It's granted more freely to those who get more coverage, have more followers on social media—and to those who are white. Despite the fine, the Norwegian beach handball team found immediate support for wanting to be more comfortable, and the world applauded the statement by the majority-white German gymnastics team, who preferred a more modest uniform. But for women athletes who wear the hijab, the right to compete in a uniform that makes them feel comfortable is still controversial if not outright forbidden. Hijab bans in sports are sometimes justified as being a matter of safety—even though plenty of tight-fitting options specifically designed for competition exist, and no sport federation has produced any evidence that wearing a hijab increases the risk of injury. What these bans actually accomplish is keeping Muslim women and girls out of sports. In 2014, the entire Qatari women's basketball team was forced to withdraw from an international competition because the International Basketball Federation banned the hijab. In 2019, high school runner Noor Alexandria Abukaram was disqualified from her track meet for her decision to wear the head covering. In 2022, soccer players in France were still not allowed to compete in the hijab despite FIFA, the sport's international governing body, overturning its hijab ban in 2014. These instances all made headlines but didn't spark nearly the same level of feminist outrage as we tend to see over the policing of what white women wear, pointed out sports journalist and activist Shireen Ahmed. "While the policing of white women's bodies at the Olympic Games is no different from the policing of Muslim women's bodies, what clearly varies is the level of rage we feel depending on the color of female athletes' skin," wrote *USA Today* opinion contributor Anushay Hossain.[23] For things to change, it takes women to speak up, yes. But it also takes a public who respects women—of all races and identities—enough to listen. If the Norwegian handball players and German gymnasts deserve to wear what makes them feel comfortable (and be applauded for it), so too do France's Les Hijabeuses.

All of this—the obsession with commenting on women's bodies, the tendency to focus on sex appeal rather than skill, the policing of what women are allowed to wear—helps feed a culture of abuse. "When we view an objectified woman, we tend to view her as a collection of body parts rather than a whole," says Heldman. When men see images of sexually objectified women, she explains, brain scans show the same part of the brain lights up as when they're about to use a tool. It's a primal dehumanization, she says. "We know from historical accounts and research that dehumanization is the first step in violence toward a group," Heldman continues. "So it doesn't at all surprise me that women are facing epidemic levels of domestic and sexual violence." Or as writer Lindy West put it, "the relentless coding of women as sex things puts women in lifelong, simmering, physical danger."[24]

This culture makes for a lot of abuse in sports. To be crystal clear, a uniform or photograph in a magazine is never the cause of abuse—it is *never* about what she was wearing, or how she was posing, or how her hair was styled, or what she was doing, or her sexual history, or what she ate for breakfast that morning, for that matter. But abuse grows like mold in an environment where women are routinely reduced to their bodies. More than one in ten elite athletes, across all sports, have experienced some form of sexual abuse, according to a 2021 survey by the World Players Association. Half reported experiencing emotional abuse. Other studies estimate abuse in sports is even more common: a 2017 study of elite athletes in Germany found that over a third had experienced at least one instance of sexual violence.

Gymnastics became a painful example of what this looks like when hundreds of gymnasts bravely came forward with their stories in 2016 and 2017. As Joan Ryan, the author of *Little Girls in Pretty Boxes* and the first journalist to begin widely reporting on the culture of abuse in women's sport nearly thirty years ago, described, the explicit ideal for gymnasts and figure skaters was to emulate the prepubescent body of a girl. "Aesthetics" are important in competition, one coach said, and another described the sentiment as "we prefer not to have mature body types."[25] For decades, women and girls in elite gymnastics were objectified, reduced to how they looked, and stripped of their confidence to meet these standards. "The culture was created to exploit these girls," Ryan told me. "I'm really surprised so little has changed."

Sexualizing and objectifying women athletes devalues women in a way that has ripple effects far beyond sports. There is a strong link between the objectification of women in the media and sexual violence. A 2018 study published in the *Journal of Interpersonal Violence* found that when women are objectified, it makes all of us less likely to recognize abuse. In two experiments, researchers showed groups of participants (one group of women only and one group that also included men) a fictional newspaper article describing a case of sexual harassment at work. Two versions of the article were distributed: one that included a photo of the victim in "sexualized clothing," with another version showing the victim in nonsexualized clothing. In both groups, people were less willing to help the victim when she was presented in a sexualized way. And in the group that included both men and women, researchers found that "endorsement of traditional masculine norms" made the participants even more biased against the victim.[26]

These violent effects of the male gaze undermine women's safety and economic empowerment. Up to 85 percent of women will report experiencing sexual harassment at work. And the pandemic may have made it even more common: a survey by Project Include found that in a new working environment with many women more likely to be working from home—where boundaries are blurred and there are often no witnesses to interpersonal interactions with colleagues—25 percent of respondents said they'd experienced an increase in gender-based harassment.

It's a huge contributing factor to the pay gap, the financial ramifications of which are chillingly quantifiable. "When we think about sexual harassment, the framing is usually around the emotional cost—we don't spend a lot of time thinking about what women lose economically when they are harassed," says C. Nicole Mason, president and CEO of the Institute for Women's Policy Research. But the cost is huge. Harassment can lead to debilitating conditions like depression and PTSD, both of which can impact earning potential; it can prevent women from getting career-changing mentorship and force them to step away from game-changing opportunities; it can mean lost earnings for women forced to leave before finding another opportunity and financial stress that can last for years. (Women who experience harassment at work are 6.5 times more likely to leave their jobs.) Together, these things cost women who have been sexually harassed—anywhere from a mere $600 to $1.3 million in lost earnings over a lifetime, according to an analysis published by Time's Up and the Institute for Women's Policy Research in 2021, which tallied the costs of sixteen individual case studies.[27] "And who do you go to see about these costs?" challenges Mason.

Outside of gender-based violence, this sexualized system also creates a complicated and well-documented beauty paradox that directly affects how much money women make. On one hand—as we see so often with women in sports—sexual attractiveness undermines women's competence. Attractive women are perceived not just as less capable skiers or hurdlers or racecar drivers, but as less trustworthy leaders. It's what Leah Sheppard, an associate professor at Washington State University's Carson College of Business, calls the "femme fatale effect," according to her research published in the journal *Sex Roles*. Attractive men in business don't suffer from the same superficial penalty that influences the ability to rise at work.[28]

Even more insidiously, these sexualized stereotypes can also influence performance, shaping how we present ourselves and messing with our minds. "The more likely we are to buy into this idea that our bodies are the most important thing about us, the higher our rates of what's called 'self-objectification,'" explains Heldman, referring to what happens when we start to internalize the toxic misogynistic sludge that transforms women into objects. "Seeing yourself as a sex object has been linked to eating disorders, higher rates of anxiety, higher rates of depression, lower self-esteem, lower personal efficacy—the belief that you can bring about change and that you're effective in the world—and lower political efficacy," Heldman says. "Across the board, the more a girl or woman sees herself as a sex object, the more profoundly negative the internal effects are." In a 2019 study, researchers asked one hundred women to sign up for an experimental website by submitting a photo and a personal description. They received feedback from a fictitious male user that was either neutral, related to their personal description, or related to their appearance. Those in the last group—what researchers described as the "objectifying" condition—believed they had less personal free will and saw themselves, unsurprisingly, as more object than person. Self-objectification is so damaging it actually diminishes cognitive performance, hijacking a woman's brainpower.[29] "When you cue women to think about their body in a way that is objectifying, meaning they're concerned about how they appear to the outside world, it adds to their cognitive load and it slows down their speed and messes with their accuracy," says Heldman. This bullshit, in other words, literally makes women less capable.

For Telfer, the pressure to be feminine can hold her back on the track. "As an athlete, you should just be thinking about execution, but every time I put on my athletic wear, I'm thinking 'Are my boobs big enough? I'm too tall, I'm too muscular,'" she says. "I'm holding myself back at this point. I'm not trying to achieve my full potential because I'm trying to be that soft girl, that slender girl that women are supposed to be. It's already tough competing, let alone having to match society's perfect image of what a female should look like." Vonn knows what this feels like too. Early in her career, she focused on what her body was doing for her—the number on the scale never mattered much. "But once I started doing red carpets and things like that, I realized that I was thirty, forty, fifty pounds heavier than everybody else there. People would comment about my thighs and say that I'm not pretty and that I shouldn't be there. It derailed me," she says. Feeling self-conscious, she tried to lose weight and it wound up hurting her performance for the next year, she says. "I ended up losing the overall title by three points. And I blamed that squarely on myself. I let it affect me."

Here is where the beauty paradox gets really messy: sex appeal also has a well-documented history of paying off for women. At least, financially. Look no further than the fallen Victoria's Secret Angels—some of the highest-paid models in history. For years, these women made jaw-dropping sums of money—Adriana Lima made over $10 million in 2016—by turning the male gaze into a female fantasy and selling the perfect (read: actually very damaging) ideal of feminine sex appeal. Victoria's Secret's standards for its "beautiful young girls" were notoriously high, creating a hotness hierarchy even among its genetically blessed cohort of models— the more attractive you were, according to the definitions of men like Ed Razek (the man behind the Victoria's Secret fashion show, who has been accused of misconduct), the more money you made. The same twisted logic also applies to mere mortals in much more mundane workplaces. Studies have long shown an unsurprising if maddening truth: hot people make more money. An analysis by the National Bureau of Economic Research confirmed there is indeed a beauty premium when it comes to paychecks in jobs where attractiveness is seen as a tangible asset, such as a job with a lot of interpersonal interactions (or, you know, one that requires attracting thousands of fans). An important caveat: what constitutes "attractiveness" likely has more to do with submitting to the male gaze than any biological traits. A 2016 study from researchers at the University of Chicago and the University of California–Irvine found getting glammed up—wearing makeup and doing their hair—accounted for essentially all of an attractiveness-fueled salary boost for women.[30]

Be attractive enough to cash in on that beauty premium, but not so sexy as to undermine your competence—it's a nasty double bind that gets simultaneously more complex and more explicit in sports. "I remember when I was covering a lot of tennis, and the Women's Tennis Association would put out a calendar of really sexy pictures of their tennis players to get coverage," says Ryan. "Obviously, men never, ever, ever had to do that." "It's really messed up standards," adds Vonn. "Women are only marketable if they're winning *and* good-looking. Men are marketable either way—as long as they win, it doesn't matter if they're good-looking." For years, playing up a woman athlete's sex appeal was the only way to get them any attention, says Lindsay Kagawa Colas, the agent at Wasserman who represents some of the biggest stars in basketball. "The directive was always 'We need to make it sexy.' What they meant was hetero-normatively sexy by some traditional Western standard," she says.

≈ ≈ ≈

THESE COMPLEX, OFTEN conflicting dynamics have put women athletes—tasked with drawing attention to their underresourced, underfunded sports—in some pretty morally sticky positions and sparked debates about whether they're the victims or the perpetrators. That unbelievable news segment about Danica Patrick didn't end with the "I'm sexy and I know it!" tirade. In the full clip, the lone woman anchor on set with her two male colleagues points out that Patrick is a woman breaking gender barriers. Perhaps trying to recover, Shimabuku—the reporter who all but called Patrick a bitch just seconds before—tries to change the subject to a male driver, but the second male anchor on set can't resist chiming in. "Hey, back to Danica Patrick for a second," he says. "If she's trying to lose the sexy image, the GoDaddy commercials don't exactly further that cause."

If you ever watched a Super Bowl between 2007 and 2015, and honestly even if you didn't, you'll likely remember these commercials. They are probably some of the best examples of misogynistic advertising in media history, more softcore porn than ads for a web domain-hosting platform. Patrick starred in them for years and made bank doing it, playing the object of tech nerd fantasies: showering with another woman, re-creating that iconic water scene from *Flashdance*, directing model Bar Refaeli to make out with the nerdy IT guy, and even getting a strip tease from a sexy lady cop dying to be a "GoDaddy Girl" in one particularly gross installment. The commercials are so raunchy that some of them sit behind age-restriction firewalls on YouTube. They are sexy in the very worst way.

We love to blame women for this. *Lindsey Vonn posed in three Sports Illustrated swimsuit issues—talking about her butt is fair game. Danica Patrick made millions playing up her hotness—she's a bitch for not liking it when people call her sexy.* They're easy arguments. Watch a GoDaddy commercial, tweet at Patrick for being the worst kind of role model, move on. Maybe that's a fair assessment. Maybe she is both a pioneer for women and a person who has reinforced sexist stereotypes—not every barrier breaker is a feminist hero. But it's not entirely fair to forget the fact that women's economic potential is governed by a strict and deeply sexist double bind. It creates real internal tension. Mary Jo Kane, the researcher on women in sport, conducted a study in which she and her coauthors presented women athletes with three categories of images: action shots of women athletes on the court, all-American girl-next-door photos, and what Kane describes as images of "off the court 'sexy babes.'" They asked how the women wanted to be seen. The athletes "overwhelmingly" chose the athletic images as the ones they felt best represented them and were most likely to increase respect for their sport. But nearly half felt that the "soft porn" portrayals were the images most likely to increase interest in their sport.[31]

For men, this duality is okay. David Beckham, for example, is allowed to cash in on his ample sex appeal, showing off his divinely sculpted body in underwear ads that will make you blush, without it negatively affecting his career or sparking online outrage about the way he's representing men. For Beckham, sex appeal is all upside—confirmation of his raw physical power and position at the top of the desire food chain. Looking at his seductively posed bod probably made many people think he was an even better soccer player. But for women, sex appeal is a sick catch-22: women fight to be taken seriously in a culture that tells them the most valuable thing about them is their appearance while simultaneously using their appearance to objectify and undermine them. "We are rewarded for buying into a system that defines us as lesser than," says Heldman. "The problem is the game, not the players."

Women can of course present themselves as both sexy and serious—but doing so is filled with landmines. In 2015, Serena Williams was named Sportsperson of the Year by *Sports Illustrated*. It was a big honor—Williams was the first solo woman to receive the title since 1983. She is arguably the greatest player tennis has ever seen and she had *dominated* that particular year—she won three of the four Grand Slams and finished the season ranked as the number one player in women's tennis in the world. So it was fitting that she'd be portrayed as the Queen of the Court—owning her image, taking up space, and totally in command. The image on the cover of *SI* is definitely . . . powerful. It's "what my students called a 'beaver shot' of her," says Kane. Williams, in a black lace bodysuit and patent leather stilettos, is draped seductively over a golden throne, thighs open to the camera. "I mean, it's almost like a caricature of our research," Kane says. Probably anticipating another Vonn

PR crisis, *Sports Illustrated* tweeted that the art direction for the cover was Williams's idea "to express her own ideal of femininity, strength and power."* "I can't tell you the number of female athletes who've said to me, 'What's wrong with being portrayed this way? I'm very proud of my body and I want to show my body off,'" Kane says.[32]

For as long as feminism has been a movement, this has remained one of the most hotly contested debates: *Can a woman reclaim the male gaze by portraying herself as a sex object? And is there ever anything truly empowering about that?* Something tells me David Beckham doesn't have to ask himself these questions before he appears in his underwear, but women athletes do. Given everything we know about how the world responds when it sees a woman portrayed in a sexual way, there's not a simple answer. Yes, it can undermine women's worth. And yes, it can also symbolize a woman's control over her body.

Williams looks unquestionably in control in her cover shot. And in an equitable world, that would be the whole story: woman owns her own image, everybody else shuts up about it. But we do not live in an equitable world. We live in a world where Raymond Moore, then CEO of the Indian Wells tennis tournament, said women "ride on the coattails of the men." He continued: "If I was a lady player, I'd go down on my knees every night and thank God that Roger Federer and Rafa Nadal were born, because they have carried this sport."[33] He said this in 2016 just before "lady player" Serena Williams won the tournament (and after the future president of the United States Donald Trump made a similar statement about the fantasy of seeing professional women drop to their knees). Ev-

---

* The photo wasn't the only reason Williams's cover was controversial: in a readers' choice poll that same year, *SI* readers overwhelmingly voted for American Pharoah, the winner of the Triple Crown—who is a horse—as sportsperson of the year. Williams came in eleventh out of twelve in the readers' choice poll, in case you needed further proof that women in sports are grossly underappreciated.

ery image, every word, every move a woman makes happens in a world where men like Moore and Trump are allowed to say things like this but women like Williams and Vonn and Patrick aren't allowed to decide what makes them feel powerful without the whole world weighing in. "It's an added burden," says Kane. And until women get respect, they'll continue to carry it.

CHAPTER 9

GOOD FOR A GIRL

AS WOMEN MAKE GAINS—THE KIND THAT COME WITH long-overdue money and power—the ways in which they are constantly belittled become more obvious. The impulse to objectify and sexualize is the tip of the iceberg, just the public-facing misogyny that tends to make the most headlines. The most damaging prejudice lurks out of sight, embedded into institutions and internalized as a simple belief: that men are inherently superior to women. That they're bigger, stronger—*better*.

"Sports have always served as 'empirical proof,' that men are naturally, meaning physically, superior to women. As long as we can establish that men are naturally superior to women in sports, then that can be generalized beyond sports to the broader population," says Mary Jo Kane, the researcher on gender in sports. "But if we see women outperforming men, then that upsets the whole apple cart, doesn't it?"

When that happens, things get ugly. After the 2019 World Cup, US Soccer found themselves backed into a corner. Here were the facts: Since the Women's National Team was founded in 1985, they have won four World Cups and six Olympic medals. The Men's National Team has won zero of either since they played their first game in 1916.[1] In other words, when the WNT faces the best women from around the world, they most often win, and when the MNT faces the best men, they often fail to make the cut. If the metric for performance given to both teams was to win, the WNT would undisputedly be the more successful team, and thus should be getting paid not equal to the MNT but even more. (Wins, as we've discussed, aren't the only metric of success—it's a complicated soup of revenue generation and publicity. But wins on the international stage are undoubtedly part of that, and the optics of comparing both teams' records with their pay aren't great for US Soccer's defense.) So in the months following the WNT's epic victory and the outpouring of global support for equal pay, US Soccer reached for the oldest, basest argument in the book to defend themselves in their ongoing lawsuit. The women of the WNT shouldn't be paid the same as the men's team because of their—wait for it—biological inferiority.

There is a "materially higher level of speed and strength required to perform the job of a [Men's National Team] player," the court document, filed in 2020, reads. That isn't a "sexist stereotype," the brief assures, "it is indisputable 'science.'" They didn't stop there. The brief continued, "Even assuming there are [Women's National Team] players who could perform the job of MNT player (contrary to plaintiff's own testimony), that is not the point. The job of an MNT player (competing against senior men's national teams) requires a higher level of skill based on speed and strength than does the job of a WNT player." These facts are, again, "undisputed," US Soccer said. There's more: "Plaintiffs also fail to demonstrate, as a matter of undisputed fact, that the job of WNT player and the job of MNT player carry equal 'responsibility,'" the documents read.[2] "MNT players have responsibility for competing in multiple soccer tournaments with the potential for generating a total of more than $40 million in prize money for U.S. Soccer every four years. WNT players compete in only one soccer tournament every four years that has the potential to generate any prize money at all and most recently that amounted to one-tenth of the amount the MNT players could generate."

Perhaps instead of using the sexist architecture of soccer to paint the US women as less "responsible," the federation could have focused their efforts on leveling the international playing field. If the women had the opportunity to win the same prize pool as the men just in the last two World Cups alone, they would have made $73 million for US Soccer. The men earned nada during that period.

The filing predictably triggered internet-melting outrage. In their justification for why the women should be paid less, lawyers for the federation made it clear that they are not only failing to invest equally in the women's game as a matter of principle (and law), but also failing to invest in the players, male or female, with the most proven record. Instead, they doubled down on the losing team, working against their own business interests rather than choosing to elevate their best players. It was a "throwback to the worst stereotyped justifications for gender discrimination," the players stated in their own court document filed in response.[3]

Women are not paid less because they are weaker, less intelligent, or less capable. Women are paid less because men control the system—and they're threatened. "The bottom line is that women's economic subordination comes from the power men have to make women work, in service to them, for less or no pay. The cause is male aggression and control of resources rather than men's natural superiority as stronger, braver, more important beings," economist Linda Scott writes in *The Double X Economy: The Epic Potential of Women's Empowerment*.[4]

US Soccer became an easy target in making its own toxic internal culture extremely public in their fight against the women.

Fans Twitter-ranted, sponsors bristled, the president of US Soccer was forced to resign, the federation issued a public apology, and, ultimately, the lawyers responsible for the brief requested to withdraw from the case.[5] But this isn't just a soccer problem. Sexism is part of sport DNA—it has for centuries been the arena where men get to become gods and women get left on the sidelines. The myth that women are the weaker sex is the primal core of the pay gap, the investment gap, and the motherhood penalty; it drives abuse and objectification, sustains transphobia and homophobia, and keeps women out of the seats of power. "To be degraded and to be marginalized and to be devalued over and over again is exhausting—it's *exhausting*," says Kendall Coyne Schofield, captain of the US Women's National Hockey Team. "[The attitude is] you should just be thankful and grateful that you have an opportunity to play." Once that mindset begins to change, she says, "conversations about equal investment, support, and resources start to change too."

~ ~ ~

THE CAMPAIGN TO keep women in the role of second-class champions relies on questioning women's capabilities, if they're allowed to play at all. Women weren't allowed to compete in the Olympics until 1900 (largely thanks to the lobbying of women athletes like French rower Alice Milliat) and even then, it was only in events suited for their "femininity and fragility," like sailing and croquet. But the belief that women aren't serious competitors never fully went away; even as activists fought for more Olympic events for women, IOC officials worked hard to define which sports were "suitable" for the so-called weaker sex, with the debate bleeding into public discourse. "There's just nothing feminine or enchanting about a girl with beads of perspiration on her alabaster brow, the result of grotesque contortions in events totally unsuited to female architecture," read a *New York Times* article published in 1953.

Decades later, women were still being treated as biologically and socially unfit. At the inaugural FIFA Women's World Cup held in 1991, the matches were eighty minutes rather than the traditional ninety because officials were afraid those extra ten minutes would be too strenuous for the fragile girls prancing around the field.* "They were afraid our ovaries were going to fall out," team captain April Heinrichs later reflected.[6]

There are still different rules for men and women who compete in the same sports at the Olympics. It wasn't until 2014 that women were permitted in the ski jumping competition after decades of being barred from the slopes due at least in part to the false belief that the hard landings might make the sport medically unsuitable for ladies' delicate frames. It wasn't until the Tokyo Olympics in 2021—the most "gender-equal" Olympics ever—that women were allowed to compete in the grueling 1500-meter swimming freestyle event (Katie Ledecky dominated). And to this day, women still aren't allowed to compete in the Olympic decathlon—a series of ten track-and-field events that encapsulate so many skills it's often referred to as the producer of the "world's greatest athlete"—because the event is thought to be too strenuous for women to handle. "This overemphasis on protecting girls from strain or injury and underemphasis on developing skills and experiencing teamwork fits neatly into the pattern of the second sex. Girls are the spectators and the cheerleaders. . . . This is perfect preparation for the adult role of women," Kathryn Clarenbach, founding chairperson of the National Organization for Women, once said.[7]

Since the founder of the International Olympic Committee first declared the participation of women to be "uninteresting," we've seen women best men, shatter records once held by men, and

---

* That event, by the way, was technically called the FIFA Women's World Championship for the M&Ms Cup, the "World Cup" title thought to be too prestigious to give to lady soccer players. M&Ms, apparently, we can have.

reshape our ideas of what we thought the human body capable of when it was defined by men. We've seen women surpass men in higher education, and beat out men to run countries and Fortune 500 companies. But society and the men who run it still don't find women winning to be "enchanting."

At the 2019 Women's World Cup in France, the US Women's National Team came in hot. In their first match against Thailand, the team, coached by Jill Ellis, dominated 13–0. It was the biggest win, by the biggest margin, in World Cup history—men's or women's. People did not take kindly to this. Some felt the women had won by *too much*, showing off and running up the score after it was clear they'd won the match. Others criticized the women for celebrating their goals on the field, calling the team "classless."[8] These women did nothing wrong. In fact, they did their job, which is to win soccer matches. It's important to understand that their high score does in fact matter. In the event of a World Cup tie in the first elimination round, FIFA uses total goals scored by each team as a tiebreaker for who advances—a polite 2–0 win is not the same as a 13–0 shutout. But more importantly, this score made history. It was a chance to prove that the women's team—who, let's not forget, was in the midst of an equal-pay lawsuit to prove their worth— were the best competitors with the most potential to grow the game in the United States. Should they have held hands and made flower crowns in the grass after goal number five?

The problem was that the women of the US Women's National Team dared to defy gender expectations. It is men who are expected to dominate, to conquer. Women are expected to play nice. Imagine the media calling Michael Jordan and the Dream Team "classless" for winning too many championships. Imagine commentators shaking their heads in disappointment when Michael Phelps thrust his freakishly long arms into the air, index fingers raised to indicate his status as number one, as he did with so many of his twenty-three Olympic gold medals.

There is a premium on niceness for women that simply does not exist for men. Like the beauty paradox, women face a no-win set of contradicting rules. Add too many exclamation points to your email and risk not being taken seriously. Write like a man, and get called a bitch. Women pay an assertiveness penalty not just in sports or entertainment but in every profession on the planet. A *Wall Street Journal* investigation of seventy-one studies examining the assertiveness penalty found that women are "particularly penalized for direct, explicit forms of assertiveness, such as negotiating for a higher salary." In 2021, Scarlett Johansson sued Disney over their decision to release her film *Black Widow* on Disney+ in addition to in theaters, significantly cutting into her potential theatrical earnings, the suit, which has since been settled for an undisclosed sum, alleged. Johansson was standing up for her contractually guaranteed earning potential—a shrewd move men are routinely applauded for—but Disney hit back in a filing that Time's Up called "a gendered character attack." Disney's response called Johansson's defense of her rights "callous" in light of the pandemic and, in the words of the joint statement released by Time's Up, Women in Film, and ReFrame, attempted to "characterize Johansson as insensitive or selfish for defending her contractual business rights," and contributed to "an environment in which women and girls are perceived as less able than men to protect their own interests without facing ad hominem criticism."[9] To get any recognition at all, women are expected to fight to prove their worth—but only to a point.

Then, of course, there's the routine infantilization of women. The 2015 Australian Open became mired in a controversy known as "Twirlgate" when a sideline announcer asked Serena Williams and Eugenie Bouchard to give the cameras a twirl to show off their outfits. It's hard to imagine Roger Federer or Rafael Nadal being asked to show off their cute 'lil tennis shorts, but for women—who are more often stereotyped as sweet young girls than as sports gods—it's just another day on the court. "The standard progression of any sort of social justice—whether it's racial justice, disability justice, gender justice—is that overt bias or discrimination tends to be the first thing that disappears. What lingers, and how these systems maintain themselves, is through more subtle or covert ways like framing," explains Caroline Heldman, director of the Representation Project. In their analysis of media coverage of the Tokyo Olympics, the Representation Project found that women were seven times more likely to be referred to using "gender diminutive language" like "girl" or "chick."[10] "A girl is a child," Heldman says. "We do not call male athletes 'boys'—it would be jarring if we did, which kind of reveals how insidious this is."

Joan Ryan, the journalist who first wrote about the culture of abuse in gymnastics, theorized this is at the heart of why gymnasts and figure skaters have historically been such popular athletes. "Gymnasts, like figure skaters, are 'acceptable' female athletes who are brave but not macho, muscled but not bulky, competitive but still vulnerable. . . . Gymnasts are beacons of feminine simplicity and innocence," she wrote in *Little Girls in Pretty Boxes*.[11] "They've got sparkles in their hair," she tells me now. "You're never going to find a more fiercely competitive athlete than an elite gymnast—fearless, those women. Yet, because they're wearing basically a bathing suit and their hair is in a ponytail, you don't get that ferocity." The more we think of these powerhouse athletes simply as girls tumbling around after school—innocent, vulnerable, controllable—the less likely they are to upset that apple cart.

Another way to discredit women is to plant the idea that they are emotional, unreliable drama queens who need the stabilizing influence of level-headed men—a dangerous misconception that has defined gender roles for centuries. "With my injuries, one thing that really bothered me was everyone saying I was dramatic," says Vonn. "Have they ever said that about a man? Absolutely not. I'm in a dangerous sport—people blow their knees out every single day. Because I did it so many times and because there was media attention around it, that's dramatic? No. People write articles because it gets people's attention and that's not my doing. I'm just out there trying to win races and yes, I crashed. And I also recovered and I got back up."

For Black women, being depicted as dramatic, emotional, or unstable in competition takes on another layer of significance. One of the most famous examples is the way Serena Williams was treated when she lost the 2018 US Open final to Naomi Osaka. Umpire Carlos Ramos issued Williams a warning after he believed her coach was signaling to her from the sidelines (a big no-no in tennis). Williams took offense at the accusation. "I have a daughter and I stand for what's right," she said. "I have never cheated." Things escalated from there, with Williams losing another point for smashing her racket in frustration and finally losing the match when she demanded Ramos apologize. There's a solid argument to be made that the call against Williams for protesting was sexist—"I will admit I have said worse and not gotten penalized," former tennis pro James Blake tweeted after the match. But the public piled on by harping on Williams's behavior, calling it the "mother of all meltdowns." "When a woman is emotional, she's 'hysterical' and she's penalized for it," Billie Jean King tweeted after Williams's loss. "When a man does the same, he's 'outspoken' and there are no repercussions." That's true, but race undoubtedly played a role here too. Stories on Black athletes are more likely to focus on crime, domestic violence, and moral failings and less likely to focus on training, work ethic, dedication, and accomplishments, according to research published by Cynthia Frisby, who studies bias in media coverage. Williams was certainly no exception. After the controversial Open, a political cartoon depicting the final published in a major Australian newspaper went viral. Mark Knight drew on overtly racist stereotypes for his depiction of a brutish Williams, whom he depicted as a hulking beast/baby, wide mouth curled into an enraged cry, powerful hands tightened into fists—an angry Black woman mid-tantrum. In the background, Williams's slender, white, blonde opponent—who couldn't possibly have been the Japanese-Haitian Naomi Osaka—stands demurely.[12]

When women athletes don't fit any of our dominant narratives—weak, obedient, dramatic, demure—we simply omit them. In this universe, men are so superior that women are invisible. After tennis player Andy Murray won his second Olympic gold in 2016, sports reporter John Inverdale asked how it felt to be the "first person ever" to do so. It was a fairly innocuous question—except for the fact that Murray was very obviously not the first person to win multiple Olympic golds in tennis. "Venus and Serena have won about four each," Murray promptly replied. It's a pretty wild oversight. Who forgets Venus and Serena Williams? They are two of the rare athletes who have transcended their sport to become cultural icons; they've founded businesses, walked red carpets, amassed tens of millions of followers on social media. Their dominance in tennis is well-known by people who have never watched a single match—there's only one reason why a sports reporter, whose job it is to know this stuff, would overlook it.

That same year, swimmer Simone Manuel won gold in the 100-meter freestyle, becoming the first Black woman to medal in any individual swimming event in Olympic history. For her achievement, the *San Jose Mercury News* published a story with the headline "Michael Phelps Shares Historic Night with African-American."[13] These tiny erasures are like drops of water—easy enough to brush aside as sloppy errors or honest mistakes in the moment but powerful enough to erode a canyon through women's credibility over time.

Or perhaps we simply attribute women's accomplishments to the men behind them. Society has for centuries tried to suppress the idea that women can be competent in their own right without some thanks owed to a man. This happens all the time in sports where male coaches and partners get credit for women's wins. In

2011 when Lindsey Vonn divorced her former husband Thomas Vonn, *Bleacher Report* published an article with the headline "Lindsey Vonn: Impending Divorce Will Ruin American Skier's Career." Sportswriter Adam Wells (because, again, of course this came from a male journalist) wrote, "Thomas played an integral part in Lindsey's success on and off the slopes. He did everything he could to help keep her mind on her craft and made sure she had nothing to worry about when she prepared to race." He continued that losing that kind of "stabilizing force" could have a "devastating effect" on Vonn's career, ultimately predicting that "all of her hard work and dedication are going to come crashing down on her. It is sad to say, but the end of Vonn's marriage also signals the end of her career as a dominant skier."[14]

For a man who is neither a psychologist who studies the psychosocial effects of divorce, nor a champion skier who understands the focus it takes to complete a title-winning run, nor an expert on this woman's personal life in any way, shape, or form, to sound the death knell of her career with such authority would be absurd if it wasn't so objectively gross. Wells talks about one of the greatest athletes of all time like she's an unstable teenager incapable of getting herself together in the morning. And he wasn't the only writer to make such sexist suggestions. The coverage about her post-divorce career still has Vonn seething. *Chicago Tribune* published a similarly insulting piece in which (oh, you guessed it) a male sportswriter asked "whether she will continue to ski like the same Lindsey Vonn who became the world's most successful active racer and the greatest U.S. skier in history during her four-year marriage."[15] Writer Philip Hersh went so far as to include a list of quotes from Vonn praising her husband when they were still married as if to justify his deeply sexist appraisal of her career.

Vonn has never forgotten the writers who asked whether she could succeed "'without a man by her side,' because, it was initially my dad who was coaching me and then it was my ex-husband," she says. "I think that it's completely absurd that anyone would ever say that." Obviously, no woman is an island—every athlete has coaches and supportive people in their lives who help make it possible for them to be superhuman. But "I don't see anyone else but myself standing in the starting gate," Vonn says. "No one's doing it for me." That doesn't stop male journalists from acting like this is a valid question, pushing the narrative that a woman's success must be, in some way, dependent on a man, and legitimizing the idea that women athletes are inherently worth less than the men in their lives. In the 2012 Olympics, the words most commonly used to describe male athletes were "fastest" and "strongest." For women athletes? "Married" and "unmarried."[16] This kind of conversation literally devalues women—they're not taken as seriously and they pay for it.

For the record, Vonn wasn't the same skier "without a man by her side." She was better. She went on to win eleven world titles after her divorce. "Those comments motivated me for many, many years. It definitely spurred me to push myself even harder to prove them wrong," she says. "That year was the best, biggest of my career. So I definitely got them back."

~ ~ ~

DESPITE THE ATTEMPTS to keep them on the sidelines, to belittle their performances, to cast them as unstable, to falsely attribute their accomplishments to men, to demonize them when they do succeed, women continue to prove that they are competition to be taken seriously. As all the aforementioned means of keeping women in their "natural" place fail to keep women from rising, the haters turn to the kind of base biological-differences arguments that showed up in US Soccer's highly controversial filing. To protect the status quo, those in power assert that their place as the reapers of all the cash and opportunity is a biologically divine right. The archaic arguments about women's physical frailty still routinely show up in sports, keeping women out of the game. As of this writing, there were no women Formula 1 drivers on the grid, due in part to the incorrect belief that women's bodies aren't strong enough to withstand the G-forces experienced by drivers. (Women fighter jet pilots, who withstand eight or nine G-forces to do their jobs, would likely have something to say about that.)

It's not just sports where this argument refuses to die. In 2017, a software engineer at Google published a now infamous manifesto titled "Google's Ideological Echo Chamber," claiming the reason women are so underrepresented in the tech industry is not systemic sexism but biological differences. Women, he feebly argues, just don't have what it takes to thrive in the highly analytical field; men prefer the logic of coding, while women prefer "aesthetics." Ignoring these so-called innate gender differences, he argues, is "compassion for the weak," making efforts to close the gender gap in tech "unfair, divisive, and bad for business." These are the rantings of one individual (which Google quickly condemned), but attitudes like this contribute to lower numbers of women entering an industry notorious for othering women. Half of women who start their careers in tech leave by thirty-five, according to a study published by Accenture and Girls Who Code in 2021; only one in five women—and fewer than one in ten women of color—viewed the tech industry as a place where they could thrive. Across levels, women hold between a quarter and a third of jobs in tech and are paid less than their male counterparts doing the same jobs 59 percent of the time.[17] Such workplace hostilities are a much stronger explanation for the pipeline problem, keeping the number of women in certain industries low, than any sort of biologically governed natural selection process.

I would wager that many of the people who reach for this idea to justify the second-class treatment of women see themselves as delivering an inconvenient but necessary truth. There's an air of martyrdom to these arguments, a sense that it may not be socially popular or politically correct but someone needs to stand up to the woke police and say it: most men *are* bigger, faster, stronger— and therefore better—competitors than women. There are biological differences between the brains of women and men that make each sex better suited to different roles . . . right? Perhaps a part of you thinks this too, even if you're disinclined to admit it. It would be understandable, even expected—the idea of male dominance rooted in a fixed biologically ordained supremacy is the sociocultural bedrock of the gender gap. There are obviously loosely generalizable differences between men and women. But those who lazily reach for the weaker sex argument overlook two critical points: first, whether these differences are really biologically hardwired rather than culturally conditioned, and therefore malleable, and second, how you define which set of so-called biological traits is superior.

To the first point, from a cognitive perspective, "there are no essential male or female characteristics" in the brain, argues Cordelia Fine, PhD, a professor at the University of Melbourne who studies biological explanations of behavioral sex differences.[18] She writes,

Neither sex has the monopoly on characteristics like competitiveness, promiscuity, choosiness, and parental care. The particular pattern . . . depends on the animal's ecological, material, and social situation. This suggests that even within a particular species, the effect of the genetic and hormonal facets of sex on brain and behavior must not inflexibly inscribe or "hardwire" particular behavioral profiles or predispositions into the brain; not even those more common in one sex or the other. Instead, they are drawn out to a greater or lesser degree, as circumstances dictate.[19]

Take, for example, empathy—a trait popularly understood to be associated most abundantly with the female brain. Fine devotes an entire chapter of her book *Delusions of Gender: How Our Minds, Society, and Neurosexism Create Difference* to understanding the incredibly nuanced science surrounding empathy and gender. It proves to be very instructive in explaining how the science of so-called biological differences is shaped by the culture in which it's conducted. She cites a series of studies conducted in the 1990s by social psychologist William Ickes designed to measure the real-world empathetic ability of men and women. Here's a quick recap: Two participants are left in a room to interact naturally. Their exchange is filmed and played back for each participant individually, who is then asked to note down all the instances where they could recall having a feeling and whether that feeling was neutral, negative, or positive. In the final phase of the experiment, the video is played back to each participant again. This time, each participant is tasked with decoding the tone of the other person's feelings.

In the first seven iterations of the study, conducted in different geographic locations and sociocultural settings, no gender difference in empathetic ability was observed. Men and women were equally good at demonstrating this trait. Fascinating! Yet, it gets more interesting: several years later, the researchers repeated the experiment, except this time, they *did* observe gender differences. Why? The culprit, according to the researchers, was a minor change in the instructions given to the participants as they reviewed the video the second time. Instead of simply asking them to guess their conversation partner's feelings, they were also asked to rate how accurate they thought their guess was. This seemingly insignificant prompt, Ickes suggested, reminded women that they *should* be better at empathy. And therefore they were. While "women, on average, do not appear to have more empathetic *ability* than men, there is compelling evidence that women will display greater accuracy than men when their empathetic *motivation* is engaged by situational cues that remind them that they, as women, are expected to excel at empathy-related tasks," Ickes wrote. Proving the point, subsequent research found men's empathetic motivation, and therefore ability, can be just as easily manipulated by tying empathetic accuracy to measures men believe they should perform well, like sexual desirability.[20] The point of all this? A modern understanding of developmental neuroscience suggests observed differences between the loosely generalizable skill sets of men and women aren't biologically hardwired at all, but socially conditioned, and therefore adaptable.

But what about *physical* biological differences? Surely, scientists agree that there are indeed "indisputable" hardwired physical differences between men and women (beyond the genitalia and sex organs) that make men as a group tougher competitors than women. There are very few opportunities to actually put this theory to the test in sports. With most types of competition segregated by gender, you can compare women's records with men's, but that leaves room for subjective sexist arguments that the men's game is inherently harder than the women's game, as alleged by US Soccer's controversial legal brief. But there is one sport in which you can compare the physical skill of men and women with some objectivity: running.

Running is a beautifully impartial sport, uninterested in most qualitative nuances of performance and grounded firmly in quantitative outcomes. No matter the distance, or the conditions on race day, arbiters of running supremacy only care about one thing: how fast an athlete got their ass across the finish line. Sports lore tells us that men are faster than women as a rule. Sure, there are exceptions based on training and level of fitness—Allyson Felix is always going to beat Justin Bieber in a race—but an elite male runner should always beat an elite female runner thanks to his biological advantages, right? Allyson Felix, in other words, is always going to lose to Usain Bolt, the fastest human on record.

Actually, it depends on the race.

Bolt holds the record for the 100-meter dash, a distance he ran in a stunning 9.58 seconds in 2009. In the 100-meter, he remains the uncontested champion. In the 800-meter dash, however, he's a self-admitted slowpoke. When asked why he never competed in that particular race, Bolt admitted his personal record of 2 minutes and 7 seconds was "really slow, like, a woman could beat me." As Jordan-Young and Karkazis point out, this is an epic understatement. A ranking of the best recorded times in history for the women's 800-meter run reveals there are literally thousands of women who could and did beat Bolt's time handily. Bolt wasn't fast enough to even qualify for the rankings—the slowest time of 1 minute and 58.99 seconds has been achieved by fifteen women who are currently tied for 2,105th place.[21]

Bolt is of course just one man—one who proves a different set of skills is required to run very fast for 100 meters than the one required to run very fast for 800 meters. This is the point. If a mere 700 meters can bring the notion of absolute male athletic superiority to its knees, it forces a reexamination of the stories we tell about what constitutes athletic skill. Alex Schmider, from GLAAD, offers himself as an example. He's short-statured, compact, muscular. He would likely make a great gymnast, or jockey, or coxswain in crew (with a little practice and persistence). "My body is well-positioned to achieve in these sports," he says. LeBron James, at six foot nine and 250 pounds, is probably not going to make the cut as a jockey or gymnast.

"What we have always said is that athletic superiority is defined as bigger, stronger, faster," says Kane. "You see men jumping higher, being physically stronger, out-hitting women in sports like baseball, right? And you say, 'Oh, well, it's not some backroom conspiracy, it's the natural order." Running provides a perfect opportunity to talk about the biological *similarities* of elite athletes rather than their differences. But even if you've never watched a race before, you can probably guess that's not what happens, regardless of who wins. "Typically in a marathon, the first thirty-five to forty finishers are male, although that gender gap is narrowing. But once the first woman crosses the finish line, we compare her to the men who finished ahead of her," says Kane. "What we never do is say, 'This woman, or these front-running women, who just crossed the finish line are outperforming the thousands of men who are right behind them.'" It's not that we should ignore the thirty-five men who crossed the finish line first, but framing is everything. "If you just focus on the fact that a woman was outperformed by thirty-five men, the punchline is, 'No matter how good a woman is, she can never beat a man,'" Kane says. Focus on the fact that she beat the vast majority of the elite male runners in the race and the story changes—it becomes about what women *can* do. In fact, women are narrowing the gap in ultramarathons—races over the standard 26.2 miles. An analysis of finishing times from ultraruns over the past twenty years found that the longer the race, the shorter the gap between the average pace of male and female runners.[22] We, of course, almost never hear the story told that way. We get the version where women's power is erased and men's power is confirmed—where men are superior athletically and, therefore, superior period. "As a sociologist, I always go back to whose interests are being served when that happens," Kane says. "And it is certainly not women's interests."

This is the crux of why sports is the most important tool we have for shaping gender roles. If you change the definition of athletic superiority—agility over explosive power, balance over strength, 800 meters over 100 meters—the whole sexist house of cards comes crumbling down. What if, instead of size and strength being the be-all and end-all of athletic eminence, it was the ability to do a backflip on a balance beam? "If that were the definition—and it could be," says Kane, "then who would be the naturally superior athletes?"

Mixed-gender competitions offer an opportunity to shake things up. "The argument about why we segregate sports is that it's about protecting women and their interests, meaning their bodies," says Kane. "I have argued that no, sex segregating sports is about protecting men's interests." Vonn fought for years to race against men, to go head-to-head, to see if she could cast some doubt on the notion of male superiority. She often trained with men, and at first, they were better than she was. "That's why I would train with them, because I wanted to be better and I wanted to be faster. And eventually, I was," she says. "I was beating men all the time and it really pushed me—I wanted to race against them so that I could see where I strapped up." It wasn't likely that Vonn would win a men's ski race—she herself told me she "wasn't even close to thinking that." But even letting Vonn compete on the same course, under the same conditions, would mean admitting that maybe men and women have more similarities than differences. That maybe the strengths most commonly associated with women are just as valuable as those claimed by men. "It's always, 'good *for a woman.*' We're always less than," says Vonn.

Competing together likely would have made the men she raced against better competitors. That was the effect desegregation had on Norway's universally feared and respected ski jumping team. The Winter Olympics powerhouse team began training as one mixed-gender unit as a competitive strategy. The way they saw it, men ski jumpers had just as much to learn, if not more, from women ski jumpers as the other way around. Teaming up gave them the ability to pick each other's brains, share data, and analyze performance in new ways. The results spoke for themselves. After the gender divide fell, Norway's ski jumping team went on to win five medals in a single Olympics—the most for any country in the history of the sport.[23]

More important than medals, mixed-gender competition creates the opportunity to see women as equals. When men in typically male-dominated fields, such as the military, live and work along-side women, their attitudes become more egalitarian, according to research from the National Bureau of Economic Research.[24] Imagine the impact.

~ ~ ~

THE WAY OUR culture talks about, represents, and publicly penalizes women naturally shadows them as they step up to the negotiating table. Jessica Nordell, author of *The End of Bias: A Beginning*, set out to quantify exactly how much sexist undermining costs women in terms of time and career advancement. She partnered with a computer science professor from the University of Buffalo to build a simulation of everyday office interactions in a fictional company they dubbed NormCorp. They baked gender bias into the model in all its many incarnations: "the expectation that [women] be unfailingly helpful; the golf rounds and networking opportunities they're not invited to; the siphoning off of credit for their work by others; unfair performance reviews that penalize them for the same behavior that's applauded in men; the 'manterrupting.'" After simulating ten years of promotion cycles, Nordell found that if a woman's performance is undervalued by just 3 percent, it will take her over twice as long as a male colleague to work her way up the ladder from entry-level employee to executive (eight and a half years vs. four).[25]

The constant casting of women as inferior also costs them straight-up cash. Sexism plays a measurable role in driving the wage gap. To understand how much, the National Bureau of Economic Research (NBER) quantified the role of individual drivers of the gender wage gap—differences in education, hours worked, concentrations of men vs. women in high-paying industries—and found that 38 percent of the pay gap cannot be explained by any sort of measurable differences between men and women.[26] One plausible conclusion: 38 percent of the pay gap is caused by labor market discrimination—in this case, straight-up sexism.

As the authors of the NBER report noted, it's very possible sexism also influences the "explained" drivers of the pay gap, by showing up in explicit ways. An MBA program may have a biased admissions process, meaning fewer women can obtain an advanced degree from that school, for example, or a woman may cut back at work after having a baby because our cultural narrative tells her it's her destiny to be the primary caregiver and the market tells her she'll be hit with a motherhood penalty anyway. Sexism also influences the explained drivers of the pay gap in more subtle ways—a young woman in her first job out of college receives less mentorship than the guy in the cubicle next to her and isn't promoted as quickly, for example, or perhaps she never applies for that high-paying finance job in the first place because she subconsciously feels the industry is hostile to women.

After all these factors are accounted for, we're still left with the fact that when a woman makes $83,000 for doing the exact same job as her male coworker who gets paid $100,000, economists are left with a murky explanation for at least $6,460 of that gap. It doesn't matter what type of work, or what level of skill, or what country, or what source of data you look at, structural sexism costs women. And as we've seen throughout this book, it also costs the institutions that perpetuate it. So why choose, season after season, to forgo the returns from taking women seriously? Why continue to belittle women's accomplishments, credit their wins to the success of men, and undermine them as sex objects or hysterical girls at every opportunity when building them up as champions would be so much more valuable?

Kane believes it comes down to one simple question: What motive do those in power have that overrides the fact that they're actively hurting their own economic interests? "If you believe that ultimately men want to maintain power," says Kane, "then that's the way that you do it."

CHAPTER 10

IF YOU CAN SEE IT

Billie Jean King's culture-defining victory in the Battle of the Sexes was successful for one reason: millions of people around the world got to watch her.

Without a platform, King's definitive dismantling of Bobby Riggs's proud chauvinism may have eventually been forgotten—transformative for the few thousand people in the stands and fodder for headlines that would now be buried in library archives, but ultimately not a culture changer.

But the match did air—in prime time, with the full support of one of the biggest broadcast networks in television. (Though that only happened, King is sure to point out, because the match was held in a men's sports arena and most men assumed the result would be confirmation of their superiority. "The media was controlled by men and the powerful group loves to talk about itself to perpetuate their power," she tells me. Amen, Billie Jean.) Because the network gave the match a platform, more people watched King win the Battle of the Sexes than watched any other tennis match in history—ninety million people. Ninety million people saw with their own eyes how capable women were—and how irrelevant the male chauvinist pig had become. It was more than enough to seed a cultural reckoning on women's perceived power and strength, and to usher in a new era of respect for women.

A version of this happens every time we see women compete. Every time a WNBA game is played in a bar at happy hour, or women's Olympic events get prime-time coverage, or cities host viewing parties for the Women's World Cup, respect for women's worth grows. Seeing women in their fierce, sweaty, laser-focused glory chips away at the primitive stereotypes still trying to convince us that men are superior. Seeing women in sports succeed challenges the idea that women aren't worthy of investment; it obliterates assumptions about pregnancy and parenthood; reinforces the power of the collective; gives the most marginalized a microphone for activism and validation; showcases women's superior performance as leaders; amplifies the power of ownership; counteracts the effects of sexualization; and exposes the basest manifestations of sexism for what they are—thinly veiled power grabs.

But you have to *see* it. For women's sports to have the power to change culture, we have to be able to actually watch them. And that's still much harder than it should be.

~~~

ONE OF THE most important things we can do to further women's equality is to watch women's sports. Yet, in spite of the incontestable excellence of women athletes the world over, there is still a massive disparity in the coverage they receive—one that directly impacts the power women in sports have to build a more equitable world for us all.

Much has been written about a particularly disturbing statistic: that women receive just 4–5 percent of sports media coverage. But perhaps just as disturbing is another fact. "Over the past 30 years, we have not seen meaningful change in the amount of coverage women athletes receive," said Cheryl Cooky, a professor at Purdue University and lead author of a landmark study that's been tracking the gender gap in sports coverage for over three decades.[1] The study, conducted jointly with researchers at the University of Southern California, has been releasing findings every five years since it began tracking both the quantity and quality of sports coverage by major networks in 1989. It's been consistently dismal.

The study's latest findings as of this writing, which were released in 2021 and included viewership data through the 2019 women's World Cup, showed little improvement. Women athletes received just 5.4 percent of airtime on affiliate news shows and ESPN's *SportsCenter*. That's up—barely!—from 5 percent in 1989 and 5.1 percent in 1993. Women's sports have *exploded* in those thirty years—in 1989 there was no WNBA, no NWSL, and barely a US Women's National Hockey or Soccer Team—flooding sports broadcasters with tens of thousands of hours of potential content. Yet they've only gained 0.4 percent more airtime? Meanwhile, 80 percent of the sports news and highlight shows the researchers analyzed for the most recent study included no mention of women's sports at all.[2]

If you look closer at the data, there's evidence that the coverage of regular-season women's sports has actually decreased. When researchers removed coverage of the 2019 women's World Cup from the data set, the total airtime for women's sports that year dropped to 3.5 percent. Even when global events like the World Cup break the sports-coverage glass ceiling, they are still "eclipsed by the steady stream of men's sports, which are covered in season, out of season, [and] with more energy," Cooky said. This tokenization was typical of coverage throughout the study. When women's sports were included in sports broadcasts, they were shorter than the average segment on men's sports, shuffled in between stories of male sporting excellence. Women's sports segments were also more likely to get cut. The researchers cited one example in which a blandly delivered twenty-three-second-long segment on a regular-season WNBA game included in a 6 p.m. news broadcast was axed to make room for a baseball recap in the 11 p.m. segment—a story about a hotdog-eating contest, however, stayed.[3]

The quantity of the coverage isn't the only issue. Over thirty years, sexism in media coverage of women's sports has evolved—moving from a climate of sexualizing comments about women's bodies to framing women athletes in relation to the men in their lives—but never disappeared. Every time we've seemingly eradicated one incarnation of bias, another one appears. The current version is what researchers have dubbed "gender-bland sexism." In this iteration of inequality, coverage of women's sports is just plain boring, devoid of the passion and energy that make sports interesting in the first place. "Men's sports are the appetizer, the main course and the dessert, and if there's any mention of women's sports it comes across as begrudging 'eat your vegetables' without the kind of bells and whistles and excitement with which they describe men's sports and athletes," said Michael Messner, a professor of sociology and gender studies at USC and a coauthor of the study.[4] (Even the technical quality of women's sports coverage is subpar, featuring lower-quality production value.)

Like the pay gap, it feels like the coverage gap should be changing based on how much we hear about it. We spend a lot of time talking about women's equality, but much of the time it turns out to be just that—talk. Even the researchers of the USC/Purdue study thought that, surely, including digital media in their analysis would change the percentage of coverage women's sports received. But it didn't. Not meaningfully. Even in the age of social media, where women athletes are building valuable followings, coverage of women's sports by traditional media companies and sports networks is abysmal. The researchers analyzed content in daily online newsletters and Twitter feeds from CBS Sports,

NBC Sports, ESPN, and espnW. Even with espnW—which covers women's sports almost exclusively—in the mix, women's sports coverage accounted for just 9 percent of newsletter content and 10 percent of Twitter posts. Once espnW was removed, the coverage gap returned to around 5 percent. On Instagram, the numbers weren't much better; in 2021 women's sports accounted for 3 percent of *SportsCenter*'s coverage, 8 percent of ESPN's coverage, 4 percent of *Sports Illustrated*'s coverage, and 3 percent of coverage from *Bleacher Report*, per an analysis from Shot:Clock Media. "There just isn't a compelling excuse for that absence," Cooky said, pointing out that creating content for the internet is a lot cheaper and easier than producing a broadcast segment.[5]

Omitting women from the conversation obviously shapes our perceptions. Cheryl Cooky called out a particularly shameful example in her recent research: not only are women's athletic accomplishments glossed over, the more explicit culture-shaping work they do, such as fighting for social justice, is omitted too. The near-exclusive coverage of the activism of male athletes creates a distorted and incorrect perception that they are the leaders of social justice movements in sports. To be clear, their work is also admirable and important. But it becomes an issue when the media creates the perception that it is the *only* admirable and important activist work happening in sports. The "hypervisibility" of the NFL, for example, "has produced a story in which [Colin] Kaepernick is an icon of racial activism, but . . . erases the labor and activism that WNBA athletes had and have been performing for years before," Cooky said.[6] Kaepernick's activism is worthy of headlines—but so is the work of the women of the WNBA.

~ ~ ~

FOR THINGS TO change, two things need to happen: media outlets need to step up their storytelling and networks need to put women's sports on TV. "People need to know who these women are and what's at stake," says Haley Rosen, founder and CEO of Just Women's Sports, a media outlet that covers . . . just women's sports. For some fans, that's the whole game—they follow Serena Williams because of who she is and what she stands for without knowing the first thing about tennis. But champions of women's equality in sports argue we also "have to watch these women play," says Rosen. "The product is amazing and we don't get to see it enough—all these games are buried on back channels or behind multiple subscriptions." Media outlets have the power to change things. "You can't buy tickets to games that you don't know are happening, you can't tune in to games that aren't easily accessible, you can't buy merch for players that you don't know are out there," Rosen says. "It all starts with media."

For Rosen, this is all personal. She played soccer for Stanford, turning briefly pro before injuries forced her to retire. Once she stopped playing, Rosen wanted to keep up with the careers of her friends and former teammates but couldn't find stats, game recaps, or information about trades anywhere. "When I started actively seeking out this content, everything I was seeing on women's sports was really young, it was hyper-feminine—a lot of lifestyle content," she says. She wanted the highlights, the stats, the deals, the *sports*.

When she started pitching the idea for a media outlet that covered exclusively women's sports in 2020, the feedback was "not good," she says. Investors were skeptical and tried to push her toward changing her audience to younger girls, focusing on glossy lifestyle content or, worst of all, making JWS a nonprofit, dredging up the sexist idea that for women's sports to get money it has to be in the form of a charitable donation. Rosen was undeterred. "I lived this journey," she tells me. "It sucks playing professional [women's] soccer. It sucks putting your whole life into something knowing there's no future. It sucks getting treated like shit, it sucks having no power—it's fucking bullshit." Just like Megan Rapinoe and nearly every athlete interviewed for this book, that's why she does this work. "I want female athletes to get paid. I want this to be big business. I want millions and millions of people watching regular season games," she says. "This is a massive business opportunity. And we want to be right there."

~ ~ ~

THE IDEA THAT women's sports are inherently less watchable than men's sports has persisted for good reason: it fits in neatly with sexist stereotypes that nobody is interested in women's stories. "It took me a while to realize that the reference for 'nobody' is all of them [men], not all of us," says Mary Jo Kane, the researcher on gender in sport. "Women and many men are actually deeply interested."

Don't take her word for it—look at the data. Viewership of women's sports has been booming in recent years—even eclipsing audience size for men's sports. In 2015, the women's World Cup drew a then record audience of thirty million US viewers, over 50 percent more than the average number who watched the NBA finals that year, which saw Steph Curry go head-to-head with LeBron James. In 2020, the WNBA was the only major team sport—men's or women's—to come out of the pandemic with audience growth, measuring a 38 percent increase in viewership during regular and postseason games while other leagues suffered from pandemic-induced backslides. In 2021, 3.4 million people tuned in to watch rookies Emma Raducanu and Leylah Fernandez face off in the US Open final, which surpassed the peak viewership for the men's final that year (2.7 million viewers), a significant match in which Novak Djokovic was gunning for a historic twenty-first Grand Slam title. That same year, CBS reported a decline in viewership for the men's March Madness tournament, while ESPN reported the audience for the women's championship had increased 9 percent. In 2022, 23.3 million people—*nearly one-third of the United Kingdom's population*—tuned in to watch the BBC's broadcast of the

UEFA Women's Euro finals between the UK and Germany, shattering viewership records and making the women's football match the UK's most watched program of the year.[7]

The data are clear and yet the valuation for women's sports broadcasting rights is still trying to tell a different story. In 2022, 456,000 people tuned in to a match between Angel City FC and their fellow newly launched NWSL team, the San Diego Wave. That was on par with the most viewed Major League Soccer game that season (475,000 viewers), yet Goals Sports founder Caroline Fitzgerald reported the broadcast rights for the NWSL were valued at just $1.5 million per year, while the MLS media rights were valued at $90 million.[8] "The power of sexism in this culture is such that assumptions around audience, around value, are so strong, that even when you can make the economic argument that media entities are ignoring audiences and leaving money on the table, they're so blinded by their own viewpoint, that they don't actively go out and seek new business," says Ellen J. Staurowsky, the professor of sports media at Ithaca College. "Which completely defies all logic."

There are many ways to grow women's sports and to increase their power to change our perceptions of women's worth. They all start with people believing that women's sports are compelling content. Critics of giving women's sports a platform assume that they're not, arguing leagues and brands need to up their investment in women's sports to improve the product enough to earn more media coverage. But it's actually the opposite that's true: 84 percent of global sports fans say they are interested in women's sports. It's the lack of media coverage of games and players that prevents them from watching.[9]

The solution is infuriatingly simple: when we give more women more coverage, more people watch them. When more people engage with women, more brands will want to invest. When more brands invest, leagues will make more money. And when leagues make more money, women will get paid. The data are practically begging to be acted upon—one report on investment in women's sport found that in the UK alone, women's sport had the ability to generate $1.4 billion in annual revenue by 2030. They just needed one thing to reach that billion-plus payday: "increased visibility of female athletes and teams."[10]

A mini version of this happened in Australian sport. Commonwealth Bank, the country's national cricket sponsor, conducted a study and found increased coverage of the women's game resulted in 48 percent increased interest in women's sports, with 53 percent of Australians subsequently watching women's games live or on TV. Australia tested a similar strategy with the launch of a women's Australian Football League (AFLW) in 2017, with free to attend games and a broadcast strategy that involved simply giving potential fans opportunities to see the women play through free local and national TV coverage. The result? Forty-one percent of Australians are now AFLW fans, and when the players signed a new contract in 2022, it included a 94 percent raise.[11] When we do give women a platform—one that carries the same weight and respect as the one we give men—everyone wins.

∼ ∼ ∼

THE GENDER GAP—AND how it affects the way women receive money, power, and respect—is a beast of a problem. Its solutions are complex, incremental, often achingly slow. But in sports, there is an opportunity to create real change. And so much reason for optimism. In the darkest moments for women, I think of Billie Jean King and the way her strength gave Missy Park the confidence to play to her full potential against the boys. I think of Hilary Knight, skating with her AirPods in, convincing every women's hockey player in the country to stand with the National Team in their fight for equality. I think of Alysia Montaño being brave enough to call out the biggest brands in the business, knowing it might cost her her livelihood. I think of the US Women's National Team refusing to bow to their employers even when they tried to convince the world they were biologically inferior. I think of Jess Smith's fire when people laughed at her for daring to think the women of Angel City could be worth more. I think of the women of the WNBA, who stand united to keep doing the work. And I think of CeCé Telfer, who keeps showing up even when competing as her true self becomes increasingly dangerous. I think of these women, and I am reminded that as important as it is to celebrate the wins, there is more work to do. "Nothing can be taken for granted in terms of women's lives and equity," says Staurowsky. "Understanding the history as well as I do, I know that all of these areas have been and will remain vulnerable. As we make progress, we also have to be absolutely mindful that we cannot take anything for granted."

So . . . LFG.

ACKNOWLEDGMENTS

If my work on women's equality in sports has taught me one thing, it's that visibility matters. This book would not be complete without saying a huge thank-you to the village of people who made it possible.

First to Ashley Lopez, my incredible agent at Waxman Literary Agency. Her immediate belief in this story when it was little more than a rant helped will this work into being. I am equally grateful to Emma Berry, my incredible editor at Seal Press, for immediately understanding that sports were indeed the next feminist frontier. Her thoughtful edits made me a better writer and this book is undoubtedly better for it. Thank you both for getting it.

I am forever thankful for the wonderful women writers and editors I get to call friends. Special thanks to Christine Yu, Mattie Kahn, and Jessica Radloff for their commiseration and cheerleading as they finished their own books; to Emma Hinchcliffe for having a crystal-clear read on how any given issue impacts women, always pushing my thinking; and to my *Glamour* family for first giving me the space to cover women's sports.

This book would not exist without the generous contributions of so many women in sports and business (and the men who champion them). A special thank-you to Billie Jean King, Stef Strack, Allyson and Wes Felix, Lindsay Kagawa Colas, Kendall Coyne Schofield, Allison Galer, Mary Jo Kane, Nathalie Molina Niño, Missy Park, the Institute for Women's Policy Research, VOICEINSPORT, Athlete Ally, Angel City FC, and Athleta.

This book was shaped not only by the stories of professional athletes but also by my own experiences with the power of sports to change the way we see girls and women. I have seen that nowhere more powerfully than as a coach for Girls on the Run. Thank you for continuing to empower girls through sports.

I am so grateful for the support of my McAnearney family. To Nika and John, for always taking interest in what I do (and sourcing some of the best women's sports books in Australia); to Lisa and Phil, for your constant positivity and congratulations every step of the way; and to Anne and Michael, for being the most supportive in-laws and for raising a son who is a true partner.

To my dad, thank you for being the kind of father who taught his daughter that girls could do anything and never to let anyone tell me otherwise. And for taking the time to send me a text every International Women's Day—it always makes me smile. To my mom, who has done the invisible unpaid labor of motherhood for most of her life, thank you for always encouraging me to be curious and to stand up for what I believe in.

More than anyone, I owe this book to the women in my life whom I most admire. To Stephanie, Emily, and Sarah, you have made me the woman and writer I am. My constant inspirations, I love you. To Suzee, my soul sister, running buddy, fellow adventurer, you make me more ambitious and for that I am forever grateful. To Jenny and Rebecca, how lucky to find two best friends who get it on every level and serve as the best damn journalistic sounding board a gal could have. To Sam, my fellow seeker, thank you for always believing in my wildest dreams. And to Naomi, whose fierce feminism I've always admired and whom I am lucky to call a friend.

And finally, to Stephen. I'd thought I would write that I could have written this book without you (that seemed like the feminist thing to say). But the truth is that I couldn't have written something that I put my whole self into if I didn't have a partner who supported me so fully. Thank you for making dinners, for taking care of the dog, for vacuuming. Thank you for sending me every feminist thing you read on Twitter, for helping me find clarity in the most challenging ideas in these pages, and for being my earliest reader. And thank you most of all for being my best friend, my partner, and my home. I couldn't have written this book without you.

NOTES

INTRODUCTION

1. "France 2019: Global Broadcast and Audience Report," FIFA press release, October 18, 2019, www.fifa.com/tournaments/womens/womens worldcup/france2019/news/fifa-women-s-world-cup-2019tm-watched-by -more-than-1-billion; Abigail Johnson Hess, "US Viewership of the 2019 Women's World Cup Final Was 22% Higher Than the 2018 Men's Final," CNBC, July 10, 2019, www.cnbc.com/2019/07/10/us-viewership-of-the -womens-world-cup-final-was-higher-than-the-mens.html.

2. Theodoric Meyer, "U.S. Soccer Hires Lobbyists to Argue Women's National Team Isn't Underpaid," *Politico*, August 7, 2019, www.politico.com /story/2019/08/07/us-soccer-lobbyists-womens-national-team-not-underpaid -1452331#; Document Cloud, USSF Arguments, www.documentcloud.org /documents/6807270-USSF-Arguments.html.

3. Macaela MacKenzie, "She Scored. She Won. She's Going to Get Us All Paid Better," *Glamour*, October 23, 2019, www.glamour.com/story/women -of-the-year-2019-megan-rapinoe.

4. Matthew Lavietes, "Fans Heckle U.S. Soccer President, Demand 'Equal Pay' for World Cup Winners," Reuters, July 10, 2019, www.reuters.com /article/us-soccer-worldcup-usa-ceremony/fans-heckle-u-s-soccer-president -demand-equal-pay-for-world-cup-winners-idUSKCN1U52KV.

5. Institute for Women's Policy Research, "Gender Wage Gaps Remain Wide in Year Two of the Pandemic," March 2022, https://iwpr.org/wp-content/uploads/2022/02/Gender-Wage-Gaps-in-Year-Two-of-Pandemic_FINAL.pdf; Jasmine Tucker, "Native American Women Need Action That Closes the Wage Gap," National Women's Law Center, September 2021, https://nwlc.org/wp-content/uploads/2020/09/Native-Women-Equal-Pay-2021.pdf; Jasmine Tucker, "Some Asian American, Native Hawaiian, and Pacific Islander Women Lose Over $1 Million over a Lifetime to the Racist and Sexist Wage Gap," National Women's Law Center, May 2022, https://nwlc.org/wp-content/uploads/2022/05/AANHPI-EPD.pdf; Institute for Women's Policy Research, "Gender Wage Gaps Remain Wide in Year Two of the Pandemic."

6. Emily Peck, "Women in Same-Gender Partnerships Face a Double Pay Gap," *Axios*, January 21, 2022, www.axios.com/2022/01/21/women-men-same-sex-partners-wage-gap; "Being Transgender at Work," *McKinsey Quarterly*, November 10, 2021, www.mckinsey.com/featured-insights/diversity-and-inclusion/being-transgender-at-work.

7. Spotrac, "Stephen Curry," www.spotrac.com/nba/golden-state-warriors/stephen-curry-6287 (accessed September 26, 2022); Spotrac, "WNBA Salary Rankings," www.spotrac.com/wnba/rankings (accessed September 26, 2022).

8. Zaheena Rasheed, "Why Sexism Is Still a Problem at the Most 'Gender-Equal' Olympics," Al Jazeera, August 8, 2021, www.aljazeera.com/news/2021/8/8/sexism-is-still-a-problem-at-the-first-gender-equal-olympics.

9. Lakshmi Puri, speech, February 16, 2016, www.unwomen.org/en/news/stories/2016/2/lakshmi-puri-speech-at-value-of-hosting-mega-sport-event.

10. Women's Sports Foundation, "Benefits—Why Sports Participation for Girls and Women," August 30, 2016, www.womenssportsfoundation.org/advocacy/benefits-sports-participation-girls-women; Mariah Burton Nelson, *The Stronger Women Get, the More Men Love Football* (New York: Avon Books, 1995), 11.

11. Adam Williams, "An Indigenous Women's Softball Team Beats Opponents, and Machismo," *New York Times*, November 17, 2021, www.nytimes.com/2021/11/17/sports/mexico-softball-indigenous-women.html.

12. Nayanika Guha, "These Afghan Athletes Are Devastated by the Taliban's Ban on Women's Sports: 'What We Built in 20 Years Is Gone in Five Seconds,'" *The Lily*, September 9, 2021, www.thelily.com/these-afghan-athletes-are-devastated-by-the-talibans-ban-on-womens-sports-what-we-built-in-20-years-is-gone-in-five-seconds.

CHAPTER 1: EQUAL PAY FOR EQUAL PLAY

1. Mary Leisenring, "Women Still Have to Work Three Months Longer to Equal What Men Earned in a Year," US Census Bureau, March 31, 2020, www.census.gov/library/stories/2020/03/equal-pay-day-is-march-31 -earliest-since-1996.html; Susan Ware, *Game, Set, Match: Billie Jean King and the Revolution in Women's Sports* (Chapel Hill: University of North Carolina Press, 2011), 43.

2. Billie Jean King, *All In* (New York: Alfred A. Knopf, 2021), 250–251, 233.

3. Angelina Chapin, "Four Decades After the Battle of the Sexes, the Fight for Equality Goes On," *Guardian*, March 11, 2017, www.theguardian .com/sport/2017/mar/11/billie-jean-king-battle-of-the-sexes-tennis; King, *All In*, 242.

4. King, *All In*, 239.

5. Ware, *Game, Set, Match*, 2; "The Troubles, and Triumph, of Billie Jean," *New York Times*, May 6, 1981, www.nytimes.com/1981/05/06/opinion /the-troubles-and-triumph-of-billie-jean.html.

6. World Economic Forum, *Global Gender Gap Report 2022* (Geneva: World Economic Forum, 2022), www3.weforum.org/docs/WEF_GGGR _2022.pdf.

7. World Economic Forum, *Global Gender Gap Report 2022*; Women, Business and the Law 2022 (Washington, DC: World Bank, 2022), https://wbl .worldbank.org/en/wbl; World Bank, "Nearly 2.4 Billion Women Globally Don't Have Same Economic Rights as Men," press release, March 1, 2022, www.worldbank.org/en/news/press-release/2022/03/01/nearly-2-4-billion -women-globally-don-t-have-same-economic-rights-as-men; Linda Scott, *The Double X Economy: The Epic Potential of Women's Empowerment* (New York: Farrar, Straus and Giroux, 2020), 15.

8. Brynhildur Heiðarog Ómarsdóttir, "Equal Pay in Iceland: Setting a New Standard," International Alliance of Women, www.women alliance.org/equal-pay-in-iceland-setting-a-new-standard; *US Equal Employment Opportunity Commission*, Equal Pay Act of 1963, www.eeoc.gov/statutes /equal-pay-act-1963; *Equal Pay Handbook* (Commonwealth of Australia, 1998), https://humanrights.gov.au/sites/default/files/content/pdf/sex_discrim /equal_pay.pdf; Prime Legal, "The Principle of Equality and the Gender Wage Gap in India," HG.org, www.hg.org/legal-articles/the-principle-of -equality-and-the-gender-wage-gap-in-india-59945#.

9. Scott, *Double X Economy*, 193; Eric Morath and Andrew Duehren, "House Passes Paycheck Fairness Act Aimed at Closing Gender Pay Gap," *Wall Street Journal*, April 15, 2021, www.wsj.com/articles/housepasses -paycheck-fairness-act-aimed-at-closing-gender-pay-gap-11618525733; Uberto Percivalle, "EU Draft Directive Bites the Tail of the Gender Pay Gap Dragon," Society for Human Resource Management, July 14, 2021, www .shrm.org/resourcesandtools/hr-topics/global-hr/pages/eu-equal-pay -directive-proposal.aspx.

10. Fatma Abdel-Raouf and Patricia M. Buhler, *The Gender Pay Gap: Understanding the Numbers* (New York: Routledge, 2021), 61.

11. Abdel-Raouf and Buhler, *Gender Pay Gap*.

12. "2022 State of the Gender Pay Gap Report," Payscale, www.payscale .com/research-and-insights/gender-pay-gap.

13. Jeff Hayes and Heidi Hartmann, "Wage Gap Will Cost Millennial Women $1 Million over Their Careers," Institute for Women's Policy Research, April 10, 2018, https://iwpr.org/iwpr-general/wage-gap-will-cost -millennial-women-1-million-over-their-careers; Abdel-Raouf and Buhler, *Gender Pay Gap*, 36; Emily Peck, "Pandemic Could Cost Typical American Woman Nearly $600,000 in Lifetime Income," *Newsweek*, May 26, 2021, www.newsweek.com/2021/06/11/exclusive-pandemic-could-cost-typical -american-woman-nearly-600000-lifetime-income-1594655.html.

14. Stephen Curry, "This Is Personal," *Players' Tribune*, August 26, 2018, www.theplayerstribune.com/articles/stephen-curry-womens-equality.

15. Ellevest Team, "Understanding (and Closing) the Gender Investing Gap," *Ellevest*, March 28, 2022, www.ellevest.com/magazine/disrupt -money/closing-the-investing-gap; World Economic Forum, *Global Gender Gap Report 2022*; Mercer and CFA Institute, "Gender Differences in Pension Outcomes: 2021 Global Pension Index Special Chapter," www.mercer.com /content/dam/mercer/attachments/private/gl-2021-global-pension-special -chapter-gender-differences-in-pension-outcomes-mercer.pdf; Social Security Administration, "Social Security Is Important to Women," fact sheet, January 2021, www.ssa.gov/news/press/factsheets/women-alt.pdf; Abby Wambach, Barnard College commencement speech, 2018, https://barnard .edu/commencement/archives/2018/abby-wambach-remarks.

16. Valerie Wilson, "Women Are More Likely to Work Multiple Jobs Than Men," Economic Policy Institute, July 9, 2015, www.epi.org /publication/women-are-more-likely-to-work-multiple-jobs-than-men; US Bureau of Labor Statistics, Economic News Release, "Table A-16 Persons

Not in the Labor Force and Multiple Jobholders by Sex, Not Seasonally Adjusted," last modified September 2, 2022, www.bls.gov/news.release/empsit .t16.htm.

17. Matt Newman, "How Much the Average PGA Tour Pro Won in 2021," *Morning Read*, September 15, 2021, www.si.com/golf/news/how-much-the -average-pga-tour-pro-won-in-2021; Mike Hall, "How Much Does the Average LPGA Tour Pro Make?," *Golf Monthly*, May 25, 2022, www.golf monthly.com/tour/how-much-does-the-average-lpga-tour-pro-make; Jeff Rueter and Sam Stejskal, "MLS 2022 Salaries Analysis: Highest Earners, Balance Across Teams and Players," *The Athletic*, May 17, 2022, https://the athletic.com/3317383/2022/05/17/mls-salaries-2022-analysis; Abigail Gentrup, "NWSL Minimum Salaries Jump 60% with First CBA," *Front Office Sports*, February 1, 2022, https://frontofficesports.com/nwsl-minimum -salaries-jump-60-with-first-cba; Bryan Murphy, "Kane, Toews Among Highest-Paid Players in the NHL This Season," NBC Sports, October 15, 2021, www.nbcsports.com/chicago/blackhawks/who-gets-paid-most-and -least-2021-22-nhl-season; Associated Press, "Premier Hockey Federation to More Than Double Salary Cap, Add Expansion Franchises," ESPN, January 18, 2022, www.espn.com/nhl/story/_/id/33091153/premier -hockey-federation-increase-salary-cap-add-franchises-boost-women -hockey; Owen Poindexter, "Average Salaries for MLB Players Increase in 2022," *Front Office Sports*, April 17, 2022, https://frontofficesports.com /average-salaries-for-mlb-players-increase-in-2022; Snap Softball, "NPF Pay: How Much Pro Softball Players Make in 2021," www.snapsoftball .com/npf-pay-how-much-pro-softball-players-make; Shotclock_media, "Q: Is the Gender Wage Gap Real?," Instagram video, April 30, 2022, www .instagram.com/reel/Cc_bjvXDTTQ/?igshid=MDJmNzVkMjY%3D.

18. Karli Stone, "What Does Increased Viewership Mean for the Future of the WNBA?," *Talking Points Sports*, June 28, 2021, https://talking pointssports.com/wnba/what-does-increased-viewership-mean-for -the-future-of-the-wnba; Timothy Rapp, "Duncan Robinson Re-signs with Heat on 5-Year, $90M Contract; Largest Ever for UDFA," *Bleacher Report*, August 2, 2021, https://bleacherreport.com/articles/10009480-duncan -robinson-re-signs-with-heat-on-5-year-90m-contract-largest-ever-for -udfa.

19. Spotrac, "Paolo Banchero," www.spotrac.com/nba/orlando-magic /paolo-banchero-78110 (accessed September 27, 2022); Spotrac, "Rhyne Howard," www.spotrac.com/wnba/atlanta-dream/rhyne-howard-76492

(accessed September 27, 2022); "NBA Player Salaries 2019–2020," ESPN, www.espn.com/nba/salaries/_/year/2020/seasontype/4; Kim Tingley, "The W.N.B.A. Is Putting On Some of the Best Pro Basketball in America. Why Aren't More Fans Showing Up?," *New York Times*, September 2, 2019, www .nytimes.com/2019/09/02/magazine/wnba-atlanta-dream.html; Jabari Young, "WNBA Agrees to 53% Pay Raise, Maternity Benefits for Players in New Collective Bargaining Agreement," CNBC, January 14, 2020, www .cnbc.com/2020/01/14/wnba-agrees-to-53percent-pay-raise-maternity-benefits -for-players-in-new-collective-bargaining-agreement.html.

20. Ben Rothenberg, "Roger Federer, $731,000; Serena Williams, $495,000: The Pay Gap in Tennis," *New York Times*, April 12, 2016, www.nytimes .com/2016/04/13/sports/tennis/equal-pay-gender-gap-grand-slam-majors -wta-atp.html; Ben Miller, "Wimbledon Prize Money 2022: How Much Will the Winner Make? Total Purse, Breakdown," *Sporting News*, July 10, 2022, www.sportingnews.com/us/tennis/news/wimbledon-prize-money -2022-winner-breakdown/zwzdg723ailgoubfnpy7q5ht#; Cindy Shmerler, "Even in Flush Tennis, Equal Pay Is a Struggle," *New York Times*, May 29, 2022, www.nytimes.com/2022/05/29/sports/tennis/women-tennis-equal -pay.html.

21. Brett Knight, "The Highest-Paid Female Athletes Score a Record $167 Million," *Forbes*, January 13, 2022, www.forbes.com/sites/brettknight /2022/01/13/the-highest-paid-female-athletes-score-a-record-167-million /?sh=5a58648a78cc.

22. Will Pry, "From $15 a Day to Equal Pay: Celebrating U.S. Soccer's New Deal," National Soccer Hall of Fame, June 1, 2022, www.national soccerhof.com/news/2022/06/hall-of-famers-celebrate-equal-pay.html; Anne M. Peterson and Ronald Blum, "US Soccer Equalizes Pay in Mile-stone with Women, Men," AP, May 18, 2022, https://apnews.com/article /us-soccer-equal-pay-65070ae0dfb82598b2815295039dfd2d.

23. Juliet Macur, "On Artificial Turf Issue, U.S. Women Dig In at Last," *New York Times*, December 8, 2015, www.nytimes.com/2015/12/09/sports /soccer/on-turf-us-women-dig-in-their-heels-at-last.html; Bill Chappell, "U.S. Women's Soccer Team Members File Federal Equal-Pay Complaint," NPR, March 31, 2016, www.npr.org/sections/thetwo-way/2016/03/31 /472522790/members-of-u-s-women-s-national-team-file-federal-equal-pay -complaint.

24. Michael McCann, "Inside USWNT's New Equal Pay Law-suit vs. U.S. Soccer—and How CBA, EEOC Relate," *SI*, March 8, 2019,

www.si.com/soccer/2019/03/08/uswnt-lawsuit-us-soccer-equal-pay-cba
-eeoc-gender-discrimination.

25. Caitlin Murray, "USWNT, USMNT Pay Gap Explained: Comparing Their U.S. Soccer Contracts as Both Sides Negotiate New CBAs," ESPN, February 10, 2022, www.espn.com/soccer/united-states-usaw/story/4589310 /uswntusmnt-pay-gap-explained-comparing-their-us-soccer-contracts-as -both-sides-negotiate-new-cbas; McCann, "Inside USWNT's New Equal Pay Lawsuit vs. U.S. Soccer."

26. Rachel Bachman, "U.S. Women's Soccer Games Outearned Men's Games," *Wall Street Journal*, June 17, 2019, www.wsj.com/articles/u-s -womens-soccer-games-out-earned-mens-games-11560765600.

27. Theodoric Meyer, "U.S. Soccer Hires Lobbyists to Argue Women's National Team Isn't Underpaid," *Politico*, August 7, 2019, www.politico .com/story/2019/08/07/us-soccer-lobbyists-womens-national-team-not -underpaid-1452331; Tyler Conway, "US Soccer, USWNT Mediation over Equal Wages Breaks Down," *Bleacher Report*, August 14, 2019, https:// bleacherreport.com/articles/2849679-us-soccer-uswnt-mediation-over -equal-wages-breaks-down.

28. Franklyn Cater, "Federal Judge Dismisses U.S. Women's Soccer Team's Equal Pay Claim," NPR, May 2, 2020, www.npr.org/2020/05/02 /849492863/federal-judge-dismisses-u-s-womens-soccer-team-s-equal-pay -claim.

29. Rachel Bachman, "U.S. Women's Soccer Equal Pay Appeal Focuses on Superior Performance," *Wall Street Journal*, July 23, 2021, www .wsj.com/articles/u-s-womens-soccer-equal-pay-appeal-11627048834; Molly Hensley-Clancy, "U.S. Men's Soccer Team Backs Women in Equal-Pay Fight, Saying USWNT Should Have Been Paid More," *Washington Post*, July 30, 2021, www.washingtonpost.com/sports/2021/07/30/usmnt -supports-uswnt-equal-pay.

30. Richard Fry, "Young Women Are Out-Earning Young Men in Several U.S. Cities," Pew Research Center, March 28, 2022, www.pewresearch .org/fact-tank/2022/03/28/young-women-are-out-earning-young-men-in -several-u-s-cities.

31. National Committee on Pay Equity, "The Wage Gap over Time: In Real Dollars, Women See a Continuing Gap," www.pay-equity.org /info-time.html; Earlene K. P. Dowell, "Gender Pay Gap Widens as Women Age: Women Consistently Earn Less Than Men," US Census Bureau, January 27, 2022, www.census.gov/library/stories/2022/01/gender-pay-gap -widens-as-women-age.html.

32. Quentin T. Wodon and Bénédicte de la Brière, *Unrealized Potential: The High Cost of Gender Inequality in Earnings* (Washington, DC: World Bank, 2018), www.worldbank.org/en/topic/gender/publication /unrealized-potential-the-high-cost-of-gender-inequality-in-earnings; Kweilin Ellingrud, Anu Madgavkar, James Manyika, Jonathan Woetzel, Vivian Riefberg, Mekala Krishnan, and Mili Seoni, "The Power of Parity: Advancing Women's Equality in the United States," McKinsey Global Institute, April 7, 2016, www.mckinsey.com/featured-insights/employment -and-growth/the-power-of-parity-advancing-womens-equality-in-the -united-states#:~:text=.

33. Saijel Kishan, "Economist Found $16 Trillion When She Tallied Cost of Racial Bias," Bloomberg, October 20, 2020, www.bloomberg .com/news/articles/2020-10-20/racism-and-inequity-have-cost-the-u-s-16- trillion-wall-street-economist-says?; Statista, "Gross Domestic Product (GDP) at Current Prices in China from 1985 to 2021 with Forecasts Until 2027," www.statista.com/statistics/263770/gross-domestic-product-gdp-of -china.

34. Camonghne Felix, "Simone Biles Chose Herself: 'I Should Have Quit Way Before Tokyo,'" *The Cut*, September 27, 2021, www.thecut.com/article /simone-biles-olympics-2021.html; Nina Banks, "Black Women in the United States and Unpaid Collective Work: Theorizing the Community as a Site of Production," *Review of Black Political Economy* 47, no. 4 (2020), https:// doi.org/10.1177/0034644620962811.

35. Organisation for Economic Co-operation and Development, "Investing in Women and Girls: The Breakthrough Strategy for Achieving the MDGs," www.oecd.org/dac/gender-development/investinginwomen andgirls.htm.

36. Gemma Clarke, *SoccerWomen: The Icons, Rebels, Stars, and Trailblazers Who Transformed the Beautiful Game* (New York: Bold Type Books, 2019), 3–4.

37. Meg Linehan, "USWNT Players Reach Settlement with U.S. Soccer for Total of $24 Million in Pay Discrimination Lawsuit," *The Athletic*, February 22, 2022, https://theathletic.com/news/uswnt-players-reach -settlement-with-us-soccer-for-total-of-24-million-in-pay-discrimination -lawsuit/BXmnGmymxK4b; US Soccer, "US Soccer Federation, Women's and Men's National Team Unions Agree to Historic Collective Bargaining Agreements," May 18, 2022, www.ussoccer.com/stories/2022/05/ussf -womens-and-mens-national-team-unions-agree-to-historic-collective -bargaining-agreements.

CHAPTER 2: PUT YOUR MONEY WHERE YOUR MOUTH IS

1. Ali Kershner, Instagram, March 18, 2021, www.instagram.com/p/CMkRJ2LswFp.

2. Abel Shifferaw, "Players Call Out NCAA for Disparities in Men's and Women's Weight Rooms (UPDATE)," Complex Networks, March 18, 2021, www.complex.com/sports/players-call-out-ncaa-for-dispairites-in-mens-womens-weight-rooms-training-facilities; Sedona Prince (@sedonaprince_), Twitter [video], March 18, 2021, https://twitter.com/sedonaprince_/status/1372736231562342402.

3. Charlotte Carroll, Chantel Jennings, Dana O'Neil, and *The Athletic* staff, "'Time's Up': Head Coaches Respond Following NCAA Tournament Disparities," *The Athletic*, March 20, 2021, https://theathletic.com/news/we-fell-short-ncaa-acknowledges-disparity-in-mens-and-womens-amenities/MiF7SffY1PtD; Juliet Macur and Alan Blinder, "Anger Erupts over Disparities at N.C.A.A. Tournaments," *New York Times*, March 19, 2021, www.nytimes.com/2021/03/19/sports/ncaabasketball/women-ncaa-tournament-weight-room.html; Meredith Cash, "Photos of the Bewildering March Madness Swag Bags Show the NCAA Even Gave the Women Inferior Puzzles Compared to the Men," *Insider*, March 19, 2021, www.insider.com/march-madness-puzzles-ncaa-500-150-pieces-men-women-sexism-2021-3; Brenna Greene (@BrennaGreene_), Twitter [video], March 21, 2021, https://twitter.com/BrennaGreene_/status/1373845665038565378.

4. Stanford Women's Basketball (@StanfordWBB), Twitter, March 20, 2021, https://twitter.com/StanfordWBB/status/1373454377445425152?s=20.

5. Henry Bushnell, "NCAA Reveals Budget, Revenue Gulfs Between Men's and Women's Basketball Tournaments," Yahoo Sports, March 26, 2021, www.yahoo.com/video/ncaa-revenue-budget-march-madness-mens-womens-basketball-tournaments-202859329.html.

6. Kaplan Hecker & Fink, LLP, "NCAA External Gender Equity Review," 2021, https://ncaagenderequityreview.com.

7. Rachel Bachman, Louise Radnofsky, and Laine Higgins, "NCAA Withheld Use of Powerful 'March Madness' Brand from Women's Basketball," *Wall Street Journal*, March 22, 2021, www.wsj.com/articles/march-madness-ncaa-tournament-womens-basketball-11616428776.

8. US Department of Justice, Title IX of the Education Amendments of 1972, www.justice.gov/crt/title-ix-education-amendments-1972; US Department of Education, Office for Civil Rights, Sex Discrimination Frequently Asked Questions, www2.ed.gov/about/offices/list/ocr/frontpage

/faq/sex.html; King, *All In*, 210; Sherry Boschert, "The True Mother of Title IX. And Why It Matters Now More Than Ever," *Washington Post*, June 22, 2022, www.washingtonpost.com/outlook/2022/06/22/true-mother-title -ix-why-it-matters-now-more-than-ever.

9. US Department of Education, Office for Civil Rights, Sex Discrimination Frequently Asked Questions.

10. National Federation of State High School Associations (NFHS), "2018–19 High School Athletics Participation Survey," www.nfhs.org /media/1020412/2018-19_participation_survey.pdf; Billie Jean King, "Title IX: 37 Words That Changed Everything," www.billiejeanking.com /equality/title-ix; Women's Educational Equity Act Equity Resource Center, "Report Card—Athletics," www2.edc.org/womensequity/resource/title9 /report/athletic.htm.

11. US Department of Education, Office for Civil Rights, "Letter to Chief State School Officers, Title IX Obligations in Athletics," www2.ed.gov /about/offices/list/ocr/docs/holmes.html; NFHS, "2018–19 High School Athletics Participation Survey"; Women's Sports Foundation, "50 Years of Title IX: We're Not Done Yet," May 2022, www.womenssportsfoundation .org/wp-content/uploads/2022/05/13_Low-Res_Title-IX-50-Report.pdf.

12. Susan Ware, *Game, Set, Match: Billie Jean King and the Revolution in Women's Sports* (Chapel Hill: University of North Carolina Press, 2011), 62.

13. Ware, *Game, Set, Match*, 54–55; *SI* Staff, "Sports Equity," *SI*, January 28, 1974, https://vault.si.com/vault/1974/01/28/scorecard; Congresswoman Jackie Speier, "Speier, Sherrill Introduce Resolution Affirming the NCAA Is Subject to Title IX; Must Work to Prevent Sex Discrimination Against Women Athletes," press release, June 29, 2021, https://speier.house.gov /press-releases?id=DC2A490F-42C0-4A1B-A3EE-F07F3C51DAF7#.

14. Paul Newberry, "Summer of Women: Females Stole the Show at 1996 Olympics," ABC News, August 13, 2020, https://abcnews.go.com /Sports/wireStory/summer-women-females-stole-show-1996-olympics -72357572.

15. Women's Sports Foundation, "50 Years of Title IX: High School Participation," fact sheet, 2022, www.womenssportsfoundation.org/wp -content/uploads/2022/04/FINAL6_WSF-Title-IX-Infographic-2022.pdf; Women's Sports Foundation, "We're Not Done Yet"; National Federation of State High School Associations (NFHS), "2018–19 High School Athletics Participation Survey."

16. Women's Sports Foundation, "High School Participation"; Women's Sports Foundation, "We're Not Done Yet."

17. Kimberle Crenshaw, "Demarginalizing the Intersection of Race and Sex: A Black Feminist Critique of Antidiscrimination Doctrine, Feminist Theory and Antiracist Politics," *University of Chicago Legal Forum* 1989, no. 1 (1989), https://chicagounbound.uchicago.edu/cgi/viewcontent.cgi?article=1052 &context=uclf; Women's Sports Foundation, "We're Not Done Yet"; National Women's Law Center (NWLC) and Poverty and Race Research Action Council (PRRAC), "Finishing Last: Girls of Color and School Sports Opportunities," 2015, https://prrac.org/pdf/GirlsFinishingLast_Report.pdf.

18. Ware, *Game, Set, Match*, 71.

19. James Bowman, "Why Women's College Basketball Might Be Stuck in the Red," SB Nation, November 12, 2013, www.swishappeal.com /2013/11/12/5090384/ncaa-womens-college-basketball-profits-donations; Women's Sports Foundation, "We're Not Done Yet."

20. David Leonhardt, "Massages for Men, Doubleheaders for Women," *New York Times*, June 4, 2021, www.nytimes.com/2021/06/04/briefing /college-sports-gender-inequality.html; Clare Brennan, "Women's College World Series Tops College World Series in Viewership," Just Women's Sports, July 7, 2021, https://justwomenssports.com/womens-college-world -series-tops-college-world-series-in-viewership; Caitlin Murray, "New Turf Fight Has U.S. Soccer and Women's Team at Odds Again," *New York Times*, September 21, 2017, www.nytimes.com/2017/09/21/sports/soccer /uswnt-us-soccer-artificial-turf.html; Katerina Kerska, "Injuries Related to Artificial Turf," National Center for Health Research, www.center4 research.org/injuries-related-to-artificial-turf; Megan Rapinoe, *One Life* (New York: Penguin, 2020), 98.

21. Caitlin Murray, *The National Team: The Inside Story of the Women Who Changed Soccer* (New York: Abrams, 2019), 16; Vanessa Friedman, "Women Finally Get Their Own World Cup Soccer Style," *New York Times*, March 11, 2019, www.nytimes.com/2019/03/11/style/womens-world-cup-kit-nike.html.

22. Darran Simon, "Megan Rapinoe Says Fight for Equal Pay Is About More Than Money. It's About Investment in Women's Soccer," CNN, July 10, 2019, www.cnn.com/2019/07/09/us/megan-rapinoe-interview/index .html.

23. Jordan Rubio and Priyamvada Mathur, "An Exceptional Year for Female Founders Still Means a Sliver of VC Funding," PitchBook, January 10, 2022, https://pitchbook.com/news/articles/female-founders-dashboard -2021-vc-funding-wrap-up; UBS, "The Funding Gap: Investors and Female Entrepreneurs," March 3, 2021, www.ubs.com/global/en/wealth-management /women/insights/2021/funding-gap.html; Affirmative Finance Action for

Women in Africa (AFAWA), "Why AFAWA?," www.afdb.org/en/topics
-and-sectors/initiatives-partnerships/afawa-affirmative-finance-action
-for-women-in-africa/why-afawa; Rohit Arora, "The Lending Gap Narrows
for Women Business Owners, but It's Still 31% Less Than for Men," CNBC,
March 7, 2019, www.cnbc.com/2019/03/07/the-lending-gap-narrows-for
-women-business-owners-nationwide.html; Emma Hinchliffe, "The Number of Black Female Founders Who Have Raised More Than $1 Million
Has Nearly Tripled Since 2018," *Fortune*, December 2, 2020, https://fortune
.com/2020/12/02/black-women-female-founders-venture-capital-funding
-vc-2020-project-diane.

24. Dianna Chane, "The Power of Female Mentors: Why We Need
More Women Leading Today's Workforce," Forbes Business Council, February 10, 2020, www.forbes.com/sites/forbesbusinesscouncil/2020/02/10
/the-power-of-female-mentors-why-we-need-more-women-leading-todays
-workforce/?sh=4e629a462d89; Christine Silva, "Mentoring: Necessary but
Insufficient for Advancement," Catalyst, December 1, 2010, www.catalyst
.org/research/mentoring-necessary-but-insufficient-for-advancement.

25. Michael Long, "'I Like to Feel We Can Do It Differently': What if
Women's Sport Went Its Own Way?," *SportsPro*, November 1, 2021, www
.sportspromedia.com/from-the-magazine/just-womens-sport-media
-investment-nwsl-wnba; "Naomi Osaka," *Forbes* profile, www.forbes.com
/profile/naomi-osaka/?list=athletes&sh=68013894384e; Brett Knight, "The
World's 10 Highest-Paid Athletes [2022]," *Forbes*, www.forbes.com/sites
/brettknight/2022/05/11/the-worlds-10-highest-paid-athletes-2022/?sh
=30e90fc1f6c9.

26. Lindsay Kagawa Colas, "Commentary: Why Brittney Griner Was
in Russia, and What It Says About Women's Sports in the U.S.," *Los Angeles
Times*, April 26, 2022, www.latimes.com/sports/story/2022-04-26/brittney
-griner-russia-pay-gap.

27. Bill Simmons, "LeBron James's Life Is Constructed to Keep Him on
the Court," *The Ringer*, June 8, 2016, www.theringer.com/2016/6/8/16040612
/nba-lebron-james-bill-simmons-malcolm-gladwell-5369d6959c67#
.c7xotcum2.

28. Doug Feinberg, "Explainer: Why WNBA Players Go Overseas to
Play in Offseason," AP, March 6, 2022, https://apnews.com/article/russia
-ukraine-business-sports-europe-sue-bird-b634587c62d9bdc61b4c596
fd37c5a86; John Marshall, "Taurasi to Skip WNBA Season; Russia Offers
Money to Rest," AP, February 3, 2015, https://apnews.com/article/c24a337

fdbc345ff827148274a6ed858; Mike Prada, "A Russian Team Paid Diana Taurasi to Sit Out 2015 WNBA Season," SB Nation, February 3, 2015, www.sbnation.com/nba/2015/2/3/7973177/diana-taurasi-sit-out-wnba-season-russian-salary; Alexa Philippou, "Where Are All the Players? WNBA Teams Hindered with Stars Arriving Late to Training Camp, Season Openers Due to Overseas Commitments," *Hartford Courant*, May 12, 2021, www.courant.com/sports/hc-sp-connecticut-sun-20210513-20210513-z3fuq73uyfcf3nbegqbanwql6u-story.html.

29. Wajih AlBaroudi, Isabel Gonzalez, and Shanna McCarriston, "Brittney Griner Situation Explained: Oct. 25 Set as Date for Appeal of Nine-Year Prison Term in Russian Court," CBS Sports, October 5, 2022, www.cbssports.com/wnba/news/brittney-griner-situation-explained-wnba-star-communicating-via-email-letters-while-in-jail-per-report; "Russia Sentences Griner to 9 Years in Prison, White House Calls for Her Release," Reuters, August 5, 2022, www.reuters.com/world/basketball-star-brittney-griner-awaits-fate-russia-drugs-trial-2022-08-03; "Russian Court Rejects Griner Appeal of Her 9-Year Sentence," AP, October 25, 2022, https://apnews.com/article/brittney-griner-russia-prison-appeal-denied-0baf45ba608ec4231642c3d0fe3d1522.

30. Colas, "Commentary: Why Brittney Griner Was in Russia."

31. Alan Blinder, "N.C.A.A. Expands Division I Women's Basketball Tournament," *New York Times*, November 17, 2021, www.nytimes.com/2021/11/17/sports/ncaabasketball/ncaa-womens-basketball-tournament-68-teams.html; Liz Clarke, "After Social Media Shaming, NCAA Tries to Get Gender Equity Right for 2022 March Madness," *Washington Post*, March 11, 2022, www.washingtonpost.com/sports/2022/03/11/ncaa-womens-tournament-changes.

32. "Sports Global Market Report 2022," PR Newswire, March 10, 2022, www.prnewswire.com/news-releases/sports-global-market-report-2022-301500432.html; Ross Andrews, "Women's Sports Popularity Is Growing, According to Nielsen Study," *Global Sport Matters*, November 13, 2018, https://globalsportmatters.com/business/2018/11/13/womens-sports-popularity-is-growing-according-to-nielsen; Paul Lee, Kevin Westcott, Izzy Wray, and Suhas Raviprakash, "Women's Sports Gets Down to Business: On Track for Rising Monetization," *Deloitte Insights*, December 7, 2020, www2.deloitte.com/xe/en/insights/industry/technology/technology-media-and-telecom-predictions/2021/womens-sports-revenue.html.

33. Shot:Clock, The Collective, and GOALS, "The Goal Post: Tracking Key Moments in Women's Sports, March Madness Edition," https://static1 .squarespace.com/static/5d14bd1dc71e6a0001e78970/t/624ee65d1119662990 57c818/1649337954699/The+Goal+Post+-+March+Madness.pdf.

34. The Fan Project, www.thefanproject.co/thefanprojectreport.

35. The Fan Project, "How Women's Sports Will Lead the Sports Industry into the Future," https://assets.ctfassets.net/40abn7j4v349/XWdrSe E0YWHefrzMlSVnq/277baf2fdcda326672da90a683538daa/SIL_The _Fan_Project_Report.pdf; Joshua Hodson, "Women's Sports Drives Better Sponsorship Outcomes," Ministry of Sport, April 26, 2021, https://ministry ofsport.com/womens-sports-drives-better-sponsorship-outcomes.

36. FIFA, "Arkema, First National Supporter of the FIFA Women's World Cup France 2019™," press release, April 6, 2018, www.fifa.com /tournaments/womens/womensworldcup/france2019/media-releases /arkema-first-national-supporter-of-the-fifa-women-s-world-cup-france -2019tm; Madison Williams, "NWSL's Challenge Cup Achieves Pay Equity with Historic UKG Deal," *SI*, May 6, 2022, www.si.com/soccer/2022/05/06 /nwsl-challenge-cup-achieves-pay-equity-historic-ukg-deal.

37. Meredith Cash, "Gatorade Commits $10 Million to Breaking Down the Barriers Keeping Young Women and Minorities out of Sports," *Insider*, February 16, 2022, https://frontofficesports.com/gatorade-dropping -nhl-to-focus-on-college-womens-sports; Madison Williams, "Pepsi Will No Longer Sponsor Super Bowl Halftime Show," *SI*, May 24, 2022, www.si.com /nfl/2022/05/25/pepsi-no-longer-sponsor-super-bowl-halftime-show; Jeff Kearney, "Gatorade Parts Ways with NHL, Reinvents Marketing Playbook," LinkedIn, May 31, 2022, www.linkedin.com/posts/jeff-kearney -3894a17_gatorade-parts-ways-with-nhl-reinvents-marketing-activity -6937453716706926593-FuDP; Owen Poindexter, "Gatorade Dropping NHL to Focus on College, Women's Sports," *Front Office Sports*, June 1, 2022, https://frontofficesports.com/gatorade-dropping-nhl-to-focus-on-college -womens-sports.

38. Shalini Unnikrishnan and Cherie Blair, "Want to Boost the Global Economy by $5 Trillion? Support Women as Entrepreneurs," Boston Consulting Group, July 30, 2019, www.bcg.com/publications/2019/boost -global-economy-5-trillion-dollar-support-women-entrepreneurs; Katie Abouzahr, Matt Krentz, John Harthorne, and Frances Brooks Taplett, "Why Women-Owned Startups Are a Better Bet," Boston Consulting Group, June 6, 2018, www.bcg.com/publications/2018/why-women-owned-startups -are-better-bet.

CHAPTER 3: THE MOTHERHOOD PENALTY

1. Macaela MacKenzie, "The Women's World Cup Is a Pivotal Moment for Women in Sports," *Glamour,* June 10, 2019, www.glamour.com/story /the-world-cup-is-a-pivotal-moment-for-women-in-sports.

2. Alysia Montaño, "Nike Told Me to Dream Crazy, Until I Wanted a Baby," *New York Times,* May 12, 2019, www.nytimes.com/2019/05/12 /opinion/nike-maternity-leave.html.

3. Olena Mykhalchenko and Isabel Santagostino Recavarren, "In 38 Countries, Women Can Still Be Fired for Being Pregnant," *Let's Talk Development* (blog), May 13, 2021, https://blogs.worldbank.org/developmenttalk /38-countries-women-can-still-be-fired-being-pregnant.

4. Janet Paskin, "Having Kids Is Terrible for Women's Earning Power," Bloomberg, April 10, 2019, www.bloomberg.com/news/articles/2019-04-10 /the-pay-check-what-having-kids-does-to-women-s-pay; Safia Samee Ali, "'Motherhood Penalty' Can Affect Women Who Never Even Have a Child," NBC News, April 11, 2016, www.nbcnews.com/better/careers/motherhood -penalty-can-affect-women-who-never-even-have-child-n548511.

5. Allyson Felix, "Allyson Felix: My Own Nike Pregnancy Story," *New York Times,* May 22, 2019, www.nytimes.com/2019/05/22/opinion/allyson -felix-pregnancy-nike.html.

6. Claire Cain Miller, "The World 'Has Found a Way to Do This': The U.S. Lags on Paid Leave," *New York Times,* October 25, 2021, www.nytimes .com/2021/10/25/upshot/paid-leave-democrats.html; AEI-Brookings Working Group on Paid Family Leave, "Paid Family and Medical Leave: An Issue Whose Time Has Come," Brookings, May 2017, www.brookings.edu /research/paid-family-and-medical-leave-an-issue-whose-time-has-come; Paid Leave for the United States, "Paid Family Leave: Messages That Resonate," https://drive.google.com/file/d/1HZ3LKmTDhkRFVG7zTkHVt53 Wwi2dyrAd/view; Kathryn Dill and Angela Yang, "Companies Are Cutting Back on Maternity and Paternity Leave," *Wall Street Journal,* August 22, 2022, www.wsj.com/articles/the-surprising-benefit-some-companies -are-taking-awayparental-leave-11661125605.

7. Mariam Khan, Allison Pecorin, and Libby Cathey, "Pelosi Says Democrats Adding Paid Family Leave Back into Social Spending Bill, Fate in Senate Unclear," ABC News, November 3, 2021, https://abcnews.go.com/Politics /pelosi-democrats-adding-paid-family-leave-back-social/story?id=80950206.

8. Gianna Melillo, "US Ranks Worst in Maternal Care, Mortality Compared with 10 Other Developed Nations," *American Journal of Managed*

Care, December 3, 2020, www.ajmc.com/view/us-ranks-worst-in-maternal -care-mortality-compared-with-10-other-developed-nations; Donna L. Hoyert, "Maternal Mortality Rates in the United States, 2020," National Center for Health Statistics, Centers for Disease Control and Prevention, February 2022, www.cdc.gov/nchs/data/hestat/maternal-mortality/2020/maternal -mortality-rates-2020.htm.

9. Allyson Felix, transcript of testimony to US House of Representatives, May 16, 2019, https://docs.house.gov/meetings/WM/WM00/20190516 /109496/HHRG-116-WM00-Wstate-FelixA-20190516.pdf.

10. March of Dimes, "Stress and Pregnancy," fact sheet, January 2015, www.marchofdimes.org/materials/Maternal-Stress-Issue-Brief -January2015.pdf; Roosa Tikkanen, Munira Z. Gunja, Molly FitzGerald, and Laurie Zephyrin, "Maternal Mortality and Maternity Care in the United States Compared to 10 Other Developed Countries," Commonwealth Fund, November 18, 2020, www.commonwealthfund.org/publications /issue-briefs/2020/nov/maternal-mortality-maternity-care-us-compared -10-countries; Centers for Disease Control and Prevention, "Working Together to Reduce Black Maternal Mortality," April 6, 2022, www.cdc.gov /healthequity/features/maternal-mortality/index.html; Susanna Trost, Jennifer Beauregard, Gyan Chandra, Fanny Njie, Jasmine Berry, Alyssa Harvey, and David A. Goodman, "Pregnancy-Related Deaths: Data from Maternal Mortality Review Committees in 36 US States, 2017–2019," Centers for Disease Control and Prevention, September 19, 2022, www.cdc .gov/reproductivehealth/maternal-mortality/erase-mm/data-mmrc.html.

11. Robyn Horsager-Boehrer, "Postpartum Exercise: When It's Safe to Start Running and Lifting After Pregnancy," *MedBlog*, UT Southwestern Medical Center, May 11, 2021, https://utswmed.org/medblog/workouts -after-pregnancy; Montaño, "Nike Told Me to Dream Crazy."

12. David Cox, "Does Childbirth Improve Athletic Ability?," *The Running Blog* (*Guardian*), November 4, 2014, www.theguardian.com/lifeandstyle /the-running-blog/2014/nov/04/does-childbirth-improve-athletic-ability; Maggie Mertens, "Maternity Leave—Not Higher Pay—Is the WNBA's Real Win," *The Atlantic*, February 1, 2020, www.theatlantic.com/culture /archive/2020/02/why-wnbas-new-maternity-leave-policy-revolutionary /605944; J. R. Thorpe, "The Science Behind Allyson Felix's Stunning Postpartum Athletic Performance," *Bustle*, October 4, 2019, www.bustle.com /p/postpartum-athletic-performance-is-individual-experts-say-18845932; Francine Darroch, Amy Schneeberg, Ryan Brodie, Zachary M. Ferraro,

Dylan Wykes, Sarita Hira, Audrey Giles, Kristi B. Adamo, and Trent Stellingwerff, "Impact of Pregnancy in 42 Elite to World-Class Runners on Training and Performance Outcomes," *Medicine and Science in Sports and Exercise*, August 22, 2022, https://pubmed.ncbi.nlm.nih.gov/35975937.

13. Talya Minsberg, "Keira D'Amato and Sara Hall Rewrite the Distance Running History Books," *New York Times*, January 19, 2022, www.nytimes .com/2022/01/19/sports/keira-damato-sara-hall-american-marathon -record.html.

14. Matthias Krapf, Heinrich W. Ursprung, and Christian Zimmer-mann, "Parenthood and Productivity of Highly Skilled Labor: Evidence from the Groves of Academe," Federal Reserve Bank of St. Louis Working Paper 2014-001, January 2014, https://s3.amazonaws.com/real.stlouisfed .org/wp/2014/2014-001.pdf.

15. Scott Cacciola, "From Athens to Tokyo, Allyson Felix's Journey to the Olympic Record Books," *New York Times*, August 7, 2021, www .nytimes.com/2021/08/07/sports/olympics/allyson-felix-olympic-medals .html; Adam Kilgore, "Allyson Felix Bids a Joyful Goodbye to Track and Field," *Washington Post*, July 16, 2022, www.washingtonpost.com/sports /olympics/2022/07/16/allyson-felix-world-championships.

16. Kim Gaucher (kgaucher), Instagram [video], June 23, 2021, www .instagram.com/p/CQe6gi8Lb5e.

17. Dave Sheinin, "Nursing Olympians No Longer Have to Choose Be-tween the Tokyo Games and Their Babies," *Washington Post*, June 30, 2021, www.washingtonpost.com/sports/olympics/2021/06/30/nursing-moms -babies-tokyo-olympics; Rachel Axon, "Nursing Moms Face Difficult Deci-sion When Coming to Tokyo Olympics to Compete, *USA Today*, July 25, 2021, www.usatoday.com/story/sports/olympics/2021/07/25/2021-olympics -nursing-moms-face-tough-decision-when-coming-tokyo/8080047002.

18. Molly Dickens, "The Mothers Are Missing: Can Changing the Sports Industry Bring Them Back?," Medium, May 7, 2021, https://medium.com /and-mother/the-mothers-are-missing-8fb09e49358.

19. Sarah Jane Glynn, "An Unequal Division of Labor: How Equi-table Workplace Policies Would Benefit Working Mothers," Center for American Progress, May 18, 2018, www.americanprogress.org/article /unequal-division-labor; United Nations Department of Economic and Social Affairs, "Women's Job Market Participation Stagnating at Less Than 50% for the Past 25 Years, Finds UN Report," www.un.org/en/desa /women%E2%80%99s-job-market-participation-stagnating-less-50

-past-25-years-finds-un-report; UN Women, "The COVID-19 Pandemic Has Increased the Care Burden, but by How Much?," December 3, 2020, https://data.unwomen.org/features/covid-19-pandemic-has-increased-care -burden-how-much-0; Oxfam, "Time to Care: Unpaid and Underpaid Care Work and the Global Inequality Crisis," January 19, 2020, www.oxfam america.org/explore/research-publications/time-care.

20. Shelley J. Correll, Stephen Benard, and In Paik, "Getting a Job: Is There a Motherhood Penalty?," *American Journal of Sociology* 112, no. 5 (March 2007): 1297–1338, www.jstor.org/stable/10.1086/511799?seq=1 #metadata_info_tab_contents; Patrick Ishizuka, "The Motherhood Penalty in Context: Assessing Discrimination in a Polarized Labor Market," *Demography* 58, no. 4 (2021): 1275–1300, https://read.dukeupress.edu /demography/article/58/4/1275/174038/The-Motherhood-Penalty-in-Context-Assessing; Sara Savat, "Mothers May Face Increased Workplace Discrimination Post-Pandemic, Research Warns," *Newsroom* (Washington University in St. Louis), July 20, 2021, https://source.wustl.edu/2021/07 /mothers-may-face-increased-workplace-discrimination-post-pandemic -research-warns.

21. Correll, Benard, and Paik, "Getting a Job: Is There a Motherhood Penalty?"; Michelle J. Budig, "The Fatherhood Bonus and the Motherhood Penalty: Parenthood and the Gender Gap in Pay," Third Way, September 2, 2014, www.thirdway.org/report/the-fatherhood-bonus-and-the -motherhood-penalty-parenthood-and-the-gender-gap-in-pay; Claire Ewing-Nelson, "Even Before This Disastrous Year for Mothers, They Were Still Only Paid 75 Cents for Every Dollar Paid to Fathers," National Women's Law Center fact sheet, May 2021, https://nwlc.org/wp-content/uploads/2021 /04/EDPFS.pdf.

22. Budig, "The Fatherhood Bonus and the Motherhood Penalty."

23. Julie Kashen, Sarah Jane Glynn, and Amanda Novello, "How COVID-19 Sent Women's Workforce Progress Backward," Center for American Progress, October 30, 2020, www.americanprogress.org/article /covid-19-sent-womens-workforce-progress-backward; Charles Kenny and George Yang, "The Global Childcare Workload from School and Preschool Closures During the COVID-19 Pandemic," Center for Global Development, June 25, 2021, www.cgdev.org/publication/global-childcare-workload -school-and-preschool-closures-during-covid-19-pandemic.

24. Jazmin Goodwin, "Women Lost $800 Billion in Income Last Year. That's More Than the Combined GDP of 98 Countries," CNN Busi-

ness, April 28, 2021, https://edition.cnn.com/2021/04/28/success/women -economic-impact-coronavirus/index.html.

25. Simon Workman, "The True Cost of High-Quality Child Care Across the United States," Center for American Progress, June 28, 2021, www.americanprogress.org/article/true-cost-high-quality-child -care-across-united-states; NCT, "Average Childcare Costs," www.nct .org.uk/life-parent/work-and-childcare/childcare/average-childcare -costs; Danielle Wood and Tom Crowley, "New Data a Reminder That High Childcare Costs Continue to Bite in Australia," Grattan Institute, January 26, 2021, https://grattan.edu.au/news/high-childcare-costs -continue-to-bite; "Jessica McDonald, FIFA World Cup Champion," Into the Gloss, 2019, https://intothegloss.com/2019/07/jessica-mcdonald-world -cup.

26. Molly Hensley-Clancy, "Parenting in the Bubble: 'This Is Mom's Job. You Have to Work with Me,'" *New York Times*, July 16, 2020, www.nytimes .com/2020/07/16/sports/soccer/parenting-bubble-nwsl-wnba.html.

27. Hensley-Clancy, "Parenting in the Bubble."

28. Michael Madowitz, Alex Rowell, and Katie Hamm, "Calculating the Hidden Cost of Interrupting a Career for Child Care," Center for American Progress, June 21, 2016, www.americanprogress.org/issues/early -childhood/reports/2016/06/21/139731/calculating-the-hidden-cost-of -interrupting-a-career-for-child-care; Center for American Progress, "The Hidden Cost of a Failing Childcare System," https://interactives.american progress.org/childcarecosts/?_ga=2.230476186.706783556.1666816183 -177708099.1666816183.

29. OlympicTalk, "Allyson Felix Breaks Usain Bolt Record for World Titles, Gets First Gold as a Mom," NBC Sports, September 29, 2019, https://olympics.nbcsports.com/2019/09/29/allyson-felix-usain-bolt-world -championships-record.

30. Sarah Jane Glynn, "Breadwinning Mothers Continue to Be the U.S. Norm," Center for American Progress, May 10, 2019, www.american progress.org/article/breadwinning-mothers-continue-u-s-norm; Institute for Women's Policy Research, "Breadwinner Mothers by Race/Ethnicity and State," September 2016, https://iwpr.org/wp-content/uploads/2020/08 /Q054.pdf; Tiffany Burns, Jess Huang, Alexis Krivkovich, Ishanaa Rambachan, Tijana Trkulja, and Lareina Yee, "Women in the Workplace 2021," McKinsey & Company, September 27, 2021, www.mckinsey.com /featured-insights/diversity-and-inclusion/women-in-the-workplace.

31. Lenore M. Palladino, Anwesha Majumder, and Jessica Forden, "Paid Leave Pays Dividends: How a National Paid Leave Policy Will Benefit the Economy," Time's Up Foundation, September 2021, https://timesupfoundation .org/wp-content/uploads/2021/09/TimesUp-Paid-Leave-Report_v1.pdf.

32. Eliana Dockterman, "42% of Women Say They Have Consistently Felt Burned Out at Work in 2021," *Time*, September 27, 2021, https:// time.com/6101751/burnout-women-in-the-workplace-2021/; Misty Heggeness and Palak Suri, "Telework, Childcare, and Mothers' Labor Supply," Federal Reserve Bank of Minneapolis Institute Working Paper 52, November 16, 2021, www.minneapolisfed.org/research/institute-working-papers /telework-childcare-and-mothers-labor-supply; Katherine Gallagher Robbins and Anwesha Majumder, "Transformative Caregiving Proposals Would Increase GDP by at Least $330 Billion," Time's Up Foundation, September 19, 2021, https://timesupnow.org/transformative-caregiving-proposals.

33. Abha Bhattarai, "Congresswomen Press Nike About Its Treatment of Pregnant Athletes," *Washington Post*, May 21, 2019, www.washingtonpost .com/business/2019/05/21/congresswomen-press-nike-about-its-treatment -pregnant-athletes; Adam Kilgore, "Under Fire, Nike Expands Protections for Pregnant Athletes," *Washington Post*, August 16, 2019, www.washingtonpost .com/sports/2019/08/16/under-fire-nike-expands-protections-pregnant -athletes; Jen A. Miller, "Maternity Leave for Sponsored Runners," *New York Times*, May 18, 2019, www.nytimes.com/2019/05/18/well/move/maternity -leave-for-sponsored-runners.html.

34. &Mother, "Resource Guide," https://andmother.org/resources.

35. Athleta, Power of She Fund, https://athleta.gap.com/browse/info .do?cid=1175290.

36. Sean Gregory, "Allyson Felix Is Launching an Initiative to Provide Free Childcare for Athletes," *Time*, June 21, 2022, https://time.com/6189321 /allyson-felix-free-childcare-athletes.

37. Gabriel Fernandez, "New WNBA CBA Brings Salary Bumps, and Maternity Leave Among Other Major Changes," CBS, January 14, 2020, www.cbssports.com/wnba/news/new-wnba-cba-brings-salary-bumps-and -maternity-leave-among-other-major-changes; Gabriela Weigel, Usha Ranji, Michelle Long, and Alina Salganicoff, "Coverage and Use of Fertility Services in the U.S.," Kaiser Family Foundation, September 15, 2020, www .kff.org/womens-health-policy/issue-brief/coverage-and-use-of-fertility -services-in-the-u-s; Percy Allen, "'We're Betting on Ourselves': Why WNBA's Landmark New Deal Is a Huge Win for Women's Professional Sports," *Seattle Times*, January 14, 2020, www.seattletimes.com/sports

/storm/storms-sue-bird-on-landmark-wnba-collective-bargaining-agreement
-were-going-to-be-looked-at-as-pioneers-in-the-sports-world.

CHAPTER 4: STRONGER TOGETHER

1. Seth Berkman, "U.S. Women's Hockey Team Plans to Boycott World Championship over Pay Dispute," *New York Times*, March 15, 2017, www.nytimes.com/2017/03/15/sports/hockey/team-usa-women-boycott -world-championships.html; Alex Azzi, "The Current State of Professional Women's Hockey, Explained," NBC Sports, January 19, 2021, https:// onherturf.nbcsports.com/2021/01/19/the-current-state-of-professional -womens-hockey-explained.

2. Cammi Granato, "What U.S. Women's Team Accomplished Is Nothing Short of Heroic," ESPN, March 28, 2017, www.espn.com/espnw/voices /story/_/id/19027162/us-women-hockey-team-why-cammi-granato-proud -women-landmark-deal; John Buccigross, "Buccigross: Granato Deserved Better Ending," ESPN, August 29, 2005, www.espn.com/nhl/columns /story?columnist=buccigross_john&id=2145917.

3. Seth Berkman, "U.S. Women's Team Strikes a Deal with U.S.A. Hockey," *New York Times*, March 28, 2017, www.nytimes.com/2017/03/28 /sports/hockey/usa-hockey-uswnt-boycott.html.

4. Berkman, "U.S. Women's Team Strikes a Deal."

5. Macaela MacKenzie, "Broadcast Wasn't Built for Chiney Ogwumike. That's Not Stopping Her," *Glamour*, October 5, 2020, www.glamour.com /story/broadcast-wasnt-built-for-chiney-ogwumike-thats-not-stopping-her.

6. Amanda Fins, Sarah David Heydemann, and Jasmine Tucker, "Unions Are Good for Women," National Women's Law Center fact sheet, July 2021, https://nwlc.org/wp-content/uploads/2021/07/Union -Factsheet-7.27.pdf; Chabeli Carrazana, "'This Is Our Time': How Women Are Taking Over the Labor Movement," The 19th, June 1, 2022, https://19th news.org/2022/06/women-labor-unions-movements-pandemic; Chuxuan Sun, Acadia Hall, and Elyse Shaw, "Stronger Together: Union Membership Boosts Women's Earnings and Economic Security," Institute for Women's Policy Research, September 1, 2021, https://iwpr.org/iwpr-publications /stronger-together-union-membership-boosts-womens-earnings-and -economic-security; K. Bronfenbrenner, "Organizing Women: The Nature and Process of Union Organizing Efforts Among US Women Workers Since the Mid-1990s," *Work and Occupations* 32, no. 4 (2005): 1–23, https:// ecommons.cornell.edu/bitstream/handle/1813/75931/Bronfenbrenner3 _OrganizingWomenPostPrint_1.pdf?sequence=1&isAllowed=y.

7. "The 1975 Women's Strike: When 90% of Icelandic Women Went on Strike to Protest Gender Inequality," *Iceland Magazine*, October 24, 2018, https://icelandmag.is/article/1975-womens-strike-when-90-icelandic-women -went-strike-protest-gender-inequality.

8. Kirstie Brewer, "The Day Iceland's Women Went on Strike," BBC News, October 23, 2015, www.bbc.com/news/magazine-34602822; World Economic Forum, *Global Gender Gap Report 2021* (Geneva: World Economic Forum, 2021), www3.weforum.org/docs/WEF_GGGR_2021.pdf.

9. Melissa Murphy, "Original 9 Trailblazers Stood for Tennis Equality in 1970," AP, September 23, 2020, https://apnews.com/article/new-york-billie -jean-king-virginia-us-open-tennis-championships-wimbledon-ec4f2a 1684a5efd286cbfb31a7611764; Matt Trollope, "Aussies Dalton and Reid Recall Original 9 Breakthrough," Australian Open, September 22, 2020, https://ausopen.com/articles/news/aussies-dalton-and-reid-recall-original -9-breakthrough.

10. Brett Knight, "The Highest-Paid Female Athletes Score a Record $167 Million," *Forbes*, October 5, 2020, www.forbes.com/sites/brettknight /2022/01/13/the-highest-paid-female-athletes-score-a-record-167-million/?sh =297a26e778cc.

11. Mike Murphy, "NWHL Releases Salary Details for 2017–2018 Season," *The Ice Garden* (SB Nation), October 20, 2017, www.theicegarden .com/2017/10/20/16508376/nwhl-releases-salary-details-for-2017-18-season -womens-hockey-pay-players-tiers-compensation-nwhlpa; Seth Berkman, "C.W.H.L. Folds, Leaving North America with One Women's Hockey League," *New York Times*, March 31, 2019, www.nytimes.com/2019/03/31 /sports/cwhl-womens-hockey.html.

12. "Billie Jean King Among Group Exploring Launch of New Women's Pro Hockey League," AP, May 25, 2022, www.si.com/nhl/2022/05/25/billie -jean-king-mark-walter-pwhpa-womens-hockey-pro-league.

13. Paulana Lamonier, "The Business of Being a WNBA Player," *Forbes*, July 2, 2018, www.forbes.com/sites/plamonier/2018/07/02/the-business -of-being-a-wnba-player/?sh=d1772d35af12; Nneka Ogwumike, "Bet on Women," *Players' Tribune*, November 1, 2018, www.theplayerstribune.com /articles/nneka-ogwumike-wnba-cba-bet-on-women.

14. Michael Baker, Yosh Halberstam, Kory Kroft, Alexandre Mas, and Derek Messacar, "Pay Transparency and the Gender Gap," National Bureau of Economic Research Working Paper 25834, December 2021, www.nber .org/system/files/working_papers/w25834/w25834.pdf.

15. Jami Farkas, "How Much Do WNBA Players Make?," Yahoo, July 16, 2021, www.yahoo.com/video/much-wnba-players-210001886.html; Erica L. Ayala, "As W.N.B.A. Players Call for Expansion, League Says Not Now," *New York Times*, January 10, 2022, www.nytimes.com/2022/01/10/sports /basketball/wnba-expansion.html; Women's National Basketball Association Collective Bargaining Agreement, https://wnbpa.com/wp-content /uploads/2020/01/WNBA-WNBPA-CBA-2020-2027.pdf.

16. Gemma Clarke, *SoccerWomen: The Icons, Rebels, Stars, and Trailblazers Who Transformed the Beautiful Game* (New York: Bold Type Books, 2019), 161; Aimee Lewis, "Norway's Footballers Sign Historic Equal Pay Agreement," CNN, December 14, 2017, www.cnn.com/2017/12/14/football/norway -football-equal-pay-agreement/index.html; Karen Zraick, "Australian Women and Men's Soccer Teams Reach Deal to Close Pay Gap," *New York Times*, November 6, 2019, www.nytimes.com/2019/11/06/sports/soccer/australia -soccer-matildas-equal-pay.html; "England Men's and Women's Teams Receive Equal Pay, FA Announces," Sky Sports, September 3, 2020, www.skysports .com/football/news/12016/12062579/england-mens-and-womens-teams -receive-equal-pay-fa-announces; "Brazil Announces Equal Pay for Men's and Women's National Soccer Teams," Reuters, September 4, 2020, www .weforum.org/agenda/2020/09/soccer-brazil-equal-pay-mens-and-womens- teams-gender-parity; Ryan Lenora Brown and Whitney Eulich, "More Nations Ending Soccer's Gender Wage Gap: 'This Could Change Things,'" *Christian Science Monitor*, September 28, 2020, www.csmonitor.com/World/2020/0928 /More-nations-ending-soccer-s-gender-wage-gap-This-could-change -things; "Republic of Ireland Women's and Men's Senior Teams Agree Equal Pay Deal with FAI," Sky Sports, August 31, 2021, www.skysports.com /football/news/12020/12395328/republic-of-ireland-womens-and-mens -senior-teams-agree-equal-pay-deal-with-fai; Meredith Cash, "Dawn Staley Credited Megan Rapinoe and the US Women's Soccer Team's Equal Pay Fight for Helping Her Get a Historic Payday," Yahoo News, October 20, 2021, https://news.yahoo.com/dawn-staley-credited-megan-rapinoe-175323598 .html.

17. Marisa Kwiatkowski, Mark Alesia, and Tim Evans, "A Blind Eye to Sex Abuse: How USA Gymnastics Failed to Report Cases," *IndyStar*, August 4, 2016, www.indystar.com/story/news/investigations/2016 /08/04/usa-gymnastics-sex-abuse-protected-coaches/85829732; Mark Ale- sia, Marisa Kwiatkowski, and Tim Evans, "Rachael Denhollander's Brave Journey: Lone Voice to 'Army' at Larry Nassar's Sentencing," *IndyStar*,

January 24, 2018, www.indystar.com/story/news/2018/01/24/larry-nassar
-usa-gymnastics-sexual-abuse-rachael-denhollander-mckayla-maroney-aly
-raisman/1060356001.

18. Tim Evans, Mark Alesia, and Marisa Kwiatkowski, "Former USA
Gymnastics Doctor Accused of Abuse," *IndyStar*, September 12, 2016,
www.indystar.com/story/news/2016/09/12/former-usa-gymnastics
-doctor-accused-abuse/89995734; Bryan Armen Graham, "Michigan State
Reaches $500 Million Settlement with Survivors of Larry Nassar Abuse,"
Guardian, May 16, 2018, www.theguardian.com/sport/2018/may/16
/michigan-state-university-larry-nassar-settlement-gymnastics; Scott Cacciola and Victor Mather, "Larry Nassar Sentencing: 'I Just Signed Your
Death Warrant,'" *New York Times*, January 24, 2018, www.nytimes.com
/2018/01/24/sports/larry-nassar-sentencing.html.

19. Dan Gartland, "Report: At Least 14 People at Michigan State Ignored Larry Nassar Complaints for Years," *SI*, January 18, 2018, www.si
.com/olympics/2018/01/18/larry-nassar-michigan-state-sexual-abuse
-complaints; Louise Radnofsky and Rebecca Davis O'Brien, "FBI Agents
Disregarded Gymnasts' Complaints About Nassar, Then Made False Statements to Cover Mistakes, Report Says," *Wall Street Journal*, July 14, 2021,
www.wsj.com/articles/critical-report-fbi-failure-to-investigate-larry-nassar
-11626280355; Ian R. Tofler, Barri Katz Stryer, Lyle J. Micheli, and Lisa R.
Herman, "Physical and Emotional Problems of Elite Female Gymnasts,"
New England Journal of Medicine 335, no. 4 (1996): 281–283, www.nejm.org
/doi/full/10.1056/NEJM199607253350412; USA Gymnastics, "USA Gymnastics Statement Regarding Today's Statement by Maggie Nichols," January
9, 2018, https://usagym.org/pages/post.html?PostID=21169; Maggie Nichols statement, Judiciary Committee Hearing, September 15, 2021, www
.judiciary.senate.gov/imo/media/doc/Nichols%20Testimony.pdf.

20. *Athlete A* [documentary], June 24, 2020; Mike Davis, "Was Maggie Nichols Unfairly Left Off the Olympic Team?," *The Medal Count* (blog),
June 30, 2020, https://themedalcount.com/2020/06/30/was-maggie-nichols
-unfairly-left-off-the-olympic-team; Holly Yan, "Karolyi Ranch Produced
Champions and a Culture of Fear, Ex-Gymnasts Say," CNN, February 2, 2018,
www.cnn.com/2018/02/02/us/karolyi-ranch-gymnastics-abuse-allegations
/index.html; Rachel Blount, "Simone Biles Clinches Olympic Bid; Maggie
Nichols Left Off Team," *Star Tribune*, July 11, 2016, www.startribune.com
/biles-clinches-olympic-bid-nichols-fails-to-make-team/386230391.

21. Donald Sull, Charles Sull, and Ben Zweig, "Toxic Culture Is Driving the Great Resignation," *MIT Sloan Management Review*, January 11,

2022, https://sloanreview.mit.edu/article/toxic-culture-is-driving-the-great-resignation.

22. Alyssa Milano (@Alyssa_Milano), Twitter, October 15, 2017, https://twitter.com/alyssa_milano/status/919659438700670976?lang=en.

23. Eric Levenson, "Michigan State University Reaches $500 Million Settlement with Larry Nassar Victims," CNN, May 17, 2018, www.cnn.com/2018/05/16/us/larry-nassar-michigan-state-settlement/index.html; Juliet Macur, "Nassar Abuse Survivors Reach a $380 Million Settlement," *New York Times*, December 13, 2021, www.nytimes.com/2021/12/13/sports/olympics/nassar-abuse-gymnasts-settlement.html; Liz Brody, "The Army of Women Who Took Down Larry Nassar," *Glamour*, October 30, 2018, www.glamour.com/story/women-of-the-year-2018-larry-nassar-survivors.

24. Simone Biles (@Simone_Biles), Twitter, January 15, 2018, https://twitter.com/Simone_Biles/status/953014513837715457; Louise Radnofsky and Rachel Bachman, "Simone Biles's Ultimate Power Move: A Post-Olympics Tour of Her Own," *Wall Street Journal*, June 6, 2021, www.wsj.com/articles/simone-biles-post-olympics-tour-gymnastics-11622955616; Macaela MacKenzie, "Simone Biles Finds Her Balance," *Glamour*, June 15, 2021, www.glamour.com/story/simone-biles-finds-her-balance.

CHAPTER 5: CHANGEMAKERS

1. Adam Kilgore, "After Shaping Protest Rules in the U.S., Gwen Berry Has a New Sponsor and an Eye on Tokyo," *Washington Post*, June 21, 2021, www.washingtonpost.com/sports/olympics/2021/06/21/gwen-berry-puma-us-olympic-track-trials; Adam Kilgore, "Athlete Protests Are Now Celebrated. One Olympian Says She's Still Paying for Hers," *Washington Post*, September 16, 2020, www.washingtonpost.com/sports/2020/09/16/olympian-gwen-berry-anthem-protest.

2. International Olympic Committee (IOC) Athletes' Commission, "Rule 50 Guidelines," https://stillmedab.olympic.org/media/Document%20Library/OlympicOrg/News/2020/01/Rule-50-Guidelines-Tokyo-2020.pdf.

3. "Timeline of Events in Shooting of Michael Brown in Ferguson," AP, August 8, 2019, https://apnews.com/article/shootings-police-us-news-st-louis-michael-brown-9aa32033692547699a3b61da8fd1fc62; Gwen Berry, "This Should Make You Uncomfortable," *Players' Tribune*, October 21, 2021, www.theplayerstribune.com/posts/gwen-berry-olympics-usa-track-and-field-racial-injustice.

4. Eddie Pells, "Pan Am Games Protesters Each Get 12 Months of Probation," AP, August 20, 2019, https://apnews.com/article/race-imboden -olympic-games-co-state-wire-peru-sports-80b2fb3ee1da43c8909cb7b6a1a47454.

5. Christine Brennan, "US Olympian Gwen Berry Raises a Fist in Protest as IOC Relaxes Rules on Free Speech," *USA Today*, August 3, 2021, www .usatoday.com/story/sports/olympics/2021/08/03/us-olympian-gwen-berry -raises-fist-protest-ioc-relaxes-rules/5468362001; Nick Zaccardi, "Gwendolyn Berry Gets Apology from USOPC After Reprimand for Podium Gesture," NBC Sports, June 4, 2020, https://olympics.nbcsports.com/2020/06/04 /gwen-berry-protest/; IOC Athletes' Commission, "Rule 50 Guidelines."

6. Dave Zirin, "Interview with Ariyana Smith: The First Athlete Activist of #BlackLivesMatter," *The Nation*, December 19, 2014, www .thenation.com/article/archive/interview-ariyana-smith-first-athlete-activist -blacklivesmatter.

7. Christina Cauterucci, "The WNBA's Black Lives Matter Protest Has Set a New Standard for Sports Activism," *Slate*, July 25, 2016, https://slate.com/human-interest/2016/07/the-wnbas-black-lives-matter -protest-has-set-new-standard-for-sports-activism.html; Phil Helsel, "WNBA Rescinds Fines Issued over 'Black Lives Matter' Protest," NBC News, July 23, 2016, www.nbcnews.com/news/sports/wnba-rescinds-fines-issued-over -black-lives-matter-protest-n615536.

8. *UN Women*, "Intersectional Feminism: What It Means and Why It Matters Right Now," July 1, 2020, www.unwomen.org/en/news/stories/2020/6 /explainer-intersectional-feminism-what-it-means-and-why-it-matters; Koa Beck, *White Feminism* (New York: Simon and Schuster, 2021); Stewart M. Coles and Josh Pasek, "Intersectional Invisibility Revisited: How Group Prototypes Lead to the Erasure and Exclusion of Black Women," *Translational Issues in Psychological Science* 6, no. 4 (2020): 314–324, www.apa.org /pubs/journals/releases/tps-tps0000256.pdf.

9. Leah Asmelash, "WNBA Dedicates Season to Breonna Taylor and Say Her Name Campaign," CNN, July 25, 2020, www.cnn.com/2020/07/25/us /wnba-season-start-breonna-taylor-cnn/index.html.

10. Greg Bluestein and Bria Felicien, "Loeffler Opposes WNBA's Plan to Spread 'Black Lives Matter' Message," *Atlanta Journal-Constitution*, July 7, 2020, www.ajc.com/blog/politics/loeffler-opposes-wnba-plan-spread-black -lives-matter-message/ybTbHIpzZx7dbRlz3sfLiM; Chris Cillizza, "How Kelly Loeffler Got Backed into Admitting Donald Trump Lost," CNN, December 7, 2020, www.cnn.com/2020/12/07/politics/kelly-loeffler-donald -trump-debate/index.html.

11. Elizabeth Williams (e_williams_1), Instagram, July 10, 2020, www .instagram.com/p/CCekluqBFMW/?hl=en.

12. Angele Delevoye, "The WNBA Influenced the Georgia Senate Race, New Research Finds," *Washington Post*, November 30, 2020, www .washingtonpost.com/politics/2020/11/30/wnba-influenced-georgia-senate -race-new-research-finds.

13. Rachel Shuster, "Billie Jean King: Tennis Star Least of Her Important Roles," *USA Today*, May 22, 2013, www.usatoday.com/story /sports/2013/05/22/billie-jean-king-icons-innovators-world-team-tennis -womens-rights/2159071; Alexandra Licata, "29 of the Most Iconic Power Couples in Sports," *Insider*, August 5, 2019, www.businessinsider.com /biggest-couples-sports-2019-8#megan-rapinoe-and-sue-bird-4; Vanessa Romo, "Carl Nassib Is the First Active NFL Player to Come Out as Gay," NPR, June 21, 2021, www.npr.org/2021/06/21/1008910050/carl-nassib-is-the -first-active-nfl-player-to-come-out-as-gay.

14. Dawn Ennis, "Donald Trump, Jr. Calls Trans Athlete's Success 'Grave Injustice' to Women," *Outsports*, February 26, 2019, www.outsports.com /2019/2/26/18241404/donald-trump-junior-trans-athletes-success-injustice.

15. Freedom for All Americans, Legislative Tracker: Youth Sports Bans, https://freedomforallamericans.org/legislative-tracker/anti-transgen-der-legislation (accessed October 27, 2022); Mitch Smith, "Indiana Lawmakers Override Transgender Sports Veto," *New York Times*, May 24, 2022, www .nytimes.com/2022/05/24/us/indiana-legislature-transgender-sports-ban .html; Morgan Trau, "GOP Passes Bill Aiming to Root Out 'Suspected' Transgender Female Athletes with Genital Inspection," *Ohio Capital Journal*, June 3, 2022, https://ohiocapitaljournal.com/2022/06/03/gop-passes-bill-aiming-to-root-out-suspected-transgender-female-athletes-with-genital -inspection; "On the First Day of Pride Month, Florida Signed a Transgender Athlete Bill into Law," AP, June 2, 2021, www.npr. org/2021/06/02/1002405412/on-the-first-day-of-pride-month-florida-signed-a-transgender-athlete-bill-into-l.

16. Shoshana K. Goldberg, "Fair Play: The Importance of Sports Participation for Transgender Youth," Center for American Progress, February 8, 2021, www.americanprogress.org/article/fair-play.

17. Justin McCarthy, "Mixed Views Among Americans on Transgender Issues," Gallup, May 26, 2021, https://news.gallup.com/poll/350174/mixed -views-among-americans-transgender-issues.aspx.

18. Rebecca M. Jordan-Young and Katrina Karkazis, *Testosterone: An Unauthorized Biography* (Cambridge: Harvard University Press, 2019).

19. United States Anti-Doping Agency, "Q&A on Transgender Athletes and USADA," November 12, 2021, www.usada.org/spirit-of-sport/trans genderathletes; Jordan-Young and Karkazis, *Testosterone*, 161.

20. Jordan-Young and Karkazis, *Testosterone*, 161.

21. Dawn Ennis, "Exclusive: NCAA Champion CeCé Telfer Says 'I Have No Benefit' by Being Trans," *Outsports*, June 3, 2019, www.outsports.com /2019/6/3/18649927/ncaa-track-champion-cece-telfer-transgender-athlete-fpu -trans-testosterone; Timothy A. Roberts, Joshua Smalley, and Dale Ahrendt, "Effect of Gender Affirming Hormones on Athletic Performance in Trans- women and Transmen: Implications for Sporting Organisations and Leg- islators," *British Journal of Sports Medicine* 55, no. 11 (2021), https://bjsm .bmj.com/content/55/11/577; International Olympic Committee, "IOC Framework on Fairness, Inclusion and Non-discrimination on the Ba- sis of Gender Identity and Sex Variations," https://stillmed.olympics.com /media/Documents/News/2021/11/IOC-Framework-Fairness-Inclusion -Non-discrimination-2021.pdf?_ga=2.195521836.1048075235.1637092563 -834742310.1637092563.

22. Valerie Siebert, "Michael Phelps: The Man Who Was Built to Be a Swimmer," *The Telegraph*, April 25, 2014, www.telegraph.co.uk/sport /olympics/swimming/10768083/Michael-Phelps-The-man-who-was-built -to-be-a-swimmer.html; Erica Sullivan, "Why I'm Proud to Support Trans Athletes Like Lia Thomas," *Newsweek*, March 18, 2022, www.newsweek.com /why-im-proud-support-trans-athletes-like-lia-thomas-opinion-1689192.

23. Ennis, "Exclusive: NCAA Champion CeCé Telfer Says."

24. Robert Hart, "Canada's Quinn Makes History as First Openly Trans- gender and Nonbinary Athlete to Win Olympic Medal," *Forbes*, August 6, 2021, www.forbes.com/sites/roberthart/2021/08/06/canadas-quinn-makes -history-as-first-openly-transgender-and-nonbinary-athlete-to-win-olympic -medal/?sh=7de80ffcd61e; Cyd Zeigler and Karleigh Webb, "These 32 Trans Athletes Have Competed Openly in College," *Outsports*, April 6, 2022, www.outsports.com/trans/2022/1/7/22850789/trans-athletes-college -ncaa-lia-thomas; Katie Barnes, "Former University of Pennsylvania Swimmer Lia Thomas Responds to Critics: 'Trans Women Competing in Women's Sports Does Not Threaten Women's Sports,'" ESPN, May 31, 2022, www.espn.com/college-sports/story/_/id/34013007/trans-women -competing-women-sports-does-not-threaten-women-sports.

25. Jake Zuckerman, "She's Ohio's Only Trans Female Playing Varsity Sports; Lawmakers Want Her Out," *Ohio Capital Journal*, June 13, 2022, https://ohiocapitaljournal.com/2022/06/13/shes-ohios-only-trans-female

-playing-varsity-sports-lawmakers-want-her-out; James Factora, "There Are More Laws Banning Trans Girls in K–12 Sports Than There Are Out Trans Girls in K–12 Sports," *Them*, September 1, 2022, www.them.us/story/there-are-more-laws-banning-trans-girls-in-k-12-sports-than-there-are-trans-girls-in-k-12-sports?; Goldberg, "Fair Play: The Importance of Sports Participation for Transgender Youth."

26. Brittney Oliver, "The Women of the WNBA Are Leading the Way for Activism in Sports—and Have Been for Years," *Glamour*, September 3, 2020, www.glamour.com/story/the-women-of-the-wnba-are-leading-the-way-for-activism-in-sports-and-have-been-for-years; "Converse Will Pay Natasha Cloud Her Forfeited WNBA Salary for Opting Out of the 2020 Season," NBC Sports, June 30, 2020, www.nbcsports.com/washington/mystics/converse-will-pay-natasha-cloud-her-forfeited-wnba-salary-opting-out-2020-season; "Grade the Deal: Khris Middleton, Bucks Agree to Five-Year, $70M Contract," *SI*, July 1, 2015, www.si.com/nba/2015/07/01/milwaukee-bucks-khris-middleton-agree-five-year-70-million-contract.

27. Tiffany Burns, Jess Huang, Alexis Krivkovich, Ishanaa Rambachan, Tijana Trkulja, and Lareina Yee, "Women in the Workplace 2021," McKinsey & Company, September 27, 2021, www.mckinsey.com/featured-insights/diversity-and-inclusion/women-in-the-workplace.

28. Matthew Futterman, "Naomi Osaka Quits the French Open After News Conference Dispute," *New York Times*, May 31, 2021, www.nytimes.com/2021/05/31/sports/tennis/naomi-osaka-quits-french-open-depression.html; Juliet Macur, "Simone Biles Is Withdrawing from the Olympic All-Around Gymnastics Competition," *New York Times*, July 28, 2021, www.nytimes.com/2021/07/28/sports/olympics/simone-biles-out.html.

29. Emma Hurt, "Keisha Lance Bottoms, a Possible Biden VP Pick, Sees Profile Rise amid Crises," NPR, July 10, 2020, www.npr.org/2020/07/10/889500483/keisha-lance-bottoms-a-possible-biden-vp-pick-sees-profile-rise-amid-crises; Zak Cheney-Rice, "Why Did Keisha Lance Bottoms Quit?," *Intelligencer*, January 3, 2022, https://nymag.com/intelligencer/2022/01/keisha-lance-bottoms-atlanta-mayor-quits.html.

CHAPTER 6: PUT HER IN

1. World Economic Forum, *Global Gender Gap Report 2021* (Geneva: World Economic Forum, 2021), www3.weforum.org/docs/WEF_GGGR_2021.pdf; Motoko Rich, Hikari Hida, and Makiko Inoue, "Tokyo Olympics Chief Apologizes for Remarks Demeaning Women," *New York Times*, February 3, 2021, www.nytimes.com/2021/02/03/sports/olympics/tokyo

-olympics-yoshiro-mori.html; France 24, "Tokyo 2020 Chief Made Sexist Remarks: Report," March 3, 2021, www.france24.com/en/live-news/20210203-tokyo-2020-chief-made-sexist-remarks-report.

2. Isabel Reynolds, "Public Outrage over Sexist Comments Forces Changes at Tokyo 2020," Bloomberg, February 12, 2021, www.bloomberg.com/news/articles/2021-02-12/public-outrage-over-sexist-comments-forces-changes-at-tokyo-2020; "Disgraced Ex–Olympics Chief Yoshiro Mori Delivers Another Sexist Remark," *Japan Times*, March 27, 2021, www.japantimes.co.jp/news/2021/03/27/national/mori-sexist-remark-women.

3. Adam Grant, "Who Won't Shut Up in Meetings? Men Say It's Women. It's Not," *Washington Post*, February 18, 2021, www.washingtonpost.com/outlook/2021/02/18/men-interrupt-women-tokyo-olympics.

4. Christopher F. Karpowitz and Tali Mendelberg, *The Silent Sex: Gender, Deliberation, and Institutions* (Princeton, NJ: Princeton University Press, 2014), https://read.amazon.com/kp/embed?asin=B00KAJJCU0&preview=&reshareId=8084J5382X5GF6WYRPV7&reshareChannel=system.

5. "Hashimoto Seiko, Kotani Mikako and Takahashi Naoko: Connecting to Tomorrow, the 'Tokyo Model,'" Olympics.com, October 5, 2021, https://olympics.com/en/news/hashimoto-seiko-kotani-mikako-and-takahashi-naoko-connecting-to-tomorrow; Stephen Wade, "Tokyo Olympics Adds 12 Women to Executive Board as Gesture Towards Gender Equality," AP, March 2, 2021, https://apnews.com/article/sports-asia-tokyo-e71c892f1e051503de28dd96b0c3fed0; Ayai Tomisawa and Yuki Hagiwara, "Tokyo to Push Olympic Sponsors on Gender After Public Blunders," Bloomberg, April 26, 2021, www.bloomberg.com/news/articles/2021-04-27/tokyo-to-push-olympic-sponsors-on-gender-after-public-blunders.

6. Women's Sports Foundation, "The Foundation Position," www.womenssportsfoundation.org/wp-content/uploads/2016/07/race-and-sport-the-womens-sports-foundation-position.pdf; Johanna Adriaanse, "Women Are Missing in Sport Leadership, and It's Time That Changed," *The Conversation*, December 11, 2016, https://theconversation.com/women-are-missing-in-sport-leadership-and-its-time-that-changed-69979.

7. UN Women, "Facts and Figures: Women's Leadership and Political Participation," September 19, 2022, www.unwomen.org/en/what-we-do/leadership-and-political-participation/facts-and-figures; Talenya, "The Diversity Benchmark Report: Key Diversity and Inclusion Indicators Among Fortune 500 Companies," June 2021, www.talenya.com/bi-annual-diversity-report.

8. Doug Feinberg, "After 8 Years as NBA Assistant, Hammon to Lead Team in WNBA," AP, January 4, 2022, https://apnews.com/article/nba -sports-basketball-coaching-san-antonio-spurs-c3c9d83711d4d4046bd2c3ea 0eea2b8c; Doug Feinberg, "Hammon Hopes It Becomes Normal for Women to Get NBA Jobs," AP, August 11, 2021, https://apnews.com/article/sports -nba-portland-trail-blazers-san-antonio-spurs-ba4451e824d4f4d184918b73 be640e39.

9. Greg Ritchie, Libby Cherry, and David Goodman, "Bank of England Shortlist for Chief Economist Had More Women Than Men," Bloomberg, October 12, 2021, www.bloomberg.com/news/articles/2021-10-12/boe-s -chief-economist-shortlist-included-more-women-than-men?sref=AGY pi2Ba.

10. Jens Mazei, Joachim Hüffmeier, Philipp Alexander Freund, Alice F. Stuhlmacher, Lena Bilke, and Guido Hertel, "A Meta-Analysis on Gender Differences in Negotiation Outcomes and Their Moderators," *Psychological Bulletin* 141, no. 1 (2015): 85–104, www.apa.org/pubs/journals/releases /bul-a0038184.pdf; Kieran Snyder, "The Abrasiveness Trap: High-Achieving Men and Women Are Described Differently in Reviews," *Fortune*, August 26, 2014, https://fortune.com/2014/08/26/performance-review-gender-bias.

11. Elle Hunt, Nick Evershed, and Ri Liu, "From Julia Gillard to Hillary Clinton: Online Abuse of Politicians Around the World," *Guardian*, June 26, 2016, www.theguardian.com/technology/datablog/ng-interactive/2016/jun /27/from-julia-gillard-to-hillary-clinton-online-abuse-of-politicians-around -the-world.

12. Tyler G. Okimoto and Victoria L. Brescoll, "The Price of Power: Power Seeking and Backlash Against Female Politicians," *Personality and Social Psychology Bulletin* 36, no. 7 (2010), https://journals.sagepub.com /doi/10.1177/0146167210371949; Felicia Sonmez, "Rep. Paul Gosar Tweets Al-tered Anime Video Showing Him Killing Rep. Ocasio-Cortez and Attacking President Biden," *Washington Post*, November 8, 2021, www.washingtonpost .com/politics/republicans-gosar-trump-ocasio-cortez/2021/11/08/ead 37b36-40ca-11ec-9ea7-3eb2406a2e24_story.html; Victoria L. Brescoll, "Who Takes the Floor and Why: Gender, Power, and Volubility in Organizations," *Administrative Science Quarterly* 56, no. 4 (2011), https://journals.sagepub .com/doi/abs/10.1177/0001839212439994?.

13. Amnesty International, "Troll Patrol Findings: Using Crowdsourc-ing, Data Science and Machine Learning to Measure Violence and Abuse Against Women on Twitter," https://decoders.amnesty.org/projects/troll -patrol/findings.

14. Andreea Papuc, "Australian Companies Add Most Women to Boards in Six Months," Bloomberg, October 14, 2021, www.bloomberg.com/news /articles/2021-10-14/australian-companies-add-most-women-to-boards-in -six-months; Emma Hinchliffe, "The Female CEOs on This Year's Fortune 500 Just Broke Three All-Time Records," *Fortune*, June 2, 2021, https:// fortune.com/2021/06/02/female-ceos-fortune-500-2021-women-ceo-list -roz-brewer-walgreens-karen-lynch-cvs-thasunda-brown-duckett-tiaa; Cat Ariail, "Cashin' in at South Carolina: Dawn Staley Inks Historic Seven-Year, \$22.4 Million Contract," SB Nation, October 22, 2021, www.swishappeal .com/ncaa/2021/10/22/22734341/ncaaw-dawn-staley-south-carolina-game cocks-contract-seven-year-22-4-million-geno-auriemma-kim-mulkey.

15. Asaf Levanon, Paula England, and Paul Allison, "Occupational Femi-nization and Pay: Assessing Causal Dynamics Using 1950–2000 U.S. Census Data," *Social Forces* 88, no. 2 (December 2009): 865–891, https://academic .oup.com/sf/article-abstract/88/2/865/2235342?redirectedFrom=fulltext; "Rosie the Riveter," History.com, April 23, 2010, www.history.com/topics /world-war-ii/rosie-the-riveter; Motoko Rich, "Why Don't More Men Go into Teaching?," *New York Times*, September 6, 2014, www.nytimes.com /2014/09/07/sunday-review/why-dont-more-men-go-into-teaching.html.

16. Rhaina Cohen, "What Programming's Past Reveals About Today's Gender-Pay Gap," *The Atlantic*, September 7, 2016, www.theatlantic.com /business/archive/2016/09/what-programmings-past-reveal-about-todays -gender-pay-gap/498797.

17. Cohen, "What Programming's Past Reveals About Today's Gender-Pay Gap"; Richard E. Lapchick, "2020 Racial and Gender Report Card[TM]," Institute for Diversity and Ethics in Sport, https://43530132-36e9-4f52 -811a-182c7a91933b.filesusr.com/ugd/138a69_bee975e956ad45949456eae2 afdc74a2.pdf; Jude (@ndjrs), "Notre Dame Releases Salaries for Brian Kelly, Muffet McGraw, Mike Brey and Jack Swarbrick for 2018–19," SB Nation, May 20, 2020, www.onefootdown.com/2020/5/20/21264873/notre-dame -salaries-mike-brey-brian-kelly-muffet-mcgraw-jack-swarbrick-2018-2019 -compensation-irs; Steven Goff, "Jill Ellis Earned More in World Cup Year but Still Not as Much as Her U.S. Men's Counterpart," *Washington Post*, February 19, 2021, www.washingtonpost.com/sports/2021/02/19/uswnt-jill -ellis-earnings-ussf.

18. Ross Kerber, "Pay Gap for U.S. Female Executives Narrows but Persists," Reuters, February 17, 2021, www.reuters.com/article/us-usa -companies-compensation-women/pay-gap-for-u-s-female-executives -narrows-but-persists-idUSKBN2AH1J4; Healy Jones, "What Salaries Did

Startup CEOs Earn in 2022?," Kruze Consulting, May 9, 2022, https://kruzeconsulting.com/blog/post/startup-ceo-salary-report.

19. Catalyst, "Why Diversity and Inclusion Matter (Quick Take)," June 24, 2020, www.catalyst.org/research/the-bottom-line-corporate-performance-and-womens-representation-on-boards-2004-2008; Jeremy Barlow, "Gender Diversity on Boards and Why It Matters," *Board Effect*, August 10, 2016, www.boardeffect.com/blog/gender-diversity-board-of-directors/; McKinsey & Company, "Women Matter," October 2017, www.mckinsey.com/~/media/mckinsey/featured%20insights/women%20matter/women%20matter%20ten%20years%20of%20insights%20on%20the%20importance%20of%20gender%20diversity/women-matter-time-to-accelerate-ten-years-of-insights-into-gender-diversity.pdf; Mark Misercola, "Higher Returns with Women in Decision-Making Positions," Credit Suisse, March 10, 2016, www.credit-suisse.com/about-us-news/en/articles/news-and-expertise/higher-returns-with-women-in-decision-making-positions-201610.html.

20. PitchBook, "All In: Female Founders in the US VC Ecosystem," November 1, 2021, https://pitchbook.com/news/reports/2021-all-in-female-founders-in-the-us-vc-ecosystem.

21. Rajalakshmi Subramanian, "Lessons from the Pandemic: Board Diversity and Performance," BoardReady, July 13, 2021, https://static1.squarespace.com/static/5ab00948710699beb7a40e29/t/60edf87b6d720f75fb6366ba/1626208384888/BoardReady_Report_Final.pdf; The Pipeline, "Women Count 2021: Role, Value, and Number of Female Executives in the FTSE 350," https://execpipeline.com/wp-content/uploads/2021/07/Women-Count-2021-Report.pdf?tpcc=.

22. Dana L. Joseph and Daniel A. Newman, "Emotional Intelligence: An Integrative Meta-Analysis and Cascading Model," *Journal of Applied Psychology* 95, no. 1 (January 2010): 54–78, https://psycnet.apa.org/buy/2010-00343-013; Irwin W. Silverman, "Gender Differences in Delay of Gratification: A Meta-Analysis," *Sex Roles* 49 (2003): 451–463, https://link.springer.com/article/10.1023/A:1025872421115; Kibeom Lee and Michael C. Ashton, "Sex Differences in HEXACO Personality Characteristics Across Countries and Ethnicities," *Journal of Personality* 88, no. 6 (December 2020): 1075–1090, https://onlinelibrary.wiley.com/doi/abs/10.1111/jopy.12551; James Andreoni and Lise Vesterlund, "Which Is the Fair Sex? Gender Differences in Altruism," *Quarterly Journal of Economics* 116, no. 1 (2001): 293–312, https://academic.oup.com/qje/article-abstract/116/1/293/1939030?redirectedFrom=fulltext; BI Norwegian Business School, "Personality for Leadership: Women Better Suited for Leadership Than Men, Research

Demonstrates," *ScienceDaily*, March 20, 2014, www.sciencedaily.com
/releases/2014/03/140320101110.htm; Julia Klevak, Joshua Livnat, and Kate
Suslava, "Benefits of Having a Female CFO," SSRN, July 14, 2021, https://
papers.ssrn.com/sol3/papers.cfm?abstract_id=3887025.

23. Georgene Huang, "Men and Women Aren't Promoted by the
Same People—Here's the Difference," *Forbes*, May 10, 2018, www.forbes
.com/sites/georgenehuang/2018/05/10/men-and-women-arent
-promoted-by-the-same-people-heres-the-difference/?sh=9d9798f10ea5;
Mark Zeigler, "Women's Pro Soccer Coming to San Diego in 2022," *San
Diego Union-Tribune*, June 8, 2021, www.sandiegouniontribune.com/sports
/soccer/story/2021-06-08/soccer-nwsl-womens-pro-soccer-expansion
-team-san-diego-jill-ellis-ron-burkle-torero-stadium-wusa-spirit; "Ava Du-
Vernay Is 'Proud' of *Queen Sugar*'s All-Female Directorial Team," Oprah.
com, www.oprah.com/own-queensugar/ava-duvernay-is-proud-of-queen
-sugars-female-directorial-team; Yohana Desta, "*Insecure*: For the First
Time, Every Single Costume Was Designed by a Black Woman," *Vanity
Fair*, December 5, 2021, www.vanityfair.com/hollywood/2021/12/insecure
-episode-seven-black-female-designers; Brooke Baldwin, *Huddle: How
Women Unlock Their Collective Power* (New York: Harper Business, 2021),
89; Barbara Rodriguez, "Before Boston's Historic Mayoral Race Between
Two Women of Color, a Diverse City Council Helped Pave the Way," The
19th, November 2, 2021, https://19thnews.org/2021/11/boston-mayor-city
-council-diversity.

24. Ilene H. Lang and Reggie Van Lee, "Institutional Investors Must
Help Close the Race and Gender Gaps in Venture Capital," *Harvard Business
Review*, August 27, 2020, https://hbr.org/2020/08/institutional-investors
-must-help-close-the-race-and-gender-gaps-in-venture-capital.

25. Surf Equity, "Milestones," https://surfequity.org/milestones.

26. Andrew S. Lewis, "For Pro Women Surfers, Equal Pay Isn't Enough,"
Outside, May 6, 2019, www.outsideonline.com/outdoor-adventure/water
-activities/world-surf-league-sophie-goldschmidt-pay-equity.

27. Glynn A. Hill, "A Little Nylon Goes a Long Way: Dawn Staley Ex-
tends a Tradition with a Package of Inspiration," *Washington Post*, November 13, 2021, www.washingtonpost.com/sports/2021/11/13/dawn-staley
-south-carolina-sends-net-black-women-coaches.

28. GM, "GM in the U.S.," www.gm.com/company/usa-operations; M.
Asher Lawson, Ashley E. Martin, Imrul Huda, and Sandra C. Matz, "Hiring Women into Senior Leadership Positions Is Associated with a Reduction in Gender Stereotypes in Organizational Language," *Proceedings of the*

National Academy of Sciences 119, no. 9 (February 22, 2022), www.pnas.org /doi/10.1073/pnas.2026443119.

29. WNY Women's Foundation, "Where Will You Find Your Next Leader?," 2015, https://wnywomensfoundation.org/app/uploads/2017/11/76 .-Where-will-you-find-your-next-leader.pdf.

30. Alpine Ski Database, "Women's Super Ranking," https://ski-db.com /db/stats/f_super.php (accessed October 30, 2022).

CHAPTER 7: OWNING YOUR WORTH

1. Jeff Tracy, "Breaking Down the WNBA's New Ownership Land-scape After Sale of Atlanta Dream," *Axios*, March 1, 2021, www.axios .com/2021/03/01/wnba-owners-atlanta-dream; Emma Hinchliffe, "'It Changes Everything': Renee Montgomery on Being the First WNBA Player to Co-Own Her Team," *Fortune*, May 17, 2021, https://fortune.com /2021/05/17/renee-montgomery-co-owner-atlanta-dream-kelly-loeffler.

2. Jung Hyun Choi, Laurie Goodman, and Jun Zhu, "A Three-Decade Decline in the Homeownership Gender Gap: What Drove the Change, and Where Do We Go from Here?," Urban Institute, August 2021, www.urban .org/sites/default/files/publication/104698/a-three-decade-decline-in-the -homeownership-gender-gap_1.pdf; UN Office of the High Commissioner for Human Rights, "Insecure Land Rights for Women Threaten Progress on Gender Equality and Sustainable Development," July 2017, www.ohchr .org/sites/default/files/Documents/Issues/Women/WG/Womens landright.pdf; Statista, "U.S. Car Owners as of 2021, by Gender," www .statista.com/statistics/1041215/us-car-owners-by-sex; US Census Bureau, "Census Bureau Releases New Data on Minority-Owned, Veteran-Owned and Women-Owned Businesses," press release, October 28, 2021, www. census.gov/newsroom/press-releases/2021/characteristics-of-employer -businesses.html; US Senate Committee on Small Business and Entrepre-neurship, "21st Century Barriers to Women's Entrepreneurship," majority report, July 23, 2014, www.sbc.senate.gov/public/_cache/files/3/f/3f954386 -f16b-48d2-86ad-698a75e33cc4/F74C2CA266014842F8A3D86C3AB619BA .21st-century-barriers-to-women-s-entrepreneurship-revised-ed.-v.1.pdf.

3. Jeff Green, "Male Executives Control 99 Times More S&P 500 Shares Than Women," Bloomberg, June 6, 2022, www.bloomberg.com /news/articles/2022-06-06/male-executives-control-99-times-more-s-p-500 -shares-than-women.

4. Dana Kanze, Mark A. Conley, Tyler G. Okimoto, Damon J. Phillips, and Jennifer Merluzzi, "Evidence That Investors Penalize Female Founders

for Lack of Industry Fit," *Science Advances* 6, no. 48 (November 25, 2020), www.science.org/doi/10.1126/sciadv.abd7664.

5. Jeff Green, "Ouster of Gap CEO Syngal Follows Trend of Women Being Fired Faster," Bloomberg, July 13, 2022, www.bloomberg.com /news/articles/2022-07-13/ouster-of-gap-ceo-syngal-follows-trend-of-women -being-fired-faster.

6. Macaela MacKenzie, "Cindy Eckert Wants You to Join the Billion-Dollar Founders' Club," *Forbes*, November 30, 2017, www.forbes.com/sites /macaelamackenzie/2017/11/30/cindy-whitehead-wants-you-to-join-the -billion-dollar-founders-club/?sh=6b81f7472b5e; Sarah Berger, "The Woman Behind 'Female Viagra' Sold Her Company for $1Billion—Then Got It Back for Free," CNBC, June 21, 2018, www.cnbc.com/2018/06/21/cindy-eckert -whitehead-back-as-ceo-of-female-viagra-company-sprout.html.

7. Hannah Withiam, "Louisville's Hailey Van Lith Is Ready for Our Brave New NIL World," Just Women's Sports, August 11, 2021, https:// justwomenssports.com/louisvilles-hailey-van-lith-is-ready-for-our-brave -new-nil-world; Kendall Baker, "Eight of the 10 Most-Followed NCAA Elite 8 Basketball Players Are Women," *Axios*, March 29, 2021, www.axios .com/2021/03/29/ncaa-basketball-social-media-followings.

8. Statista, "Distribution of Influencers Creating Sponsored Posts on Instagram Worldwide in 2019, by Gender," www.statista.com/statistics /893749/share-influencers-creating-sponsored-posts-by-gender; Jacinda Santora, "Key Influencer Marketing Statistics You Need to Know for 2022," Influencer Marketing Hub, August 3, 2022, https://influencermarketing hub.com/influencer-marketing-statistics; Kareem Copeland, "Who's Making the Most from NIL? Women's Basketball Is Near the Top," *Washington Post*, March 30, 2022, www.washingtonpost.com/sports/2022/03/30 /womens-college-basketball-endorsements-nil.

9. Alan Blinder, "College Athletes May Earn Money from Their Fame, N.C.A.A. Rules," *New York Times*, June 30, 2021, www.nytimes.com /2021/06/30/sports/ncaabasketball/ncaa-nil-rules.html.

10. Carly Wanna, "Which Final Four Basketball Players Have Greatest Earnings Potential? It's the Women," Bloomberg, March 31, 2022, www .bloomberg.com/news/features/2022-03-31/female-ncaa-athletes-brand -deals-after-march-madness-may-smash-the-pay-gap; Cody Taylor, "Magic Ink No. 1 Pick Paolo Banchero to Rookie Contract," *Rookie Wire*, July 1, 2022, https://therookiewire.usatoday.com/2022/07/01/magic-ink-no-1-pick -paolo-banchero-to-rookie-contract.

11. Rachel Bachman, "Star Female Athletes Are Fighting for More Financial Control—and Winning," *Wall Street Journal*, May 26, 2022, www.wsj.com/articles/female-athletes-equal-pay-soccer-alex-morgan-11653577757.

12. "USWNTPA Launching New Online Merchandise Store Today," *Sports Business Journal*, July 14, 2022, www.sportsbusinessjournal.com/Daily/Issues/2022/07/14/Marketing-and-Sponsorship/USWNT-Players-Association-online-store.aspx; Bachman, "Star Female Athletes Are Fighting for More Financial Control"; Caitlin Murray, "Why Nike Didn't Have Enough USWNT World Cup Jerseys to Meet Demand—and What It Cost the Players and Fans," Yahoo Sports, October 10, 2019, https://sports.yahoo.com/why-nike-didnt-have-enough-uswnt-world-cup-jerseys-to-meet-demand-and-what-it-cost-the-players-and-fans-171933947.html.

13. Opendorse, "NIL: One Year of Name Image and Likeness," https://opendorse.com/wp-content/uploads/2022/07/NIL_Full_063022_3.pdf.

14. Allyson Felix (allysonfelix), Instagram, June 27, 2021, www.instagram.com/p/CQpAdkqM4s5.

15. Daphne Howland, "Gap Inc. Joins $8M Funding Round to Take Equity Stake in Allyson Felix's Saysh," *Retail Dive*, June 17, 2022, www.retaildive.com/news/gap-inc-joins-funding-round-equity-allyson-felix-saysh/625710.

16. Kimberly Weisul, "Report: Female Entrepreneurs Much More Likely to Employ Women," *Inc.*, December 20, 2018, www.inc.com/kimberly-weisul/these-entrepreneurs-hired-very-few-men.html.

17. Adam Elder, "Natalie Portman Wanted to Shift Football Culture. So She Founded Angel City FC," *Guardian*, March 18, 2022, www.theguardian.com/football/2022/mar/18/natalie-portman-wanted-to-shift-football-culture-so-she-founded-angel-city-fc; Angel City Ownership, www.angelcity.com/club/ownership; Sandra Herrera, "NWSL's Los Angeles Team Is Named Angel City FC; Billie Jean King, Candace Parker Added to Ownership Group," CBS, October 21, 2020, www.cbssports.com/soccer/news/nwsls-los-angeles-team-is-named-angel-city-fc-billie-jean-king-candace-parker-added-to-ownership-group.

18. Footy Headlines, "Ranked: The 11 Most Lucrative Shirt Sponsor Deals in Football—Barca x Spotify 3rd," www.footyheadlines.com/2022/03/ranked-11-most-lucrative-shirt-sponsor.html.

19. Emma Hruby, "Report: NWSL Expansion Team Angel City FC Valued at More Than $100 Million," Just Women's Sports, August 12, 2022, https://justwomenssports.com/nwsl-angel-city-valued-100-million-soccer-expansion.

20. Just Women's Sports (justwomenssports), Instagram, April 30, 2022, www.instagram.com/p/Cc9o7AKsJfT/?igshid=MDJmNzVkMjY%3D; David Broughton, "NBA Attendance at 92% Capacity for Regular Season," *Sports Business Journal*, April 13, 2022, www.sportsbusinessjournal.com /Daily/Closing-Bell/2022/04/13/NBA.aspx.

21. Lawson_sv, "Hollywood Comes to the NWSL / the NWSL Comes to Hollywood," SB Nation, May 1, 2022, www.allforxi.com/2022/5/1/23051349 /hollywood-comes-to-the-nwsl-the-nwsl-comes-to-hollywood.

CHAPTER 8: SEX SELLS, WOMEN PAY

1. Cody Benjamin, "Olympics: How Fast Do Downhill Skiers Go? A Guide to Lindsey Vonn's Best Event," CBS Sports, February 13, 2018, www .cbssports.com/olympics/news/olympics-how-fast-do-downhill-skiers -go-a-guide-to-lindsey-vonns-best-event; International Skiing History Association, "Stenmark vs. Vonn, Who Was Best?," June 13, 2019, https://skiing history.org/news/stenmark-vs-vonn-who-was-best; Wayne Drehs, "The Lioness in Winter," ABC News, February 21, 2018, https://abcnews.go.com/Sports /lioness-winter/story?id=53235556.

2. Jonetta Weber and Robert M. Carini, "Where Are the Female Athletes in *Sports Illustrated*? A Content Analysis of Covers (2000–2011)," *International Review for the Sociology of Sport* 48, no. 2 (April 2013): 196–203, www .researchgate.net/publication/258142706_Where_are_the_female_athletes _in_Sports_Illustrated_A_content_analysis_of_covers_2000-2011#:~:text=.

3. Dax J. Kellie, Khandis R. Blake, and Robert C. Brooks, "What Drives Female Objectification? An Investigation of Appearance-Based Interpersonal Perceptions and the Objectification of Women," *PLoS One* 14, no. 8 (2010): e0221388, www.ncbi.nlm.nih.gov/pmc/articles/PMC6707629.

4. Cynthia M. Frisby, "Sacrificing Dignity for Publicity: Content Analysis of Female and Male Athletes on 'Sports Illustrated' and 'ESPN the Magazine' Covers from 2012–2016," *Advances in Journalism and Communication* 5, no. 2 (June 2017), www.researchgate.net/publication/317275186 _Sacrificing_Dignity_for_Publicity_Content_Analysis_of_Female_and _Male_Athletes_on_Sports_Illustrated_and_ESPN_the_Magazine_Covers _from_2012-2016.

5. Jenesse Miller, "News Media Still Pressing the Mute Button on Women's Sports," USC News, March 24, 2021, news.usc.edu/183765/womens -sports-tv-news-coverage-sportscenter-online-usc-study; Jeré Longman, "For Lolo Jones, Everything Is Image," *New York Times*, August 4, 2012, www .nytimes.com/2012/08/05/sports/olympics/olympian-lolo-jones-draws

-attention-to-beauty-not-achievement.html?_r=0; Sabrina Tavernise, Tariro Mzezewa, and Giulia Heyward, "Behind the Surprising Jump in Multiracial Americans, Several Theories," *New York Times*, August 13, 2021, www .nytimes.com/2021/08/13/us/census-multiracial-identity.html.

6. Jason Horowitz, "A Surprise Sports Hero Broadens Italy's Image of Itself," *New York Times*, October 8, 2021, www.nytimes.com/2021/10/08 /world/europe/lamont-jacobs-italy-sprinter.html.

7. Jeff Goodman, "U.S. Women Appear on Letterman," AP, July 20, 1999, https://apnews.com/article/b4049c3614994a6fad645fc4f3511053.

8. "Fox5 San Diego Sports Anchor Ross Shimabuku Calls Danica Patrick a Bitch," YouTube, posted by WomensMediaCenter, February 23, 2012, www.youtube.com/watch?v=K4lzRgNUkaw.

9. Jason Whitlock, "Serena Could Be the Best Ever, But . . . ," Fox Sports, July 9, 2009, https://web.archive.org/web/20090709162516/http://msn .foxsports.com/tennis/story/9757816/Serena-could-be-the-best-ever,-but-.

10. Cynthia M. Frisby, "A Content Analysis of Serena Williams and Angelique Kerber's Racial and Sexist Microaggressions," *Social Sciences* 5, no. 5 (June 2017), www.researchgate.net/publication/316630629_A_Content _Analysis_of_Serena_Williams_and_Angelique_Kerber's_Racial_and _Sexist_Microaggressions.

11. Matthew Norman, "Serena's Loyal Supporters," *The Telegraph*, January 22, 2006, www.telegraph.co.uk/sport/tennis/australianopen/2331012 /Serenas-loyal-supporters.html; Jenée Desmond-Harris, "Despite Decades of Racist and Sexist Attacks, Serena Williams Keeps Winning," *Vox*, January 28, 2017, www.vox.com/2017/1/28/14424624/serena-williams-wins -australian-open-venus-record-racist-sexist-attacks; Stephen Rodrick, "Serena Williams: The Great One," *Rolling Stone*, June 18, 2013, www.rollingstone .com/culture/culture-sports/serena-williams-the-great-one-88694.

12. Jeroslyn Johnson, "Sha'Carri Richardson Calls Out Olympics for Racism After White Female Athlete Fails Drug Test, Allowed to Compete," *Black Enterprise*, February 14, 2022, www.blackenterprise.com /shacarri-richardson-calls-out-double-standards-after-learning-white-female -athlete-failed-drug-test-but-allowed-to-compete.

13. Susan Ware, *Game, Set, Match: Billie Jean King and the Revolution in Women's Sports* (Chapel Hill: University of North Carolina Press, 2011), 96.

14. Britni de la Cretaz, "Androgyny Is Now Fashionable in the W.N.B.A.," *New York Times*, June 18, 2019, www.nytimes.com/2019/06 /18/opinion/androgyny-wnba-fashion.html; "WNBA (2003) Television Commercial—This Is Who I Am," YouTube, posted by Analog Indulgence,

January 20, 2021, www.youtube.com/watch?v=c8KNW6LfEGg; Dr. Nef (@NefWalker), Twitter, April 11, 2022, https://twitter.com/NefWalker /status/1513664156947435521; Chris Knoester and Rachel Allison, "Sexuality, Sports-Related Mistreatment, and U.S. Adults' Sports Involvement," *Leisure Sciences* (2021), www.tandfonline.com/doi/full/10.1080/01490400 .2021.1895009.

15. "Shamil Tarpischev Fined, Banned Year," ESPN, October 17, 2014, www.espn.com/tennis/story/_/id/11718876/russian-tennis-federation -president-shamil-tarpischev-sanctioned-serena-venus-williams-gender -comments; Jacqueline Palochko, "'Gender Reveal' Sign Directed at Northampton Girl Hockey Player Shows Sexism Girls Still Face in Sports," *Morning Call*, March 13, 2020, www.mcall.com/news/local/mc-nws -northampton-parkland-hockey-sign-20200312-zivbtxuelfchhmah2tkulb 4ebu-story.html.

16. "Semenya Offered to Show Her Body to Officials to Prove She Was Female," Reuters, May 24, 2022, www.reuters.com/lifestyle/sports /semenya-offered-show-her-body-officials-prove-she-was-female-2022-05-24.

17. Human Rights Watch, *"They're Chasing Us Away from Sport": Human Rights Violations in Sex Testing of Elite Women Athletes* (New York: Human Rights Watch, 2020), www.hrw.org/sites/default/files/media_2020/12/lgbt _athletes1120_web.pdf; Alice Park, "Woman Enough? Inside the Controversial World of Olympic Gender Testing," *Time*, July 2, 2012, https://olympics .time.com/2012/07/02/how-the-ioc-tests-for-gender; Lindsay Parks Pieper, "They Qualified for the Olympics. Then They Had to Prove Their Sex," *Washington Post*, February 22, 2018, www.washingtonpost.com/news/made -by-history/wp/2018/02/22/first-they-qualified-for-the-olympics-then -they-had-to-prove-their-sex/; Ruth Padawer, "The Humiliating Practice of Sex-Testing Female Athletes," *New York Times*, June 28, 2016, www.nytimes .com/2016/07/03/magazine/the-humiliating-practice-of-sex-testing-female -athletes.html; Bruce Kidd, "Sex Testing at the Olympics Should Be Abolished Once and for All," *The Conversation*, July 11, 2021, https:// theconversation.com/sex-testing-at-the-olympics-should-be-abolished-once -and-for-all-132956.

18. Padawer, "The Humiliating Practice of Sex-Testing Female Athletes"; National Center for Transgender Equality, "Frequently Asked Questions About Transgender People," July 9, 2016, https://transequality.org /issues/resources/frequently-asked-questions-about-transgender-people; "Semenya Offered to Show Her Body to Officials to Prove She Was

Female," Reuters; Steve Brenner, "Caster Semenya: 'They're Killing Sport. People Want Extraordinary Performances,'" *Guardian*, February 25, 2021, www.theguardian.com/sport/2021/apr/23/caster-semenya-theyre-killing -sport-people-want-extraordinary-performances.

19. Karen Crouse, "Michelle Wie West Was Ready to Retire. Then She Got Mad," *New York Times*, June 3, 2021, www.nytimes.com/2021/06/03/sports /golf/lpga-michelle-wie-us-open.html; Michelle Wie (@MichelleWieWest), Twitter, February 19, 2021, https://twitter.com/MichelleWieWest/status /1362970120381886465.

20. The Representation Project, "#RespectHerGame Report," 2021, https://therepproject.org/wp-content/uploads/2021/08/Respect-Her -Game-Report.pdf.

21. European Handball Federation, "Disciplinary Commission Im- poses a Fine for Improper Clothing," July 19, 2021, https://beacheuro .eurohandball.com/news/en/disciplinary-commission-imposes-a-fine -for-improper-clothing; Caroline Radnofsky, "Norwegian Women's Beach Handball Team Fined for Not Playing in Bikinis," NBC News, July 20, 2021, www.nbcnews.com/news/sports/norwegian-women-s-beach-handball -team-fined-not-playing-bikinis-n1274453.

22. Kim Bui (_kim.bui_), Instagram, April 24, 2021, www.instagram .com/p/COC273ehezx.

23. Zainab Chaudry and Simran Jeet Singh, "Hijabs and Turbans Are Not a Threat to Sports," *Time*, August 18, 2016, https://time.com/4456128 /hijab-ban-basketball-fiba-olympics; "Asian Games: Qatar Women's Team Pull Out over Hijab Ban," BBC, September 26, 2014, www.bbc.com/sport /basketball/29342986; Maya A. Jones, "Disqualified for Running in a Hi- jab, Noor Alexandria Abukaram Turned Pain into Action," ESPN, May 31, 2022, www.espn.com/espnw/story/_/id/34015634/disqualified-running -hijab-noor-alexandria-abukaram-turned-pain-action; Constant Méheut, "The Female Soccer Players Challenging France's Hijab Ban," *New York Times*, April 18, 2022, www.nytimes.com/2022/04/18/sports/soccer/france -hijab-ban-soccer.html?; Shireen Ahmed, "'Forcing Women out of Cloth- ing Is Just as Violent as Forcing Them into It,'" TRT World, July 23, 2021, www.trtworld.com/opinion/forcing-women-out-of-clothing-is-just -as-violent-as-forcing-them-into-it-48605; Anushay Hossain, "Tokyo Olym- pics Are Not a Bikini Showcase. Let Women Athletes Wear Unitards, and Hijabs," *USA Today*, July 27, 2021, www.usatoday.com/story/opinion/2021/07 /27/tokyo-olympics-german-gymnasts-unitards-why-not-hijabs/5385281001.

24. Lindy West, "Three Things That Need to Happen Before I Defend Men from Olympic Sexism," *Guardian*, August 16, 2016, www.theguardian .com/commentisfree/2016/aug/16/olympics-women-sexism.

25. Daniel J. A. Rhind, Hayley Musson, Andrea Florence, Pamela Gilpin, and Gigi Alford, *Census of Athlete Rights Experiences Report 2021* (Nyon, Switzerland: World Players Association and UNI Global Union, 2021), https://files.cargocollective.com/c520687/World-Players_CARE-Report -2021-.pdf; Jeannine Ohlert, Corinna Seidler, Thea Rau, Bettina Rulofs, and Marc Allroggen, "Sexual Violence in Organized Sport in Germany," *German Journal of Exercise and Sport Research* 48 (2018): 59–68, https://link .springer.com/article/10.1007%2Fs12662-017-0485-9; Joan Ryan, *Little Girls in Pretty Boxes: The Making and Breaking of Elite Gymnasts and Figure Skaters* (New York: Doubleday, 1995), 189–190.

26. Sarah Gramazio, Mara Cadinu, Stefano Pagliaro, and Maria Giuseppina Pacilli, "Sexualization of Sexual Harassment Victims Reduces Bystanders' Help: The Mediating Role of Attribution of Immorality and Blame," *Journal of Interpersonal Violence* 36, nos. 13–14 (July 2021): 6073–6097, https://pubmed.ncbi.nlm.nih.gov/30539673.

27. Ariane Hegewisch, Jessica Forden, and Eve Mefferd, "Paying Today and Tomorrow: Charting the Financial Costs of Workplace Sexual Harassment," Institute for Women's Policy Research and Time's Up Foundation, July 2021, https://timesupfoundation.org/work/costs-of-workplace -sexual-harassment; Project Include, "Remote Work Since COVID-19 Is Exacerbating Harm," https://projectinclude.org/assets/pdf/Project-Include -Harassment-Report-0321-F3.pdf; Heather McLaughlin, Christopher Uggen, and Amy Blackstone, "The Cost of Sexual Harassment," *Work in Progress* (blog), August 17, 2017, https://workinprogress.oowsection.org/2017/08/17 /the-cost-of-sexual-harassment.

28. Leah D. Sheppard and Stefanie K. Johnson, "The Femme Fatale Effect: Attractiveness Is a Liability for Businesswomen's Perceived Truthfulness, Trust, and Deservingness of Termination," *Sex Roles* 81 (2019): 779–796, https://link.springer.com/article/10.1007/s11199-019-01031-1.

29. Cristina Baldissarri, Luca Andrighetto, Alessandro Gabbiadini, Roberta Rosa Valtorta, Alessandra Sacino, and Chiara Volpato, "Do Self-Objectified Women Believe Themselves to Be Free? Sexual Objectification and Belief in Personal Free Will," *Frontiers in Psychology*, August 8, 2019, www.frontiersin.org/articles/10.3389/fpsyg.2019.01867/full; Lara Winn and Randolph Cornelius, "Self-Objectification and Cognitive Performance: A

Systematic Review of the Literature," *Frontiers in Psychology*, January 28, 2020, www.frontiersin.org/articles/10.3389/fpsyg.2020.00020/full.

30. Natalie Robehmed, "The World's Highest-Paid Models 2016: Karlie Kloss and Kendall Jenner Storm Top Three with $10 Million Apiece," *Forbes*, August 30, 2016, www.forbes.com/sites/natalierobehmed/2016/08/30/the -worlds-highest-paid-models-2016-karlie-kloss-and-kendall-jenner-storm -top-three-with-10-million-apiece/?sh=7bc901d3150f; Thong Song, "Fallen Angel" [audio], 2021, https://podcasts.apple.com/us/podcast/thong-son/id1 589072529?i=1000538427052; Daniel S. Hamermesh and Jeff E. Biddle, "Beauty and the Labor Market," National Bureau of Economic Research Working Paper 4518, November 1993, www.nber.org/papers/w4518; Todd R. Stinebrickner, Ralph Stinebrickner, and Paul J. Sullivan, "Beauty, Job Tasks, and Wages: A New Conclusion About Employer Taste-Based Discrimination," National Bureau of Economic Research Working Paper 24479, April 2018, www.nber.org/system/files/working_papers/w24479/w24479.pdf; Jaclyn S. Wong and Andrew M. Penner, "Gender and the Returns to Attractiveness," *Research in Social Stratification and Mobility* 44 (June 2016): 113–123, www.sciencedirect.com/science/article/abs/pii/S0276562416300518.

31. Mary Jo Kane, Nicole M. LaVoi, and Janet S. Fink, "Exploring Elite Female Athletes' Interpretations of Sport Media Images: A Window into the Construction of Social Identity and 'Selling Sex' in Women's Sports," *Communication and Sport* 1, no. 3 (September 2013): 269–298, https://journals .sagepub.com/doi/10.1177/2167479512473585.

32. *Sports Illustrated* (@SInow), Twitter, December 15, 2015, https:// twitter.com/SInow/status/676703283965227008?; "American Pharoah a Runaway Choice in Readers' Sportsman of the Year Poll," *SI*, December 11, 2015, www.si.com/sportsperson/2015/12/11/american-pharoah-online -readers-poll-2015-sportsman-year.

33. "Indian Wells CEO Raymond Moore Resigns After Remarks Drew Outrage," ESPN, March 21, 2016, www.espn.com/tennis/story/_/id /15039381/indian-wells-ceo-raymond-moore-resigns-remarks-drew-outrage.

CHAPTER 9: GOOD FOR A GIRL

1. US Soccer, "Timeline," www.ussoccer.com/history/timeline.

2. "USSF Arguments" [in *Alex Morgan et al. v. U.S. Soccer Federation, Inc.*], www.documentcloud.org/documents/6807270-USSF-Arguments.html.

3. "Court Dockets" [in *Alex Morgan et al. v. U.S. Soccer Federation, Inc.*], www.bloomberglaw.com/public/desktop/document/AlexMorganetalv

UnitedStatesSoccerFederationIncDocketNo219cv01717C/20?1634935825; Meg Linehan (@itsmeglinehan), Twitter, March 16, 2020, https://twitter.com /itsmeglinehan/status/1239745774306689025.

4. Linda Scott, *The Double X Economy: The Epic Potential of Women's Empowerment* (New York: Farrar, Straus and Giroux, 2020), 95.

5. Kevin Draper, "U.S. Soccer President Carlos Cordeiro Resigns," *New York Times*, March 12, 2020, www.nytimes.com/2020/03/12/sports/soccer /uswnt-carlos-cordeiro-us-soccer.html; Brakkton Booker, "U.S. Soccer Apologizes for Saying Male Players Have 'More Responsibility' Than Women," NPR, March 11, 2020, www.npr.org/2020/03/11/814656567/male -players-have-more-responsibility-than-women-u-s-soccer-says-in-court -filing; "Law Firm Criticized for Belittling USWNT Asks to Withdraw from Representing U.S. Soccer," AP, April 2, 2020, www.si.com/soccer/2020/04/02 /us-soccer-law-firm-uswnt-strategy-seyfarth-shaw-withdraw.

6. "No 'Sticking to Sports' Here," *The Gist*, July 18, 2021, www .thegistsports.com/deep-dive/0690eefc-36a7-4361-81d0-678de919d3fc; Jules Boykoff, "The Forgotten History of Female Athletes Who Organized Their Own Olympics," Bitch Media, March 18, 2019, www.bitchmedia.org /article/forgotten-history-female-athletes-who-organized-their-own-olympics; Alexander Abnos, "Start of Something Big," *SI*, www.si.com/longform /soccer-goals/goal4.html.

7. "Why Can't Women Ski Jump?," *Time*, http://content.time.com/time /specials/packages/article/0,28804,1963484_1963490_1963447,00.html; Eric Goodman, "Women's 1500m Freestyle Makes Olympic Debut as Ledecky Stars," NBC Sports, July 26, 2021, www.nbcolympics.com/news/womens -1500m-freestyle-makes-olympic-debut-ledecky-stars; Shauna Farnell, "An Olympic Hurdle: Why Is the Decathlon Only for Men?," *New York Times*, July 6, 2021, www.nytimes.com/2021/07/06/sports/olympics/us-track-field -decathlon-women-heptathlon.html?; Susan Ware, *Game, Set, Match: Billie Jean King and the Revolution in Women's Sports* (Chapel Hill: University of North Carolina Press, 2011), 124.

8. Drew Weisholtz, "US Women's National Soccer Team Criticized for Celebrating During 13–0 World Cup Win," *Today*, June 12, 2019, www .today.com/news/us-team-criticized-celebrating-during-women-s-world -cup-win-t156130.

9. Melissa J. Williams, "The Price Women Leaders Pay for Assertiveness—and How to Minimize It," *Wall Street Journal*, May 30, 2016, www .wsj.com/articles/the-price-women-leaders-pay-for-assertivenessand-how -to-minimize-it-1464660240#:~:text=; Gene Maddaus, "Scarlett Johansson

and Disney Settle 'Black Widow' Pay Lawsuit," *Variety*, September 30, 2021, https://variety.com/2021/film/news/scarlett-johansson-disney-lawsuit-settled-1235078355/; Pat Saperstein, "Scarlett Johansson Lawsuit: Disney's Response Is a 'Gendered Character Attack,' Says Time's Up, Women in Film, Reframe," *Variety*, July 30, 2021, https://variety.com/2021/film/news/scarlett-johansson-disney-lawsuit-times-up-1235031844/?.

10. Jim Caple, "Why Twirlgate Is So Much More Interesting Than Deflategate," ESPN, January 23, 2015, www.espn.com/espnw/news-commentary/story/_/id/12220097/why-twirlgate-much-more-interesting-deflategate; The Representation Project, "#RespectHerGame Report."

11. Joan Ryan, *Little Girls in Pretty Boxes: The Making and Breaking of Elite Gymnasts and Figure Skaters* (New York: Doubleday, 1995), 68.

12. Ashan Singh, Laura Coburn, and Anthony Rivas, "Serena Williams Outburst at 2018 US Open Women's Final Explored in New ESPN Series 'Backstory,'" ABC News, August 15, 2019, https://abcnews.go.com/Sports/serena-williams-outburst-2018-us-open-womens-final/story?id=65000510; James Blake (@JRBlake), Twitter, September 8, 2018, https://twitter.com/JRBlake/status/1038619979938189313?; Brian Lewis, "Serena Has Mother of All Meltdowns in US Open Final Loss," *New York Post*, September 8, 2018, https://nypost.com/2018/09/08/serena-has-mother-of-all-meltdowns-in-us-open-final-loss; Billie Jean King (@BillieJeanKing), Twitter, September 8, 2018, https://twitter.com/BillieJeanKing/status/1038613218296569856?ref_src=; Joe DeCapua, "Study Examines Racial Bias in US Sports Reporting," VOA, June 5, 2015, www.voanews.com/a/athlete-stereotyping-5jun15/2808997.html; Brooke Newman, "The Long History Behind the Racist Attacks on Serena Williams," *Washington Post*, September 11, 2018, www.washingtonpost.com/outlook/2018/09/11/long-history-behind-racist-attacks-serena-williams.

13. Laura Bates, "'Normal' in Our Society Means Male—Women Are Written Out of the Story," *Guardian*, August 17, 2016, www.theguardian.com/lifeandstyle/womens-blog/2016/aug/17/normal-society-means-male-andy-murray-venus-serena-williams; Lee Moran, "Newspaper Covers Simone Manuel's Historic Gold in Olympically Offensive Way," *HuffPost*, August 12, 2016, www.huffpost.com/entry/san-jose-mercury-news-rio-olympics-story_n_57ad7acbe4b007c36e4e2184.

14. Adam Wells, "Lindsey Vonn: Impending Divorce Will Ruin American Skier's Career," *Bleacher Report*, November 28, 2011, https://bleacherreport.com/articles/959106-lindsey-vonn-impending-divorce-will-ruin-american-skiers-career.

15. Philip Hersh, "For Vonn, Divorce Means Big Changes in Handling Ski Career," *Chicago Tribune*, November 29, 2011, www.chicagotribune.com/chi-for-vonn-divorce-means-big-changes-in-handling-ski-career-20111129-column.html.

16. The Representation Project, "#RespectHerGame Report."

17. Kate Conger, "Exclusive: Here's the Full 10-Page Anti-Diversity Screed Circulating Internally at Google," *Gizmodo*, August 5, 2017, https://gizmodo.com/exclusive-heres-the-full-10-page-anti-diversity-screed-1797564320/amp; Accenture and Girls Who Code, "Resetting Tech Culture: 5 Strategies to Keep Women in Tech," 2020, www.accenture.com/_acnmedia/PDF-134/Accenture-A4-GWC-Report-Final1.pdf; Rebecca Koehn, "Why Is There Still a Gender Gap in Tech?," *Techopedia*, March 31, 2021, www.techopedia.com/why-is-there-still-a-gender-gap-in-tech/2/34503; Carolina Gonzalez, "Men Got Higher Pay Than Women 59% of the Time for Same Tech Jobs," Bloomberg, May 19, 2021, www.bloomberg.com/news/articles/2021-05-19/gender-pay-gap-in-tech-male-job-candidates-paid-3-higher-than-women.

18. Cordelia Fine, *Testosterone Rex: Myths of Sex, Science, and Society* (New York: W. W. Norton, 2017), 23.

19. Fine, *Testosterone Rex*, 87.

20. Cordelia Fine, *Delusions of Gender: How Our Minds, Society, and Neurosexism Create Difference* (New York: W. W. Norton, 2011), 19–22.

21. Utathya Nag, "Usain Bolt's Records: Best Strikes from the Lightning Bolt," Olympics.com, March 23, 2022, https://olympics.com/en/featured-news/usain-bolt-record-world-champion-athlete-fastest-man-olympics-sprinter-100m-200m; Rebecca M. Jordan-Young and Katrina Karkazis, *Testosterone: An Unauthorized Biography* (Cambridge: Harvard University Press, 2019); Peter Larsson, "All-Time Women's Best 800m," *Track and Field All-Time Performances Homepage*, www.alltime-athletics.com/w_800ok.htm (accessed October 31, 2022).

22. Paul Ronto, "The State of Ultra Running 2020," *RunRepeat*, September 21, 2021, https://runrepeat.com/state-of-ultra-running.

23. Ben Cohen, "This Team from Norway Is Universally Feared. It's Also Unisex," *Wall Street Journal*, February 7, 2022, www.wsj.com/articles/winter-olympics-norway-ski-jumping-unisex-11644225835.

24. Gordon Dahl, Andreas Kotsadam, and Dan-Olof Rooth, "Does Integration Change Gender Attitudes? The Effect of Randomly Assigning Women to Traditionally Male Teams," National Bureau of Economic Research Working Paper 24351, February 2018, www.nber.org/papers/w24351.

25. Jessica Nordell, "This Is How Everyday Sexism Could Stop You from Getting That Promotion," *New York Times*, October 14, 2021, www.nytimes.com/interactive/2021/10/14/opinion/gender-bias.html?.

26. Francine D. Blau and Lawrence M. Kahn, "The Gender Wage Gap: Extent, Trends, and Explanations," National Bureau of Economic Research Working Paper 21913, January 2016, www.nber.org/papers/w21913.

CHAPTER 10: IF YOU CAN SEE IT

1. Cheryl Cooky, "Overlooking Her Shot: Women's Sports Need an Assist as Coverage Remains the Same as 30 Years Ago," Purdue University News, March 24, 2021, www.purdue.edu/newsroom/releases/2021/Q1/overlooking-her-shot-womens-sports-need-an-assist-as-coverage-remains-the-same-as-30-years-ago.html.

2. Cheryl Cooky, LaToya D. Council, Maria A. Mears, and Michael A. Messner, "One and Done: The Long Eclipse of Women's Televised Sports, 1989–2019," *Communication and Sport* 9, no. 3 (June 2021): 347–371, https://journals.sagepub.com/doi/full/10.1177/21674795211003524?_ga=2.63042479.1417481077.1657853899-913862602.1657853899.

3. Cooky, "Overlooking Her Shot"; Cooky et al., "One and Done."

4. Jenesse Miller, "News Media Still Pressing the Mute Button on Women's Sports," https://news.usc.edu/183765/womens-sports-tv-news-coverage-sportscenter-online-usc-study.

5. Cooky et al., "One and Done"; Shot:Clock Media (shotclock_media), Instagram, March 1, 2021, www.instagram.com/p/CL5d1JEhpDW/?utm_source=ig_embed&utm_campaign=loading; Miller, "News Media Still Pressing the Mute Button on Women's Sports."

6. Cheryl Cooky and Dunja Antunovic, "'This Isn't Just About Us': Articulations of Feminism in Media Narratives of Athlete Activism," *Communication and Sport* 8, nos. 4–5 (2020): 692–711, https://journals.sagepub.com/doi/abs/10.1177/2167479519896360; Cooky, "Overlooking Her Shot."

7. Jon Lewis (aka Paulsen), "Over 26 Million for USA's Women's World Cup Coronation," Sports Media Watch, 2015, www.sportsmediawatch.com/2015/07/womens-world-cup-record-ratings-usa-fox-largest-soccer-audience-ever-single-network; Jon Lewis (aka Paulsen), "2015 NBA Finals Most-Watched Since 1998, Highest Rated Since 2001," Sports Media Watch, 2015, www.sportsmediawatch.com/2015/06/nba-finals-ratings-highest-fourteen-years-most-watched-since-1998-warriors-cavaliers-abc; Emily Caron, "WNBA at 25 Poised for Growth After Decades of Just Getting By," Yahoo, May 14, 2021, www.yahoo.com/now/wnba-25-poised-growth-decades

-130009104.html; "US Open Women's Final Draws Bigger Audience Than Men's Decider on ESPN," Reuters, September 15, 2021, www.reuters .com/lifestyle/sports/us-open-womens-final-draws-bigger-audience -than-mens-decider-espn-2021-09-15; Jabari Young, "CBS Saw 14% Decline in Viewers for NCAA Men's Basketball Championship Game, While Ratings for Women's Title Match on ESPN Grew," CNBC, April 6, 2021, www.cnbc.com/2021/04/06/ncaa-2021-final-four-championship-ratings -mens-down-14percent-womens-up.html; "Euro 2022: England Win over Germany Watched by Record Television Audience of 17.4m," BBC Sport, August 1, 2022, www.bbc.com/sport/football/62375750#.

8. The Gist (thegistusa), Instagram, April 7, 2022, www.instagram .com/p/CcDPst2uToJ/?igshid=MDJmNzVkMjY%3D.

9. Nielsen Sports, "Global Interest in Women's Sports Is on the Rise," https://nielsensports.com/global-interest-womens-sports-rise; YouGov, "What's Stopping Consumers from Watching Women's Sports? Lack of Coverage, Not Caliber of Play," June 23, 2021, https://today.yougov.com /topics/sports/articles-reports/2021/06/23/whats-stopping-consumers -watching-womens-sports.

10. "New Research Reveals Women's Sport Will Reach £1BN Revenue if Female Athletes and Teams Are Made More Visible," Women's Sport Trust, April 20, 2021, www.womenssporttrust.com/closing-the-visibility-gap/.

11. Mike Hytner, "Research Reveals Over Half of Australians Follow Women's Sport," *Guardian*, February 15, 2019, www.theguardian.com/sport /2019/feb/16/research-reveals-over-half-of-australians-follow-womens -sport; "The Rise of Women's Sport in Australia," Physioinq (blog), May 28, 2019, https://www.physioinq.com.au/blog/rise-womens-sport-australia; Kate O'Halloran, "New CBA Sees AFLW Players Receive 94 Per Cent Pay Rise with Season Set to Start in August," ABC News, May 19, 2022, www .abc.net.au/news/2022-05-19/afl-aflpa-aflw-cba-new-season-august-pay-rise /101072676.

INDEX

ASHELY BATZ

MACAELA MACKENZIE is a journalist who writes about women and power. She covers women's equality through the lenses of sports, wellness, and the gender gap across industries. As a senior editor at *Glamour*, she directed all sports and wellness coverage. Her work has been published in *Glamour, Elle, Self, Marie Claire, Forbes*, and *Bustle*, among others. Follow her latest work at www.macaelamackenzie.com and on Instagram @macaelamac.